95 Theses for a New Reformation

95 Theses for a New Reformation

For the Church on the 500th Anniversary of the Reformation

A<small>ARON</small> B. H<small>EBBARD</small>, Editor

RESOURCE *Publications* • Eugene, Oregon

95 THESES FOR A NEW REFORMATION
For the Church on the 500th Anniversary of the Reformation

Resource Publications
An Imprint of Wipf and Stock Publishers
199 W. 8th Ave., Suite 3
Eugene, OR 97401

www.wipfandstock.com

PAPERBACK ISBN: 978-1-4982-8988-7
HARDCOVER ISBN: 978-1-4982-8990-0
EBOOK ISBN: 978-1-4982-8989-4

Manufactured in the U.S.A.   SEPTEMBER 29, 2017

Contents

Sphere II: Reforming the Family

Sphere III: Reforming the Culture

Contributors:
Twenty-First-Century Reformers

Roy Atwood (PhD, University of Iowa) is the Vice Rector for Academic and Institutional Development of Nehemiah Gateway University in Buçimas, Pogradec, Albania, where he also serves as a church planter. He is also guest lecturer at Fan Noli University in Korçë, Albania. He was previously co-founder, President, and Senior Fellow of Humanities at New Saint Andrews College, and a professor and administrator at the University of Idaho, both in Moscow, Idaho. Twice he has been a Senior Fulbright Teaching and Research Scholar at Warsaw University in Poland and the North West University in South Africa. His numerous academic articles and reviews have appeared in a variety of scholarly journals internationally. He and his wife, Beverlee, have two children and twelve grandchildren.

Joel R. Beeke (PhD, Westminster Theological Seminary) was converted at the age of fourteen, and has pastored for nearly forty years in three churches. Currently, he is president and professor of systematic theology and homiletics at Puritan Reformed Theological Seminary (since 1994), a pastor of the Heritage Reformed Congregation in Grand Rapids, Michigan (since 1986), editor of *Puritan Reformed Journal* and *Banner of Sovereign Grace Truth*, editorial director of Reformation Heritage Books, president of Inheritance Publishers, and vice-president of the Dutch Reformed Translation Society. He has written and co-authored nearly one hundred books (most recently, *A Puritan Theology: Doctrine for Life; Prepared by Grace, for Grace: The Puritans on God's Ordinary Way of Leading Sinners to Christ;* and *Debated Issues in Sovereign Predestination*), edited another one hundred books, and contributed 2,500 articles to Reformed books, journals, periodicals, and encyclopedias. He is presently working on writing a systematic theology and a book on preaching from the preacher's heart to the listener's heart. His PhD is in Reformation and Post-Reformation theology from Westminster Theological Seminary (Philadelphia). He is frequently called upon to lecture at seminaries and to speak at Reformed conferences around the world in dozens of countries. He and his wife Mary have been blessed with three children and two grandchildren.

Jerry Bridges (BS, University of Oklahoma) served with the Navigators since 1955 in a variety of positions. He also served as a Naval officer during the Korean War. He authored over twenty books including *The Pursuit of Holiness*, *The Discipline of Grace*, *Holiness Day by Day*, and *Respectable Sins*. Jerry became a widower, surviving his wife of twenty-five years, Eleanor, and is survived by two children and six grandchildren. He was remarried to Jane. Jerry Bridges passed into glory on March 6, 2016.

Scott Thomas Brown (MDiv, Talbot School of Theology, Biola University) is the President of the National Center for Family-Integrated Churches and pastor at Hope Baptist Church in Wake Forest, North Carolina. Scott graduated from California State University Fullerton with a degree in History. He gives his time to expository preaching and local pastoral ministry, as well as conferences on biblical doctrine, and church and family reformation. He and his wife Deborah have four grown children.

John M. Frame (DD, Belhaven; PhD, Whitefield Theological Seminary) currently serves as Professor Emeritus of Systematic Theology and Philosophy at Reformed Theological Seminary in Orlando, Florida, after having taught at Westminster Theological Seminary in Philadelphia and California. Dr. Frame has written numerous books and articles. He is married to Mary Grace and together they have five children.

George Grant (PhD, DLitt, Whitefield Theological Seminary; DHum Belhaven University; DMin Knox Seminary) wears many hats in his community: he is a husband, father, grandfather, mentor, president and founder of King's Meadow Study Center, the pastor of Parish Presbyterian Church, instructor at and founder of Franklin Classical School, founder of New College Franklin, writer, avid reader, runner, gardener, and barbecue master.

He is the author of over five dozen books in the areas of history, biography, politics, literature, and social criticism, and he has written hundreds of essays, articles, and columns. Dr. Grant maintains an active writing and speaking schedule in this country and around the world.

Jay Grimstead (DMin, Fuller Seminary) has worked as an Area Director for Young Life and as a theologian from 1977 to the present. In 1977 he founded and gathered a team of theologians to create the International Council on Biblical Inerrancy, which created "The Chicago Statement on Biblical Inerrancy." In 1984 Dr. Jay founded and directed the Coalition on Revival (COR), which first created "The 17 Worldview Documents" on how the Bible applies to all areas of life. Under the name of COR, Dr. Jay created the "Church Council Movement" and gathered transdenominational theologians to create the "24 Theological Documents" to be discussed at the Three Church Council Meetings in 2017 in Wittenberg, Germany, in 2019 in Zurich, and in 2021 in Worms, Germany. He co-authored *Rebuilding Civilization on the Bible* with Eugene Calvin Clingman. Dr. Grimstead and his wife, Donna, live in Murphys, California and have two adult children and three young boys as grandchildren.

Peter Hammond (DMiss, Whitefield Theological Seminary; DD, Antioch Theological Seminary) has been a pioneer missionary to some of the worst war zones in the world. For over thirty-four years Dr. Peter Hammond has served persecuted churches and pioneered evangelistic outreaches into Mozambique, Angola, Sudan, Rwanda, Congo, and Nigeria. In the course of his missionary activities, Dr. Hammond has been ambushed, come under aerial and artillery bombardments, been stabbed, shot at, beaten by mobs, arrested, imprisoned, and tortured for Christ. Dr. Peter Hammond is the Founder of Frontline Fellowship, the Reformation Society, Africa Christian Action, and William Carey Bible Institute. He is the author of numerous books including *Practical Discipleship, Answering Skeptics, The Power of Prayer, Biblical Principles for Africa,* and *Victorious Christians Who Changed the World.* Dr. Hammond has helped establish over one hundred Christian schools and numerous Bible Colleges throughout Africa. He has smuggled in and distributed hundreds of thousands of Bibles, New Testaments, and Christian books into communist and Muslim nations. Peter, and his wife Lenora, are homeschooling parents of four children.

Aaron B. Hebbard (PhD, University of Glasgow) is Founder and Fellow of Theology and the Arts at Sovereignty College, as well as professor, church planter, and pastor in Southern California. Dr. Hebbard currently serves as the Academic Dean at Community Christian College. He is the Founder, Chancellor, and First Knight of the Order of the King's Crown, a society dedicated to restoring biblical manhood. "Heb" and his wife, Nicole, have six children, one married-in daughter, and a grandson.

Nicole Hebbard is Christian wife, mother, homemaker, and homeschool educator in the Hebbard household. She blogs to encourage women of the faith to be the best they can be in their roles of wife and mother, and may be found at apouringout.blogspot.com. She married her high school sweetheart "Heb" and has been happily married since 1991, and together they have six children; three sons and three daughters, one married-in daughter, and a grandson.

Robert Herrmann (MDiv, Gordon-Conwell Theological Seminary) is an ordained minister in the Orthodox Presbyterian Church and has pastored ARP, PCA, and OPC churches across the country since 1975. He is married to Jeanne and they have two grown children and five grandchildren.

Craig D. Houston is a Christian, husband, father, and pastor. Privileged to grow up in a fourth generation Christian home, Craig was saved and baptized at an early age. Ordained to the gospel ministry in 1997, he has been seeking to preach the Word, reach the lost, and strengthen the family ever since. Craig has served as the pastor of Westside Baptist Church in Bremerton, Washington since 2002. He married his sweetheart, Emily, in 1994 and the Lord has blessed them with fourteen children.

Gary Inrig (DMin, Dallas Theological Seminary) is the lead pastor of Redeemer Fellowship in Loma Linda, California. He is a pastor, author, and conference speaker, having served in in pastoral ministry for more than forty years. He is a graduate of the University of British Columbia and Dallas Theological Seminary (ThM and DMin). He is also the author of twelve books, including *Forgiveness* and has had the privilege of speaking in more than forty countries. He and his wife Elizabeth have three children (one who is with the Lord) and eight grandchildren.

Phil Johnson is the Executive Director of Grace to You, a Christian recording and radio ministry featuring the preaching ministry of John MacArthur, with whom he has been closely associated since 1981, and edits most of MacArthur's major books. Phil pastors an adult fellowship group called GraceLife at Grace Community Church in Sun Valley, California. He is a member of the Fellowship of Independent Reformed Evangelicals (FIRE). He has a beautiful wife, Darlene, three grown sons, three fantastic daughters-in-law, and seven adorable grandchildren.

Phillip Kayser (PhD, Whitefield Theological Seminary) is Founder and President of Biblical Blueprints, and currently serves as Senior Pastor of Dominion Covenant in Omaha, Nebraska. Dr. Kayser is also Professor of

Ethics at Whitefield Theological Seminary and President of the Providential History Festival. Phillip Kayser has degrees in education, theology, and philosophy. As author of over 50 books and booklets, Dr. Kayser is passionate to see the Bible's comprehensive blueprints applied to the family, the church, civil government, education, art, science, historiography, economics, business, and every area of life. For over fifteen years, he has been involved in coaching church planters, mentoring seminary students, and teaching seminars on biblical leadership internationally. He has given leadership to the Heartland Christian Ministries Conference, Evangelical Ministries Fellowship, CELNet, the National Strategy Council, and other evangelical organizations. He and his wife Kathy have a growing family of five children and nine grandchildren who love and serve the Lord.

Steven J. Lawson (DMin Reformed Theological Seminary) is founder and president of OnePassion Ministries, a ministry designed to equip and energize a new generation of Bible expositors. He is the author of more than twenty books, including *Pillars of Grace: A Long Line of Godly Men, Volume Two*, *The Unwavering Resolve of Jonathan Edwards*, *The Expository Genius of John Calvin*, and *Foundations of Grace: A Long Line of Godly Men, Volume One*. Dr. Lawson is a Teaching Fellow with Ligonier Ministries, Professor of Preaching and Dean of the Doctor of Ministry program at The Master's Seminary, and Executive Editor for *Expositor* magazine. He is also on the board of The Master's University and Seminary, Ligonier Ministries, and Reformation Bible College. Dr. Lawson is a graduate of Texas Tech University (BBA), Dallas Theological Seminary (ThM), and Reformed Theological Seminary (DMin), has served as a pastor in Arkansas and Alabama for thirty-four years, and presently lives in Dallas, Texas. Steve and his wife Anne have three sons and a daughter.

Peter Leithart (PhD, University of Cambridge) is President of the Theopolis Institute and Teacher at Trinity Presbyterian Church, both in Birmingham, Alabama. He is the author of numerous books, most recently of *The End of Protestantism* (Baker, 2016) and a two-volume commentary on Revelation (T&T Clark, forthcoming). He and his wife Noel have ten children and nine grandchildren.

Peter Lillback (PhD, Westminster Theological Seminary) is president and professor of historical theology and church history at Westminster Theological Seminary. He also serves as the president of *The Providence Forum* and senior editor of the new *Unio cum Christo: An International Journal of Reformed Theology and Life*. Dr. Lillback has been ordained in the Orthodox

Presbyterian Church (OPC), and holds his present credentials as teaching elder in the Presbyterian Church in America (PCA). Dr. Lillback and his wife live in Wayne, Pennsylvania, and have two married daughters and two granddaughters, so far.

Richard Lusk (MA, University of Texas) pastors Trinity Presbytery Church in Birmingham, Alabama. Prior to that, he was on staff at Auburn Avenue Presbyterian Church in Monroe, LA, and Redeemer Presbyterian Church in Austin, Texas. Rich has written numerous internet and journal articles, contributed to several books, and authored *Paedofaith: A Handbook for Covenant Parents*. He is married to Jenny and together they have four children.

John F. MacArthur (MDiv, Talbot Theological Seminary) is Pastor-Teacher of Grace Community Church in Sun Valley, California. He also serves as President of both Master's University and Master's Seminary. He can be heard on his daily radio program *Grace to You*. He has authored and edited over 150 books, and notably the *MacArthur Study Bible*, *The Gospel According to Jesus*, *The Battle for the Beginning*, *Think Biblically*, and *Strange Fire*. He and his wife, Patricia, have four children and fifteen grandchildren.

R. Albert Mohler Jr (PhD, Southern Baptist Theological Seminary) is a theologian and an ordained minister, having served as pastor and staff minister of several Southern Baptist churches. He came to the presidency of Southern Baptist Theological Seminary from service as editor of *The Christian Index*, the oldest of the state papers serving the Southern Baptist Convention. Dr. Mohler also serves as the Joseph Emerson Brown Professor of Christian Theology at Southern Seminary. His writings have been published throughout the United States and Europe. In addition to contributing to a number of collected volumes, he is the author of several books, including *Culture Shift: Engaging Current Issues with Timeless Truth*; *Desire & Deceit: The Real Cost of the New Sexual Tolerance*; *Atheism Remix: A Christian Confronts the New Atheists*; *He Is Not Silent: Preaching in a Postmodern World*; *The Disappearance of God*; and *Words From the Fire*. He is currently editor-in-chief of *The Southern Baptist Journal of Theology*, a leader within the Southern Baptist Convention, a member of the Council for Biblical Manhood and Womanhood, and serves as a council member for The Gospel Coalition. He is married to Mary, and they have two children, Katie and Christopher.

Joseph Morecraft III (ThD, Whitefield Theological Seminary) is an ordained minister and has planted and pastored numerous churches in Virginia, Tennessee, and Georgia. Dr. Morecraft received his BA in History from King College, his MDiv from Columbia Theological Seminary, and his ThD from Whitefield Theological Seminary. Dr. Morecraft has lectured in such places as South Africa, England, Scotland, El Salvador, Argentina, Cypress, and many more. He has authored hundreds of articles and three books: *Liberation Theology: Prelude to Revolution, How God Wants Us to Worship Him,* and *With Liberty and Justice for All.* In 1986, Dr. Morecraft was a candidate for US Congress in the 7th Congressional District of Georgia. Dr. Morecraft is married to his wife Becky and they have four children and ten grandchildren.

Joel Pelsue (MDiv, Reformed Theological Seminary, Orlando) is the Co-Founder and President of Arts and Entertainment Ministries (www.A-E-M.org) as well as the Arts & Entertainment Institute. He is a Presbyterian minister in the PCA, pastoring now for over fifteen years in New York and in Los Angeles. Joel lives in Los Angeles with his wife Michelle, and their three children.

Joseph A. Pipa Jr (PhD, Westminster Theological Seminary; DD, Greenville Presbyterian Theological Seminary) Dr. Pipa has pastored numerous Presbyterian churches and was the Director of Advanced Studies and Associate Professor of Practical Theology at Westminster Theological Seminary in California. Dr. Pipa currently serves as the first President of Greenville Presbyterian Theological Seminary in Taylors, South Carolina. He has written Sunday School material for Great Commission Publications, and authored *Root and Branch, The Lord's Day, The Westminster Confession of Faith Study Book: A Study Guide for Churches, Galatians: God's Proclamation of Liberty,* and *Is the Lord's Day for You?* as well as numerous articles. Dr. Pipa and his wife, Carolyn, live in Greenville, South Carolina, and have two grown, married children, and eleven grandchildren.

Paul Michael Raymond (ThD, Almeda University) is the pastor of the Reformed Bible Church in Central Virginia at Appomattox, the founder and CEO of the Institute for Theonomic Reformation, and the Dean of The New Geneva Christian Leadership Academy College, Seminary, and Graduate School. He began pastoring in 1992 at the Reformed Bible Church in Suffolk County, New York until his move to Virginia in 1998. He holds an undergraduate degree from the State University of New York at Albany, and graduate degrees from Whitefield Theological Seminary and Almeda University. Pastor Raymond lives in Appomattox, Virginia with his wife Jane and has three grown children and two grandchildren.

Mark Rushdooney (BA, Los Angeles Baptist College, now The Master's University) was ordained to the ministry in 1995. He taught Christian junior and senior high school before joining the staff of Chalcedon Foundation, where he succeeded his father RJ Rushdoony as President of Chalcedon, and oversaw the integration of Ross House Books. He has written scores of articles for Chalcedon's publications, both the *Chalcedon Report* and *Faith for all of Life*. He was a contributing author to *The Great Christian Revolution* (1991). He has spoken at numerous conferences and churches in the US and abroad. Mark Rushdoony lives in Vallecito, California with his wife Darlene and their youngest son. He has three married children and seven grandchildren.

Martin G. Selbrede is the Vice-President of the Chalcedon Foundation and senior researcher for the organization's ongoing work of Christian scholarship. He has written numerous articles, essays, and position papers for such publications as *Faith for All of Life*, the *Chalcedon Report*, and *The Journal of Christian Reconstruction*. He has travelled extensively to speak on behalf of Christian Reconstruction and the Chalcedon Foundation and is considered one of the foremost experts in the thinking of R. J. Rushdoony. Martin is also an optical physicist, software engineer, novelist, and symphonic composer. He resides with his wife Kathy in Austin, Texas.

Daniel J. Smithwick founded the Nehemiah Institute in 1986, where he serves as president. Dan authored the PEERS Test and the groundbreaking study course, PILLARS, and he contributed to *The Media-Wise Family* with Dr. Ted Baehr. Dan also serves on the Executive Council of the Coalition on Revival Ministries (COR). Dan and his wife of forty-eight years (deceased 2015), are parents of five children and grandparents of twelve. Dan currently resides in Orlando, Florida.

R. C. Sproul (Drs, Free University; PhD, DD, Whitefield Theological Seminary) is the Founder and Chairman of Ligonier Ministries, which produces his daily radio teaching program *Renewing Your Mind*. He is also the Founder and Chancellor of Reformation Bible College in Sanford, Florida. Additionally, as an ordained teaching elder with the PCA, he serves as Senior Minister of Teaching and Preaching at St. Andrew's Chapel. He is the author of over one hundred books including *The Holiness of God, Willing to Believe, The Consequences of Ideas, Chosen by God, Defending Your Faith, A Taste of Heaven, What is Reformed Theology?*, and several volumes in the St. Andrew's Expositional Commentary series. In addition to these works, he has written several children's books and served as editor of the

Reformation Study Bible. He and his wife, Vesta, have two children and numerous grandchildren.

R. C. Sproul Jr. (DMin, Whitefield Theological Seminary) is a husband and the father of eight. He is a graduate of Grove City College and received his MA from Reformed Theological Seminary. He has served as an editor, a church planter, and college professor. His books include *Believing God* and *The Call to Wonder.*

Alexander Strauch (MDiv, Denver Seminary) received his undergraduate degree from Colorado Christian University For over forty years he served as an elder at Littleton Bible Chapel near Denver, Colorado. Additionally, he has taught philosophy and New Testament literature at Colorado Christian University and has helped thousands of churches worldwide through his expository writing and teaching ministry. He is the author of *Biblical Elder-ship, The New Testament Deacon, Men and Women: Equal Yet Different, The Hospitality Commands, Agape Leadership* (with Robert L. Peterson), *Meetings That Work, Leading with Love, Love or Die: Christ's Wake-up Call to the Church,* and *If You Bite and Devour One Another.* Mr. Strauch and his wife, Marilyn, reside in Littleton, Colorado, near their four adult daughters and eleven grandchildren.

Kevin Swanson (MDiv, Southern California Center for Christian Studies) serves as Director of Generations, which produces the daily radio program *Generations Radio,* geared toward fostering homeschooling and biblical worldview. He is the author of several books including his most recent *Apostate, The Second Mayflower,* and several practical commentaries in the Family Bible Study Series. Additionally, he currently serves as Pastor of Reformation Church. He and his wife, Brenda, have five children.

Paul David Tripp (DMin, Westminster Theological Seminary) is a pastor, conference speaker, and award-winning author with over thirty books and teaching series. He is the president of Paul Tripp Ministries and works to connect the transforming power of Jesus Christ to everyday life. He was a faculty member at the Christian Counseling and Educational Foundation (CCEF) for many years, a lecturer in Biblical Counseling at Westminster Theological Seminary, a Visiting Professor at Southern Baptist Theological Seminary, and a pastor at Tenth Presbyterian Church, and the Executive Director of The Center for Pastoral Life and Care. He lives in Philadelphia with his wife, Luella, and together they have four grown children.

Gene Edward Veith Jr. (PhD, University of Kansas) is a writer and a retired literature professor. He is Provost Emeritus at Patrick Henry College and the Director of the Cranach Institute at Concordia Theological Seminary in Ft. Wayne, Indiana. He has taught at Northeastern Oklahoma A&M College and was a Visiting Professor at Wheaton College, Gordon College, and Regent College (Vancouver). He was also a Visiting Lecturer at the Estonian Institute of Humanities in Tallinn, Estonia. He previously served as Culture Editor of *World Magazine* and Professor of English and Dean of the School of Arts & Sciences at Concordia University Wisconsin. He is the author of over 20 books, including *Postmodern Times: A Christian Guide to Contemporary Thought and Culture*, *The Spirituality of the Cross: The Way of the First Evangelicals*, *Classical Education*, and *God at Work: Your Christian Vocation in All of Life*. He and his wife Jackquelyn have three grown children and eleven grandchildren.

Paul Washer (MDiv, Southwestern Baptist Theological Seminary) became a believer while studying at the University of Texas. After graduating, he moved to Peru and served there as a missionary for ten years, during which time he founded the HeartCry Missionary Society in order to support Peruvian church planters. HeartCry's work now supports indigenous missionaries throughout Africa, Asia, Europe, the Middle East, Eurasia, North America, and Latin America. Paul now serves as one of the laborers with the HeartCry Missionary Society. He and his wife Charo have four children and live in Redford, Virginia.

James White (ThD, DMin, Columbia Evangelical Seminary) is the director of Alpha and Omega Ministries, a professor, and theologian. He is a graduate of Fuller Theological Seminary and Columbia Evangelical Seminary, and is currently in the PhD program at Northwest University in Potchefstroom, South Africa under well-known textual critical scholar Dr. Jorrie Jordaan. His Th.D. in Apologetics focused upon the biblical doctrine of the Trinity, and the resultant book, *The Forgotten Trinity*, has been used as a textbook in English speaking schools across the US and England. He has authored more than twenty books, including *The King James Only Controversy*, *The Roman Catholic Controversy*, *Scripture Alone*, and *What Every Christian Needs to Know About the Qur'an*. He is a professor, having taught Greek, Greek Exegesis, Hebrew, Systematic Theology, Church History, and many topics in apologetics at schools in the United States, Germany, Switzerland, Ukraine, and South Africa. He has engaged in more than 150 moderated, public debates with leading proponents of Roman Catholicism, Islam, Mormonism, and Oneness Pentecostalism. He has debated leading critics of Christianity such as Bart Ehrman, John Dominic Crossan, Shabir Ally, and others. He is an elder of the Phoenix Reformed Baptist Church. He has been married for thirty-five years to his wife Kelli, has two children, and two wonderful grandchildren.

Steve Wilkins (MDiv, Reformed Theological Seminary, Jackson, Mississippi) holds a Bachelor of Science degree in Pre-Law from the University of Alabama. He has been an ordained minister in the Presbyterian Church in America (PCA) since 1976. He has served as the pastor of Auburn Avenue Presbyterian Church of Monroe, Louisiana since 1989. Pastor Wilkins is the author of *Face to Face: Meditations on Friendship & Hospitality*; *Call of Duty: The Sterling Nobility of Robert E. Lee*, & most recently *All Things for Good: The Steadfast Fidelity of Stonewall Jackson*.

G. I. Williamson (BD, Pittsburgh-Xenia Theological Seminary) received his BA degree from Drake University in Des Moines, Iowa, and his BD degree from the Pittsburgh-Xenia Theological Seminary in Pennsylvania. He has served congregations of the old United Presbyterian Church of North America, the Associate Reformed Presbyterian Church, and the Reformed Presbyterian Church of North America, but most of his ministerial labors have been with the Reformed Churches of New Zealand and the Orthodox Presbyterian Church, in which he continues to serve. He is author of popular study guides to the Westminster Confession of Faith, the Shorter Catechism, and the Heidelberg Catechism. For fourteen years he served as editor of *Ordained Servant*, a journal for church officers. All together he has been in pastoral ministry for sixty-five years. He and his wife, Doris, have been married for seventy-three years and had three daughters (oldest died in 2001 as a victim of cancer), fifteen grandchildren, twenty-five great-grandchildren, and one great-great-grandchild.

Frank Wright (PhD, Florida Atlantic University) serves as President & Chief Executive Officer of Coral Ridge Ministries Media. Dr. Wright's prior leadership service includes serving as President & Chief Operating Officer of the Salem Media Group, President & Chief Executive Officer of the National Religious Broadcasters, and being founding Executive Director of the D. James Kennedy Center for Christian Statesmanship. Dr. Wright received his PhD in Finance from Florida Atlantic University. He and his bride Ruth have been married thirty-seven years, and they have three adult children. They reside in Palm Beach County, Florida.

Introduction

The Twenty-First-Century Reformation

The Tale of Two Churches:
The Sixteenth and Twenty-First Centuries

"It was the best of times, it was the worst of times." These are very familiar words from Charles Dickens's opening line of *A Tale of Two Cities*, but I want to tell a Tale of Two Churches: The Sixteenth and the Twenty-First-Century Churches. This opening line from Dickens is likewise apropos historically with relation to the church of the sixteenth century, and just as applicable to the church of the twenty-first century. Here we stand in an extraordinarily unique place in the grand historical continuum five hundred years after the Protestant Reformation of the sixteenth century. The day of October 31, 1517, which we mark as the starting point of the Reformation, was very subtle and not drastically eventful in and of itself. A former humble monk and local professor of Divinity named Martin Luther posted ninety-five thesis statements on the door of Wittenberg Castle Church as an open invitation to his colleagues to discuss some of the concerns that he had with regard to the misuse and abuse of papal indulgences and authority. What resulted was a politico-religious firestorm, from the ashes of which arose the true church recommitting herself to biblically-founded, Christ-centered, gospel-truth; unadulterated by manmade traditions, ideas, and practices.

The primary scope of this twenty-first-century reformation must likewise be a return to the Bible as the Word of God, which, as such, must be properly given the highest place in all of intellectual, practical, familial, professional, and devotional life, not just resigned to religious life within the four walls of a church building once a week. While the Protestant Church of the Reformation spelled out the Five Solae (*Scriptura, Fide, Gratia, Christi, Deo Gloria*), the contemporary Evangelical Church will be doing well if she

1

can once again regain her heritage in *Sola Scriptura*. If we can get this one right, the rest should naturally fall right back into their proper places. After all, we have plenty of theologically sound teachings on all our biblical doctrines, but what we lack is the church's devotion and submission to the Bible as the unparalleled, unequaled, matchless, incomparable authority of faith and practice, and life and godliness.

With that clearly stated, we have to own up to a greater culpability laid at the feet of the Twenty-First-Century Church than we could possibly ascribe to the church of the sixteenth century—as well as the earlier centuries. People suffered atrocities at the hand of the Roman Catholic Church for one main reason: the Bible was kept out of the hands and out of the tongue of the common man. Rome was able to spread her lies and manipulation because the commoner was unable to be a noble Berean; they could not search the Scriptures to see if its teaching was truly aligned with the Word of God. They were unmercifully subject to unbiblical doctrines and practices by the very same clergy who supposedly represented such truths and promoted such things in the name of God. Unbiblical distortions in both doctrine and practice spun wildly out of control and beyond the sphere of orthodoxy and orthopraxy.

So, in contrast to those who had no vernacular Bible available to them in the sixteenth century, what excuse do we offer for our sad state of affairs when the average Evangelical family has numerous copies of the Bible in a variety of translations, and even mediums, laying around and yet the Bible is not treated as if it has the preeminence of directing all of life? Admittedly, we have no excuse whatsoever. We have far less excuse to offer for our unbiblical worldview and sloppy practices than the poor pre-sixteenth century Christians who had not the Sword of the Spirit, the Word of God, available to them for consultation, direction, appeal, or authority.

Mark Twain once said, "Those who don't read have no advantage over those who can't." This is, of course, a true sentiment when it comes to advantage, but what we are dealing with here is responsibility and culpability. Prior to the introduction of vernacular translations of the Bible during the Reformation, the Medieval Church laity could not read the Bible; the contemporary church of the twenty-first century can read the Bible, but chooses not to, or at least chooses not to apply it universally to all of life and to all godliness. We rightfully fall under the criticism that James lays against those who go away, forgetting their appearance after staring intently at themselves in the mirror (1:22–24). We have gazed into the Word of God but have gone away, forgetting its rightful place of dominance, only to breathe in the air of the ever-pervasive secular nonsense that surrounds us. We have taken for granted what our forefathers in the faith fought and died for. At least in this respect, we need a reformation far more than we did five hundred years ago.

The light of Scripture was eclipsed by the darkness of the Medieval Church. To be sure, God's Word was present as the eternal light and had all the potential energy it always had, but the clergy considered themselves the sole inheritors of biblical authority while the real "Catholic Church"—the universal church of men, women, and children—was kept in the shadows cast by the clergy who stood between the people of God and the Word of God. My brothers, these things ought not to be. The Reformation mantra of *post tenebras lux*—after darkness, light—is a cliché that we think so clearly applies to *that* time and to *their* conditions, but we are so darkened that we can't see that we too are needing the light of Scripture to burst forth like the sun burning through and away the haze of our day. But this time it is not necessarily the clergy who cast the shadow now but antinomianism, pluralism, private and personal pietism, unbiblical psychology, man-centered entertainment-style worship services, political correctness, secularism, pragmatism, feminism, aggressive cultural appropriation, crass and covetous materialism, pseudo-social and pseudo-scientific evolution, postmodern relativity of truth, indiscriminate tolerance, etc. It is not the laity under the shadow but the entire church, clergy, and laity alike. We have breathed in the air of our destructive and godless culture without spiritual discernment, and we are wheezing from a lack of clean air. Both churches of the sixteenth and the twenty-first centuries are in darkness and the only cure is the light and life of Scripture.

Why This Book? What Has Happened to Evangelicalism?

The answers to the first question are actually quite simple. The first reason for this book is to commemorate and celebrate the ninety-five theses posted by Martin Luther five-hundred years ago. Such an event should be meaningful to all Protestants, and especially to Evangelicals who honestly appreciate God's movement through these Reformers, and to those who still hold a semblance of continuity to that Reformation.

The second reason is even simpler than the first: it is because the Evangelical Church today desperately needs her own reformation. By God's providence, these two events coincide—and collide. I pray that God will use the commemoration and historical interest in the Sixteenth-Century Reformation as a springboard to reviving and reforming the church of today. As the retreat to the Bible was the impetus for the revival and reformation then, let us pray the rediscovery of its wisdom for all of life will awaken the church for revival and reformation now.

So what has happened to the Evangelical Church that she is in such serious need of reform? That question is at the very heart of this book. If we see the problems of the Twenty-First-Century Church, we must address it for the sake of our Lord, Savior, King, Shepherd, and Head. If a simple answer to this complicated question were to be offered, it would boil down to the importation of surrounding secularism and its corresponding godless culture in nearly every corner of the church life. This includes simple but slippery slopes such as the belief in the basic goodness of man, and a democratized version of God and the gospel, and an anthropocentric approach to worship. The Bible—though not in theory in the Evangelical Church, but in practice—ceases to be the final authority in all matters of life and godliness, faith and practice, and to every square inch of the church's life. For some inane reason we have allowed the Bible to have unwarranted and unworthy competition. The church has lost her identity as "People of the Book," her dependence upon God's Word as her supreme manual, which leads to her loss of direction in living as salt and light in this world, and consequently her voice in creating and living out a truly biblically-conformed Christian culture, and finally as having a valid witness to the exalted Christ of the Living God. And what happens to salt after it has lost its saltiness? Jesus states with clarity that the good-for-nothing stuff is to be thrown out and be trampled underfoot (Matt 5:13).

Why is the Evangelical Church the Target Audience of These Theses?

Several times already I have delimited the target audience as being the Evangelical Church. Now, if I believe that the world at large needs repentance, and the universal church as a whole needs reformation, then why would I direct these theses only to the Evangelical Church? There are several reasons for this. Simply stated, "For it is time for judgment to begin at the household of God" (1 Pet 4:17). As opposed to the world as well as mainline and liberal Protestant churches, the Evangelical Church still believes in the Bible, and that the Bible is the Word of God, and that it has final authority in faith and practice. The problem with the world is that it fights against God and the gospel, and neither do they have the spiritual capacity to comprehend the meaning of the Bible. The problem with the mainline and liberal Protestant churches is that they do not properly hold the high status of the Bible; hence, I have nothing with which to appeal to them as a common ultimate authority. If a church or Christian does not already appeal to the Bible as the final authority—or at least in theory—there is little hope that any of these proposals will be convincing; but then again, the Holy Spirit works in the stoniest of hearts beyond our wildest imaginations.

Even if the Evangelical Church has neglected—though not rejected—the Bible as her final authority, and if she were to be confronted by exposing inadvertent secular imports vis-à-vis the eternal truth of God's Word, optimistically and prayerfully she will submit to the Word. If an "Evangelical" church does not submit to the clarity and conviction of the Word, by definition this church is not Evangelical.

In reviewing the history of the Reformation, Martin Luther had no initial intention—nor even the imagination—to break away from the Roman Catholic Church. He saw a need for internal reform of the universal church of Christ, and thus he felt the godly conviction to address the issues of his day. Of course, what consequently happened was the Protestant Church sprang forth from the Roman Catholic establishment because Rome refused to accept biblical criticism and to reform accordingly. The Protestant Church emerged from the dust as the true inheritor of biblically defined, Christ-centered, gospel-truth.

This leads naturally to the next question: will this new reformation also result in a similar break from the Evangelical Church? Like Martin Luther, we don't foresee it; we don't desire it; and we certainly don't intend for its occurrence. But unlike Luther, sadly, we can imagine it. Either those "Evangelicals" who continue to drift from conformity to the Word will have to leave Evangelicalism (as many already have), or if the majority of "Evangelicals" refuse to conform to the Word, they may expel the true Evangelicals, who will consequently emerge from the dust with a new label. Despite any novelty in label, to be sure, these twenty-first-century People of the Book will truly inherit their ancestors' deeper identity, and will retain fidelity with the Puritans of the colonial age, with the Reformers of five centuries past, and with all the Biblicists of the Middle Ages, and with Fathers of the Patristic Age, and with the Early Church two millennia ago, and with the whole people of God of all ages.

If the contemporary so-called Evangelical wing will not return to the authority of Scripture as the standard of faith and practice, to its belief in its sufficiency, to its interpretive principle of perspicuity, to its right to speak as the very voice of its Divine Author, then we also will witness a similar fracture. If Evangelicalism will continue its current path of betrayal of its own roots, the true Evangelical will be forced to bail out of this hijacked ship and chart their course properly where the nominal Evangelical movement has degenerately veered.

Our hope and prayer is that this book will help avoid this fracture and that the whole of Evangelicalism will find a course redirection, all for the sake of Christ and the purity of his Bride. So, let us be clear, unity of God's people in Christ's Church in joint obedience to Christ's directives (John 15) is the goal simply because it is the will of Christ, as seen in his Highly Priestly Prayer (John 17:21–23). And we must remember that Christ the Master Harvester will sort out the wheat from the weeds (Matt 13:30); Jesus the Good Shepherd will separate the sheep from the goats (Matt 25:32) according to his will, in his time, and by his ordained means. We pray that this book will be a means of revival, reform, purity, and unity in the Body of Christ. And if this book is divinely used for the purposes of separating wheat from weeds and sheep from goats, *soli Deo gloria*, to God alone be the glory.

To go further and more specifically, the individual target audiences are the leaders within Evangelicalism. By the term 'leaders' I do not intend to limit the audience to pastors, elders or deacons, or to the vast array of ministerial positions and titles available in the context of contemporary church ministry, or even parachurch entrepreneurs. No, a leader is one who will stand up for the reformational cause and inspire others to follow in the efforts. The priesthood of all believers will play out its powerful and important role. So while this will undoubtedly include official church leaders, it will also inevitably include lay leaders, who may be the very ones to spur their own official church leaders into the heart and action of this new reformation.

If we were to nail these ninety-five theses to the church door of today, they would not be nailed to the doors of the predominant Roman Catholic Church but on the Evangelical churches' doors on every corner of town. Yes, we are guilty in so many respects and in desperate need of reformation.

Why These Particular Ninety-Five Theses?

True enough, the contemporary Evangelical Church is in need of reform in no less than ninety-five ways. Of course, the precedent is clearly laid out in Martin Luther's ninety-five thesis statements nailed to the Wittenberg Castle Church on October 31, 1517, and in keeping with this precedent upon the five-hundredth anniversary of this monumental document, we feel it appropriate to keep the tradition of the precedent by limiting our theses to ninety-five as well. These particular ninety-five theses have been chosen for several reasons: 1) they are prioritized by the Bible, not by our modern senses of pragmatism; 2) they can be implemented across the Evangelical spectrum without being unnecessarily divisive; and 3) they touch upon a wide spectrum of the whole Christian life, with respective points needing a recalibration and re-centering on the Word of God.

Without a doubt there will be readers who may adamantly proclaim that we have forgotten something/s; and they are probably correct. All that goes to show is that such readers are ripe for this revival and reformation. If a particular area needs addressing, let the reader address it, and then let the rest of us know about it that we might practice the noble Berean exercise of testing it with the Scriptures. We are not claiming to present an exhaustive list; just ninety-five points that, if implemented, will lead to a wider-spread reformation for our Twenty-First-Century Church.

Perhaps there are other readers who may claim that their respective churches are aligned already. We do not doubt the possibility of that scenario either; so we pray that this book serves as a word of encouragement and affirmation. We hope and pray that every reader of these theses will have something to take away and implement toward reformation. Some may need to apply only one thesis, while others may need to read, think, and pray about the implementation of all ninety-five theses. For the latter, the task may seem overwhelming, but we are confident that the Holy Spirit will give the necessary strength and grace for the sake of the health of Christ's Bride.

To be honest, not all present contributors of these ninety-five theses may be in agreement with each other as to the importance, placement, or implementation of each thesis. And to be sure, not all Reformers of the sixteenth century were in agreement with each other either. But the one commonality we all share is that we must appeal to and make reformational efforts according to the dictates of Scripture. Of course, we do not just believe in *reformata*, that we stand in a reformed heritage, but we humbly admit that we need to be *semper reformanda*, always in need of and striving for further reformation, or better stated, biblical conformity.

The Face of the New Reformation

Let us firstly take a look at the truth and myth of *semper reformanda* lest we misapply constant reformational efforts in areas that may derail us from the prime objective. It is a myth that the church *reformata* (reformed) should always be in a state of reforming for the sake of reforming. No, the truth is that the Reformed Church needs to be constantly reforming where there is deformity, where there is lack of conformity to the Word of God. In other words, change for the sake of change is neither a lofty ambition nor a noble cause; as if the church would always be moving but going nowhere toward the goal of being a spotless Bride. Being progressive is no progression unless it is true spiritual sanctification. Change that comes as a result of repentance, after looking into the mirror of God's Word and being found wanting to the conformity to Christ and the Word is our humble aspiration. Again, we desire true change that emanates from the Holy Spirit, not the change reflecting the passing whims of man that will shift endlessly, vacuously, and pointlessly with no real fruit in the end.

We do not think too many critically thinking Christian leaders will deny that the church is in desperate need of a reformation, and of course, there are a few of us who are optimistically anticipating such a revival and reformation in our lifetime, and soon. Let me first make a distinction between revival and reformation in order to clarify the vocabulary as it will be used hereafter. Revival is a gift from God, who sends his Spirit to kindle the hearts of his people, who then, in turn, pray for more revival and a further opening of hearts of more of God's people. In this sense, revival is monergistic, a work of God alone. Then as revival grows, our only proper response is that we look into the mirror of God's Word and we clearly recognize our theological, cultural, ecclesiastical, familial, and personal shortcomings; and our only consequential response ought to be reformation. In this sense, reformation is synergistic, the proper response of God's people with the empowerment of God himself.

The very fact that these contributors—and thousands of others—are seeking and working toward the reformation of the church today is not coincidental, nor is it just a signpost pointing to a coming reformation, but more deeply it is an insight into the heart of God, who is the source of any and all revival in his people to inspire their God-given desire for reformation. This reformation is not man's initiative to purify the church according to the Bible, as it might appear on the surface; it is, rather, man's response to God's call of revival in purifying the church according to God's Word.

This distinction is important; when we confuse and reverse the roles of God and man—as often seen in our modern theology—we are not only left with theological bankruptcy, but more dangerously, we have robbed God of the glory due him and him alone. God must be recognized as preeminent to all holy efforts; man can only respond in obedience or disobedience, but cannot himself force God to respond to man. God alone is the source of all revival and reformation, but by all means are we to respond obediently, promptly, fervently, joyfully, and with the greatest anticipation and excitement to see what the Lord Almighty has prepared for those who love him. Let the church pray with John Calvin, "We offer you our hearts, O Lord, promptly and sincerely."

I speak now not as a prognosticator of the coming reformation but as one who has a simple inkling how this modern reformation will take hold and spread. With the advent of the five-hundredth anniversary of the Protestant Reformation, most Protestants, and especially Evangelicals, will at least give a cursory glance at the history of Reformation; and the more we promote it, the more interest will be built, the greater potential the anniversary will avail the desired effect. We believe that as the Evangelical Church comes to realize that this radical time in history was spawned as a result of believing the Bible, and only the Bible, to be the authoritative Word of God, that the church too will be reinforced in this conviction with more than mere intellectual assent. Hopefully she will rediscover the very same passion as Martin Luther, who so poignantly stated at the Diet of Worms, "Unless I can be convinced by the Word of God . . . " The church must return to the simple truth as stated by the Reformers, "The Bible alone is the Word of God." We do not deny either the natural emotional response of revival; that we, like John Wesley, will have "hearts strangely warmed" by the Word of God.

The main thrust is that we must return to the primacy of Scripture. With renewed commitments to the Word of God, the interest in the message of the Bible will be the catalyst to the reformation's full fruition; and really, any true reformation can boast the same impetus. Evangelical academics, pastors, and laymen alike will dig deeper into Scripture to find its meaning and applications for the universal church, for the local church, for the family, and for the individual, and for culture to all the ends of the earth.

We must return to a reformational approach to Scripture that refuses to bifurcate the Bible into its devotional use on one hand, and its academic investigation on the other. No, we concurrently need to treat the Bible as a treasure trove of intellectual wisdom and truth, as the practical guide to godly living, as a thrilling narrative of the drama of redemption, as a poetic expression of all human experience and conditions in light of the Living God, as manual of constructing a God-honoring culture, as a textbook of theological doctrine, and as a book of covenantal promises that are being kept and renewed every day. How can we possibly live without such a resource? We can't, that's why God gave it to us. But to our shame we must ask, with such a source granted to us by God himself, how dare we neglect to read it?! God himself declares, "so shall my word be that goes out from my mouth; it shall not return to me empty, but it shall accomplish that which I purpose, and shall succeed in the thing for which I sent it" (Isa 55:11).

The Reformation of the sixteenth century was not easy, nor will this reformation of the twenty-first century be easy. By comparison the obstacles and challenges to these reformations are radically different, but the solution remains the same: God working through his active and living Word toward revival, and the church submitting and reforming accordingly.

Why Contributions From These Particular
Authors, Church Leaders, Theologians?

Putting a proverbial finger on the pulse of the Evangelical Church will sadly reveal that such an indication of spiritual life is hard to find. Her life is, on one hand, flourishing in church membership numbers and new plants far above the declining mainline churches. On the other hand, we see our own demise and internal decay. Our "Christian" culture is silent at best; comfortably conformed to secularism in the bad cases, and reflecting and even adopting pagan beliefs and practices in the worst cases.

These contributing scholars and church leaders indeed actually have their proverbial fingers on the pulse of the church. They articulate their diagnoses, they reveal their prognoses if her condition is not addressed, and most importantly, they prescribe a full biblical dosage for her cure and restoration. In all cases for all these contributors, the cure begins with the antidote against all worldliness and spiritual disease, that is, the Bible as the Word of God and the final authority in all life and godliness. Here are the voices of our contemporary prophets, who speak the Word of God into the culture, and tell the dry bones of the church to "hear the word of the LORD" (Ezek 37:4). Let us all covenant to pray that the Lord will breathe his Spirit in us to enliven us that we should know the Lord and trust his glorious declarations. *Soli Deo gloria!!!*

SPHERE I

Reforming the Church

These ninety-five theses are divided into three spheres: reforming the church, reforming the family, and reforming the culture. Some topics clearly fall into one category or another, but there are also many topics that have blurry lines and resist clear categorization. Reforming the church naturally aids the reformation of the family, and reforming the family reforms the church, while the reformation of both the family and church is going to bring reformation to the Christian culture, which aids the reformation of the culture at large. Of course, we need the sanctifying work of the Holy Spirit on all levels, so that the Bride of Christ will be holy and without blemish, cleansed with the washing of the water of the Word (Eph 5:26–27).

The necessity to reform the church was the impetus of the Protestant Reformation five hundred years ago, and as we celebrate this five-hundredth anniversary, we too put our primary attention on the reformation of the church. We inherited a mature understanding of the church without being unnecessarily complicated. The three qualities of a true church are the preaching of the Word, especially in the purity of the gospel; the proper administration of the two sacraments, biblically prescribed as baptism and communion; and the proper exercise of church discipline, following the wisdom of biblical order. Of course, not all true churches are equally pure in being a true church. What we strive for in this reformation is not only being a true church, but being a true church in the purest expression possible. And who is the judge of such purity? Again and again emphatically, the final authority and judge of such things is the Word of God, the revealed counsel, wisdom and will of God himself.

This sphere will deal with all things that are directly related to the lifeblood of the church as the Body and Bride of Christ. We cannot help but start where we ought to start: the Bible as the final authority of faith and practice and of life and godliness, and from there we branch out into other avenues under the light of Scripture. We must submit to Scripture as it informs us how to worship, what to believe, how to defend our beliefs, how to structure church, and how we take all thoughts captive to the obedience of Christ.

The emphases of this section are on the beliefs of the church, which is critically important as foundational and fundamental to our knowledge of the faith. However, by no means should we say that proper belief is enough. Indeed, we must do well at looking into the mirror of God's Word but we must also go our way and put into action the very thing that we have come to know (Jas 1:22–24). Our intellects must inform our volitions. For the Bible believer—who must also be a Bible doer—truth is not something we merely know, but something we purposefully do (John 3:21). Christ-like integrity is defined as consistency and unity between knowledge, belief, and actions; anything less than an integral approach to belief and action is sheer hypocrisy (Matt 23:3).

1. Let the Church Read Scripture as the Very Voice of God

By faith we understand that the universe was created by the word of God,
so that what is seen was not made out of things that are visible.

—HEBREWS 11:3

In church history every great reformation of the church has been a new recognition of divinity. God has been leading the church, over and over, to a deeper recognition of himself. In the fourth century, the church came to a clearer understanding that the Son of God, Jesus Christ, was nothing less than God himself, the second person of the Trinity. In the sixteenth century, God showed the church that salvation was a *divine* work, pure grace received by faith alone, not a combined effort of God and man. As God's Son is God, so salvation is God saving us. A divine Son, a divine work.

A twenty-first-century reformation, I believe, will also be a recognition of divinity, focusing on the Scriptures. As Jesus is God's Son and salvation is God's work, so Scripture is God speaking. In a sense, this has always been the conviction of the church, but the church has sometimes compromised this understanding. In the early centuries, Christian philosophers and theologians have sometimes compromised the authority of Scripture. They sometimes tried to make Scripture conform to pagan philosophies and have sometimes made it subordinate to supposedly rational schemes.

But Scripture itself rejects such compromise. According to 2 Timothy 3:15–17, Scripture is the very breath of God, that is, God's actual speaking to us. God told Joshua, therefore, that he should do according to *all* that is written in the law (Josh 1:8). The Gospel of John (1:1) identifies Jesus as the Word of God and the Word of God with God himself: "In the beginning was the word, and the word was with God, and the word was God." So it is impossible to separate God's Word, wherever it is found, from God himself.

To encounter the Word is to encounter God. And when you despise the Word, you despise God as well.

But the church has often made the mistake of giving little honor to the written Word, while trying to give much honor to God. Many have said that Scripture is only the word of human authors (perhaps with some vague kind of divine influence) and that their writing is full of errors. That has led to movements that have denied the authority of Scripture entirely and therefore have greatly distorted the doctrines of the faith. If this error continues unopposed, little of the gospel will remain. For the gospel is nothing if it is not the promise of God himself. It is itself the Word of God; God coming to us to tell us our need and the wonderful work of Christ to supply that need. If the gospel is only a human theory, it is of little worth, and there is no reason for us to embrace it.

But if there is a reformation in the doctrine of Scripture, people will again receive the good news of Christ with assurance and joy. If the gospel is just human thoughts, it is dispensable. But if it is really God speaking to us, then it is momentous, a matter of life and death.

A twenty-first century reformation should seek to teach, through the pulpit, the Sunday schools, theologies, and seminaries that the Scriptures are nothing less than God himself speaking to us. As the fourth century learned afresh that Jesus is fully God, and the sixteenth that the work of salvation is fully a divine work, so we today must learn that the Bible is fully God's Word: not only a collection of human words, not only a collection of human words that happen to be true, but God's own speech to us.

—JOHN M. FRAME

2. Let The Church Believe and Practice the Doctrine of the Sufficiency of Scripture

Man shall not live by bread alone,
but by every word that comes from the mouth of God.

—MATTHEW 4:4

H ere is our thesis simply stated: Scripture's authority cannot be augmented or its efficacy enhanced in any way by blending biblical with human wisdom, worldly stratagems, fresh revelations, scientific discoveries, or any other addendum or innovation.

The Bible alone is the written Word of God—eternal, authoritative, and infallible, containing everything necessary for the salvation of sinners and their growth in grace. It is sufficiently clear in all that it teaches, true and trustworthy in every part, and without defect or deficiency of any kind. It is "living and active, sharper than any two-edged sword . . . discerning the thoughts and intentions of the heart" (Heb 4:12). It is the final judge of all truth-claims and the primary instrument through which the Holy Spirit enlightens our minds. In short, Scripture speaks with God's own authority and is the Christian's only infallible rule of faith, practice, and doctrine.

That's what is meant by the expression *Sola Scriptura,* sometimes referred to as the formal principle of the Protestant Reformation. In other words, this view of the Bible was the essential bedrock conviction that provided a firm foundation for the Protestant Reformation. All the other *solas* are rooted in *sola Scriptura,* because Scripture is where we are taught that redemption is not something we earn or deserve, but our justification before God is by grace alone *(sola gratia)* through faith alone *(sola fide)* in Christ alone *(solus Christus),* solely for God's glory *(soli Deo gloria).* Moreover, the authority of Scripture is where the Reformers found both the reason and the courage to stand against the self-appointed jurisdiction and spiritual tyranny of popes and councils and their religious traditions. The Reformers' stance was the same as the Apostles: "We must obey God rather than men" (Acts 5:29).

Notice: the Bible's authority is the ultimate, but not the only point. *Sola Scriptura* embraces and affirms the inerrancy, perspicuity, and sufficiency of Scripture as well. More precisely, all of those are essential features of the Bible's authority. But all of them are being subtly undermined by the drift of the Evangelical movement in our generation.

For more than a century, religious leaders captivated by modernist and rationalist skepticism have relentlessly caviled at the *inerrancy* of Scripture. More recently, the *perspicuity* of Scripture—the historic Protestant conviction that the Bible is sufficiently clear and understandable—has been questioned and attacked by people enthralled with the postmodern notion that meaning is always elusive and truth is just a matter of personal perspective.

But perhaps the most subtle and sinister attack on the Bible has been the casual denial (by modernists and postmodernists alike) of Scripture's *sufficiency.* Even most Christians no longer seem truly confident that the Bible alone is a fully sufficient resource for any soul seeking to know God, glorify Him, and pursue His will. This erosion of confidence in the sufficiency of Scripture is seen in countless ways in the mainstream of the Evangelical movement.

We see it, for example, in the widespread belief that secular psychology offers a remedy for human woes that is more potent and more reliable than Scripture. It is evident in the way managers, entrepreneurs, comedians, and showmen are seen as more effective models for church leadership than the pastor who faithfully, consistently preaches the Word. It is especially manifest in the quest for fresh revelations, personal prophecies, ecstatic experiences, and other charismatic novelties that supersede and supplant the authority of Scripture.

Quite simply: vast numbers who profess faith in Christ today do not really believe the truth contained in Scripture is sufficient to meet all our spiritual needs. That failure to affirm and defend the sufficiency of Scripture is a recipe for apostasy.

To deny the Bible's sufficiency is to subvert its authority—while opening the door for all kinds of alternative opinions and phony revelations. That in turn breeds confusion and chaos—precisely the kind of spiritual and doctrinal commotion that currently dominates the broad Evangelical movement.

As Paul reminded Timothy, "All Scripture is breathed out by God and profitable for teaching, for reproof, for correction, and for training in righteousness, that the man of God may be competent, equipped for every good work" (2 Tim 3:16–17). There is no need for us "to go beyond what is written" (1 Cor 4:6). Scripture is perfect, sure, right, pure, clean, true, and righteous altogether—adequate for every spiritual need we face, from the conversion of the soul to our perfection in glory (Ps 19:7–9). And as the hymn *How Firm a Foundation* says, "What More Can He Say Than To You He Hath Said?"

We must get back to the principle of *sola Scriptura,* and reaffirm the historic Protestant belief in the Bible's sufficiency. Until such time as that happens, the church will continue in its current backslidden, directionless, weakened state of disarray and feebleness.

—JOHN MACARTHUR

3. Let the Church Hold Fast to the Biblical Doctrines of Christ

For there is one God, and there is one mediator between God and men, the man Christ Jesus.

—1 TIMOTHY 2:5

Let the church stand in awe of the deep and abiding truths mined from the depths of scriptural reflection, dispute, and debate, which illuminate and define the God-man, the Incarnate Son of God, Yahweh in human flesh, Jesus "our great God and Savior" (Titus 2:13). The church can never be ashamed of the amazing claim we make: God of God, Light of Light, true God of true God . . . consubstantial with the Father" (Nicene Creed). The one who was in the beginning (John 1:1), Lord and God (John 20:28), entered into His own creation (John 1:14, Phil 2:6–7). This amazing declaration is at the center of all of Christian proclamation, piety, practice and thought. As soon as the church begins to draw back from the highest affirmation of the fact that the true man, the Son of Mary, was, at the same time, in truth and not just in the imagination, the same One seen by Isaiah upon the throne of heaven (Isa 6:1, John 12:41), the tightly and divinely woven fabric of Christian truth begins to fray and disintegrate.

Every element of the Christian faith is either elevated by the acceptance of the deity of Christ, or debilitated by its denial. Our proclamation begins with "Jesus Christ is Lord!" This is the essence of the Christian confession (1 Cor 12:3). But this is true of all of creation only if He was truly the Son of God who rules the nations with a rod of iron (Rev 19:15). A mere prophet, or elevated moral teacher, cannot suffice for the Christian faith. The One by whom righteous judgment will be given (Acts 17:31) must be able to fulfill His role to perfection, and only the God-Man can do so.

Consider the centrality of the deity of the Messiah to His mission at Calvary. The cross is the very center-point of history, the focus of the expression of the love of God. But what mere man could accomplish what Jesus did on the tree? To whom could the entire elect of God be joined, so that His death is their death, and His resurrection their resurrection? Who could live a perfect life, fulfilling all of God's holy law each and every day, and then give Himself voluntarily, having the authority to lay down His life and take it back up (John 10:17), so that the righteousness that would be imputed by faith to those who believe in Him would be full and complete? If we do not have a divine Savior, we have no divine gospel, no divine redemption. But if Jesus is truly the "Lord of glory," a phrase in context speaking of both His divinity and His humanity (1 Cor 2:8), we have full confidence in His ability to fulfill His role not only as sacrifice, but as mediator, intercessor, and finisher of our faith. When Jesus tells us that the Father's will for Him is to save completely all those who are given to Him (John 6:39), we can have full confidence in His ability to fulfill the Father's will, and hence we can truly have peace with God.

Believing that the God of the universe invaded His own creation in the person of an itinerant preacher in the backwaters of the Roman Empire two millennia ago will not win us a seat at the table of mankind's sages and philosophers. But the gospel that changes hearts and minds remains divine only because the One who accomplishes it is divine in the fullest sense. As the church faces hostile rejection, especially in secular cultures, the temptation to draw back in the affirmation of this central truth will be great. Let the church realize the cost of such defection, and trust the Spirit of God to make the message that is foolishness to those perishing the very wisdom of God to those being saved (1 Cor 1:18).

—James White

4. Let the Church Hold Fast to the Gospel in Purity, Power, and Clarity

For I am not ashamed of the gospel, for it is the power of God for salvation to everyone who believes, to the Jew first and also to the Greek.

—ROMANS 1:16

The gospel is the greatest treasure given to the church and is the power of God for salvation (Rom 1:16). For this reason the Apostle Paul gave the gospel the "first place" in his preaching, endeavored with all his might to proclaim it clearly, and even went so far as to pronounce a curse upon all those who would pervert its truth (1 Cor 15:3; Col 4:4; Gal 1:8–9).

Each generation of Christians is a steward of the gospel and is called to guard through the Holy Spirit this treasure that has been entrusted to it (2 Tim 1:14). If we are to be faithful stewards, we must be absorbed in the study of the gospel, take great pains to understand its truths (1 Tim 4:15), and pledge ourselves to guard its contents. In doing so, we will ensure salvation for ourselves and for those who hear us (1 Tim 4:16).

The greatest crime of this generation is its neglect of the gospel, and it is from this neglect that all our other maladies spring forth. The lost world is not so much *gospel hardened* as it is *gospel ignorant*. Absent from too many pulpits are the essential themes which make up the very core of the gospel— the justice of God, the radical depravity of man, the blood atonement, the nature of true conversion, and the biblical basis of assurance. In many cases, the gospel has been reduced to a few creedal statements, conversion has become a mere human decision, and assurance of salvation is pronounced over anyone who prays "the sinner's prayer." The result of this "gospel reductionism" is far-reaching in several ways.

Firstly, it hardens the unconverted. Few modern-day "converts" ever make their way into the fellowship of the church, and those who do often fall away or are marked by habitual carnality. Untold millions walk our streets and even sit in our pews unchanged, but are nevertheless convinced of their salvation because one time they repeated a prayer or raised their hand at an evangelistic campaign.

Secondly, such a gospel deforms the church from a spiritual body of regenerated believers into a gathering of carnal men who profess to know God but by their deeds deny Him (Titus 1:16). When the true gospel is preached, men are drawn to the church because they desire Christ and are hungry for biblical truth, heartfelt worship, and opportunities for service. When a lesser gospel is proclaimed, the church fills up with carnal men who share little interest in the things of God (1 Cor 2:14). The radical demands of the gospel must then be toned down to a more convenient morality, true devotion to Christ must give way to activities designed to meet the "felt needs" of members, and truth must be carefully filtered or repackaged so as not to offend the carnal majority.

Thirdly, such a gospel reduces evangelism to a humanistic endeavor— driven by clever marketing strategies and based on a careful study of the latest trends in culture. Many Evangelicals seem convinced that man has somehow become too complex a creature to be saved and transformed by such a simple and scandalous message as the biblical gospel. More emphasis is now given to understanding our fallen culture and its passing fads than to understanding and proclaiming the only message that has the power to save it!

Finally, such a gospel brings reproach to the name of God. Through the proclamation of a lesser gospel, the unconverted are brought into the church; and through the almost total neglect of biblical church discipline, they are allowed to stay without correction. Thus is the reputation of the church soiled and the name of God blasphemed among the unbelieving (Rom 2:24). In the end, God is not glorified, the church is not edified, the unconverted church member is not saved, and the unbelieving world has little or no gospel witness!

It does not suit us as ministers or laymen to stand so near and yet do nothing while "the glorious gospel of the blessed God" (1 Tim 1:11) is replaced by a gospel of lesser glory. As stewards, it is our duty to recover the one true gospel and proclaim it boldly and clearly to all. This is the heart of true reformation.

—PAUL WASHER

5. Let the Church Hold Fast to the Truth of Double Imputation

For our sake he made him to be sin who knew no sin,
so that in him we might become the righteousness of God.

—2 CORINTHIANS 5:21

In the sixteenth century the Protestant Reformation brought to pass the most massive split of the church in the history of Christianity. Many attempts were made to heal the rift between Rome and the Protestant Reformers. All of those attempts failed. The ultimate sticking point came down to one word. That word was *imputation*. At issue over the word *imputation* was the question of the proper grounds for our justification. That is to say, on what grounds will God declare a repentant sinner just in His sight?

The Roman Catholic Church argued that the only basis for justification in the final analysis was the acquisition of inherent righteousness. That is to say that God will only declare a person just if under divine analysis that person really is just. That is, that righteousness inheres (*inheres*). The Reformers on the other hand said that if we must wait until we are totally and inherently righteous, we will never ever be justified. The Roman Catholic Church taught that inherent righteousness could not be achieved purely by human nature working out righteousness by itself. The help of grace, faith, and Christ were all necessary to achieve that end. Righteousness comes by virtue of the infusion of divine grace into the soul, which grace the individual must give his assent and cooperation to in order to achieve inherent righteousness. If one dies with any defects in the soul, one must go for some period of time to purgatory until those remaining impurities are purged and inherent righteousness is gained. Then, and only then, will the sinner have any hope of reaching heaven.

In vivid contrast, the Reformers taught that the moment a person believes in Christ, the moment authentic faith is present, in that moment the righteousness of Christ is imputed to that person and the person is counted righteous by God. Paul's primary example of that was father Abraham, who in Genesis 15 believed God and it was counted for him to righteousness. The very word *to impute* means to consider, credit, to ascribe, or attribute something to someone. In this case what is credited or ascribed to the believer is the righteousness of Christ.

Luther spoke of that righteousness that is imputed as an alien righteousness, a righteousness that, properly speaking, is not our own. It belongs to someone else. It is a righteousness that Luther called apart from us (*extra nos*), so that the ground of our justification is not our own righteousness but the perfect righteousness of Christ. Luther's slogan to communicate the idea of justification via imputed righteousness was the phrase *simul justus et peccator*. This phrase means simply at the same time just and sinner, that in and of ourselves or inherently even after we come to faith we remain sinners. But at the same time in the sight of God we are deemed, reckoned, or considered to be just by virtue of the imputation of the righteousness of Christ.

Rome protested at this notion of the imputation of the righteousness of Christ and called it a legal fiction, that would be inappropriate for God to consider somebody to be righteous who in fact was not righteous. The Reformers countered by pointing out that the imputation of the righteousness of Christ to the sinner is not fictional. It is a real imputation. And once that imputation has been made, then God by His grace and mercy clearly does consider the sinner who possesses the imputed righteousness of Christ to be just in His sight.

Imputation of course is twofold. On the one hand, our sins are imputed to Christ in His atoning death, and His righteousness is imputed to us. In our day we face a serious loss of commitment to an understanding of this double imputation. We must not only teach and defend it . . . we must be prepared to contend for it, at all costs.

This whole concept of imputation follows a broad pattern throughout sacred Scripture via the metaphor of clothing. This principle of being clothed, to cover our nakedness, began in the Garden when, out of God's mercy toward our shame for our sense of nakedness, his first act of redemption was to provide clothing for those exposed sinners there. The whole rest of the biblical drama of redemption follows that motif, by which our filthy rags are covered and clothed by the perfect righteousness of Jesus imputed to us.

Without imputation there is no *sola fide*, and without *sola fide* there is no gospel. If we are to experience reformation for today we need to be clear from every pulpit what the essentials of the gospel are.

—R. C. Sproul

6. Let the Church Restore
the Gospel Centered Around the Five Solas

For in it the righteousness of God is revealed from faith for faith,
as it is written, "The righteous shall live by faith."

—Romans 1:17

In these present days of spiritual apostasy, the gospel of Jesus Christ has come under siege. Heretical cults are attacking the divine person and saving work of Jesus Christ. False religions are asserting that Jesus is merely one of many prophets, but nothing more. Liberal churches are assaulting his deity and mythologizing His humanity. Dissident movements are attacking the sufficiency and finality of the atoning death of Jesus by requiring self-righteousness and good works to be added to it. In this present hour, the battle for the gospel has never been more fierce.

In light of these threatening dangers, the church must be guarding the purity of the gospel message of Jesus Christ at all costs. This is a hill upon which to die. There must be a zero tolerance policy for any equivocation whatsoever on the truth of the gospel. When the purity of the gospel is lost, all is lost.

The word 'gospel' (*evangelion*) literally means good news or glad tidings. The gospel is the greatest announcement ever proclaimed to this world. It is the message from God that salvation is offered freely to a lost and perishing world in his Son, Jesus Christ. This saving truth of man's full deliverance from the fierce wrath of God is received by faith alone in Christ alone. From Genesis to Revelation, this is the central message of all of the Scripture.

The most succinct statement of this gospel message was reduced to an abbreviated form in the sixteenth century in the five *solas* of the Reformation. The word *sola* is Latin for "alone." This five-fold confession establishes the theological framework for defining the good news from God in Jesus Christ. Think of these five *solas* as an ancient temple with a firm foundation, three sturdy pillars, and a towering pinnacle.

The first *sola* is *sola Scriptura*, meaning Scripture alone, serves as the foundation for the gospel. This asserts that the entire gospel rests exclusively upon the solid foundation of what the written Word of God teaches. Five hundred years ago, the Reformers called the church back to the Scripture alone as the sole basis for saving truth. This must be preserved without any mixture of human reasonings or ecclesiastical traditions. The one, true gospel rests solely upon what is taught in the God-breathed words of Scripture.

Upon this foundation rests three sturdy pillars—*sola gratia, sola fide,* and *solus Christus,* meaning grace alone, faith alone, and Christ alone. These three massive columns are the essential truths of the gospel message itself and uphold its saving power. Anything less or anything more is not the gospel, but a soul-damning distortion of the truth.

The first pillar is *sola gratia,* which affirms that every aspect of salvation is freely provided by God. A right standing with God is entirely apart from the merit of any human works or religious rituals. Grace means the underserved favor of God is given by him to those who cannot work for it or earn it. This divine gift includes the forgiveness of sin, the righteousness of Christ, and even the repentance and faith to believe in Him.

Standing next to it is the second pillar, *sola fide,* meaning by faith alone. This next *sola* states that the perfect righteousness of God in Christ is received by guilty sinners exclusively on the basis of faith alone in Christ. This right standing before God is apart from any human works or church rituals, but is realized is by faith alone (Ephesians 2:8–9).

The third pillar is *solus Christus,* meaning Christ alone. This maintains that all saving grace is entirely *from* Christ and all faith must be exclusively *in* Him. There is no salvation outside of the person and work of Jesus. He alone is "the way, the truth, the life" (John 14:6). He is the only One whom sinners must trust for the forgiveness of sin.

When these three pillars of the gospel are squarely in place and resting upon Scripture alone, the overarching roof of this temple points upward toward the glory of God alone. This final *sola, soli Deo gloria,* avows that the highest purpose of the four initial *solas* is to promote glory to God alone. However, if there is any crack in the foundation or in these three pillars, this entire temple of gospel truth comes crashing down and robs God of his rightful glory.

In every generation, the church must teach and preach these timeless truths of the five *solas.* To be right is to be right regarding the way of salvation; but to be wrong contributes to the damnation of perishing souls. Maintaining the purity of the gospel is a battle worth fighting. Five centuries ago, the five *solas* were the rallying cry of the Reformers as they sought to restore the truth of Scripture concerning salvation. Even so, these five assertions must be our essential message as well.

—Steven J. Lawson

7. Let the Church Pray Prayerfully

Pray without ceasing . . .

—1 THESSALONIANS 5:17

"Prayer is a sincere, sensible, affectionate pouring out of the heart or soul to God, through Christ, in the strength and assistance of the Holy Spirit, for such things as God has promised, according to his Word, for the good of the church, with submission in faith to the will of God."[1] That was John Bunyan's remarkable definition of prayer in the opening sentence of his classic book on prayer. In that single sentence he packs in at least ten essential qualities of authentic prayer. Even then Bunyan only scratches the surface of the profound comprehensiveness of prayer as an intimate manifestation of our relationship with God as believers.

After studying the prayer lives of the Reformers and Puritans, I am convinced that the greatest shortcoming in today's church is the lack of such prayerful prayer. We fail to use heaven's greatest weapon as we should; and to be sure, prayer is spiritual work and spiritual warfare, and involves trials, warfare, and the enabling Spirit of God.

Does our personal use of the weapon of prayer bring us shame rather than glory? Is prayer the means by which we storm the throne of grace and take the Kingdom of heaven by violence? Is it a missile that crushes satanic powers, or is it like a harmless toy that Satan sleeps beside?

Why do the giants of church history, such as Martin Luther, John Calvin, John Knox, John Welsh, Thomas Brooks, Thomas Watson, and Charles Spurgeon dwarf us in true prayer? Is it only because they were more educated, were less distracted by cares and duties, or lived in more godly times? No; undoubtedly, what most separates them from us is that prayer was their priority; they devoted considerable time and energy to it. They were prayerful men possessed by the Spirit of grace and supplication. They were Daniels in private and public prayer. For us, prayer is too often an appendix to our lives; for them prayer was their life.

The time factor alone is not the primary problem we have. Our greater problem is the lack of quality praying. We are surrounded by a cloud of witnesses of faithful men and women whose prayers rebuke our prayerlessness.

1. Bunyan, John. *Prayer*. Reprint, Edinburgh: Banner of Truth, 2007, 1.

We must confront our prayerless praying, confess it to God, and plead for the Spirit of grace and supplication to revive our souls. But prayerlessness in any man is a tragedy and an offense to God. Every excuse not to pray—"I am too busy to pray; I am too tired to pray; I feel too dry spiritually to pray; I feel no need to pray; I am too bitter to pray; I am too ashamed to pray; I am content with mediocrity with God; we already pray as a family; God already knows what I need"—is an abomination in God's sight.[2]

Prayer is difficult and demanding work. My aim is not to discourage you but to encourage you despite your convictions about your own lack of prayer. Ask God to make you a praying Elijah who knows what it means to battle unbelief and despair, even as you strive to grow in prayer and grateful communion with God. Isn't it interesting that James presents Elijah as someone quite like you and me? He prayed in his praying, but he could also despair in his despairing. If we truly believe these things, we have sufficient motivation to undertake the journey from prayerless to prayerful praying, becoming contemporary Elijahs who truly pray in our prayers to our worthy triune God of amazing grace, who is always worthy of being worshiped, feared, and loved—even to all eternity.[3]

Luther's prayer life was legendary even in his own time, and Luther was a legend in many other ways as well. Such men were indeed Daniels, but Daniel stood head and shoulders above any other man of his generation. And all of them—Daniel, Luther, or whatever giant we may have in mind—had to start somewhere and grow into what he eventually became, often through long and hard experience. But make no mistake about it, there is tight association between the courage and work of the Reformer with his healthy prayer life as a prayer warrior. If we truly want reformation in our day, we must begin with the hard work and battle on our knees.

—JOEL R. BEEKE

2. Cf. Carson, D. A. *A Call to Spiritual Reformation*. Grand Rapids: Baker, 1992, 111–122.

3. For more meditations on how to strengthen your prayer life, see James W. Bike and Joel R. Bike, *Developing a Healthy Prayer Life: 31 Meditations on Communing with God*. Grand Rapids: Reformation Heritage Books, 2010. For a more in-depth look on prayer, see Joel R. Bike and Brian G. Najapfour, eds., *Taking Hold of God: Reformed and Puritan Perspectives on Prayer*. Grand Rapids: Reformation Heritage Books, 2011.

8. Let the Church Reform Her Worship

"But an hour is coming, and now is,
when the true worshipers will worship the Father in spirit and truth;
for such people the Father seeks to be His worshipers."

—JOHN 4:23

The reformation of worship is the beginning and goal of the renewal of culture, because the true worship of the triune God is the heart of the gospel. John Calvin wrote, "If it be inquired, then, by what things chiefly the Christian religion has a standing existence among us, and maintains its truth, it will be found that the following two not only occupy the principal place, but comprehend under them all the other parts, and consequently the whole substance of Christianity, *viz.*, a knowledge, first, of the mode in which God is truly worshipped; and, secondly, of the source from which salvation is to be obtained. When these are kept out of view, though we may glory in the name of Christians, our profession is empty and vain."[4]

For this reformation of worship to take place, the church must repent of its two most dearly held superstitions: 1) that God will bless correct rites and rituals in his worship without true repentance and devotion to him in the heart (Isa 1:10–15); 2) that God will bless actions in worship that are not commanded by him in his Word (Isa 1:12). The Lord says: "Whatever I command you, you shall be careful to do; you shall not add to nor take away from it" (Deut 12:32). In other words, worship must originate in a heart renewed by the Holy Spirit, full of faith in Jesus Christ; and everything in worship must be in obedience to what God has commanded in the Bible. As the Westminster Confession of Faith says: " . . . The acceptable way of worshiping the true God is instituted by himself, and so limited by his own revealed will, that he may not be worshiped according to the imaginations and devices of men, or the suggestions of Satan, under any visible representation, or any other way not prescribed in the Holy Scripture."[5]

Striving for the purity of worship, the church, and our society by the Word of God demands striving to end idolatrous worship and all the

4. John Calvin, *Tracts and Treatises on the Reformation of the Church*, 1:126.
5. WCF: 21.1

institutions and customs of a society that support it. Therefore, those who are striving for the purity of worship and the restoration of culture by the Word of God will be disruptive agents of social change. And, those who cling defiantly to their idolatrous worship and idolatrous culture will use political and ecclesiastical power in an attempt to silence those who are working to bring genuine Reformation to church and state. This means that until we convert Western culture to comprehensive purity, some of us may be burned at the stake, whatever that will mean in the twenty-first century. However, as Jesus said to his disciples in Matthew 5:10–16: "Blessed are those who have been persecuted for the sake of righteousness, for theirs is the kingdom of heaven. Blessed are you when men revile you, and persecute you, and say all kinds of evil against you falsely, on account of Me. Rejoice and be glad, for your reward in heaven is great, for so they persecuted the prophets who were before you. You are the salt of the earth; but if the salt has become tasteless, how will it be made salty again? It is good for nothing any more, except to be thrown out and trampled under foot by men. You are the light of the world. A city set on a hill cannot be hidden. Nor do men light a lamp, and put it under the peck-measure, but on the lampstand; and it gives light to all who are in the house. Let your light shine before men in such a way that they may see your good works, and glorify your Father who is in heaven" (NASB).

As the issue of worship was at the heart of the sixteenth century Reformation, it must necessarily be at the heart of any reformation we propose and pray for today. Again, Calvin says, "There is nothing more perilous to our salvation than a preposterous and perverse worship of God."[6] If we do not reform our worship of God, we are hopeless to reform anything at all, for the pure worship of God is our most basic duty in life.

—Joseph Morecraft III

---

6. *Letter to Cardinal Sadoleto.*

9. Let the Church Become
a True Family Again

Train up a child in the way he should go;
even when he is old he will not depart from it.

—Proverbs 22:6

In the last 150 years a massive shift occurred in church and family life, completely changing the sociology of the church. This resulted in shifting the discipleship methodology from a biblical model to a secular model patterned after public education and youth culture. This was unprecedented in the history of the church. It was so different that it transformed the nature of church discipleship, the discipleship agenda of the family, and even the entire way the family related to the church. It actually transformed the structure of the family. It was truly a mega-shift. But it happened so slowly that almost nobody noticed. What happened? Discipleship in the church gradually became age segregated, where the duties assigned to the family were handed off to church workers.

Why is the modern church age segregated? Why are the teenagers almost always worshiping and learning separately from the adults? Why are the senior citizens separated from the younger generation? Who thought it was a good idea for thirteen-to sixteen-year-olds to develop their own culture? Why is it that, in most churches today, the whole organizational structure is based on age segregation? The answer is simple: we have set aside the practices of the Word of God for the sake of our traditions.

If we only had the Bible alone as our guide, would children be separated from their parents during the meetings of the church? Would we set up children's church? Is there any biblical explicit evidence for nurseries? Did the apostles ever organize a Sunday school, a youth rally, or any kind of age-segregated gathering? Are there any commands or examples to follow in Scripture for age segregation? Of course, the answer to all of these questions is no. The disciples suffered rebuke from their Master for trying to keep the children away. Let us bring our children back into the meetings of the church in the way that is consistent with both the Old and New Testaments.

The current design for discipleship breaks the church into a fragmented sociology of interests and ages. It creates new sub-cultures. It actually raises a social structure that stands in sharp contrast to Scripture, which is the real and serious problem. How do we make our way back to a biblical model of discipleship in the church and family? We must return to the beautiful design for the church.

Think about how God has ordered His people in the church. He makes them a "family" (Matt 12:49–50; 1 Cor 1:10), "a body" (Eph 1:22–23), a "building" (1 Pet 2:5), a "flock" (Acts 20:28), a people for God's own possession (1 Pet 2:9). He gathers people from every tongue, tribe and nation, as brothers and sisters and fathers and mothers in the faith. He brings them together as "one body" (Rom 12:4–5). They are a spiritual family. He brings them together rather than separating them according to age. This is His beautiful design in so many ways.

Imagine with me a church without a generation gap, where the whole family worships together. Married couples and singles, the old and young, people from whole families and broken families all worshiping together. A little child hears the singing and preaching while in his father's or mother's arms. This is a church where the biblical pattern of age-integrated discipleship is practiced. Imagine a church, like the churches in Ephesus and Colossae, where it is assumed that the oldest to the youngest are involved together in discipleship, worship, celebration, and service (Eph 6:1–4; Col 3:20). Imagine a church where fathers and mothers are daily fulfilling their responsibility to teach their children the Word of God in their homes. Imagine a church where the excesses of youth culture are minimized and teenagers are growing wiser by walking through life with the older members of the church. Imagine a church where every fatherless boy or girl worships and serves alongside mature spiritual fathers and mothers and sisters and brothers. Imagine a church where groups of all ages talk together and minister to one another. Imagine a church where the older teach the younger, the younger appreciate the older, and the older are energized and motivated by the youth.

This is a church where Scripture is sufficient for the discipleship of all ages, where Christ is the focus, where traditions bow to the Word of God, and where the generations walk together—and love doing so. Let the church become like a family again. This is the church of the Lord Jesus Christ.

—Scott Thomas Brown

10. Let the Church's Worship Reflect the Weight of God's Glory

For my own sake, for my own sake, I do it,
for how should my name be profaned? My glory I will not give to another.

—ISAIAH 48:11

"What is the chief end of man?" "Man's chief end is to glorify God and to enjoy him forever." If an average Christian knows anything about the Westminster Standards, it is the first question and answer of the Shorter Catechism. We are called to glorify God in all we do and by the way we live. And what is the reason that God does anything? It is for his glory. In this respect, we as God's people are to be at one with God in this supreme mission, to give God the highest glory. So we have to wonder about the massive shortcoming in our modern day church in her failure to give proper weight to the glory of God.

So what is this glory we are neglecting? The Old Testament Hebrew *kabod* refers to God's glory as a matter of weightiness, abundance, immense power, and unlimited magnitude. The Septuagint's and New Testament's parallel of the Greek *doxa* puts an emphasis on the manifestation of the inherent glory of God, and Christ is that consummate manifestation.

So here is our current problem: despite the truth that we have a God of glory, who calls us to give him glory, but instead of rendering glory to God by the weightiness of our worship and doctrine, we can only muster to offer our lightweight versions of a very heavy matter, the very glory of God. Through our evangeli-light expressions of worship and doctrine, we have robbed God of his proper glory. Our post/modern doctrines have relieved God of his immense magnitude and have reduced him to unbiblical caricatures of a generous cosmic Santa Claus or the universal benevolent and indiscriminate lover of all. He certainly is not the one to fear, or one who demands repentance and obedience, or who is the judge over all, and certainly not one to damn the evildoers to hell. Our theological light-weightiness has trickled down into the church's common worship services, as we now worship a version of God that is far lighter in glory and holiness than he was seen in generations past. Worship services are designed with the worshiper in mind instead of the One whom we have come to worship. The music is also devoid of God's glory and has so much more to offer the contemporary worshiper in terms of what makes us feel good rather than what it accomplishes in rendering to God his due glory. Contrast the contemporary church that gears her songs and service toward the congregations' illicit desire for superficial feel-good entertainment to Isaiah, who encountered the Lord in the temple and heard the appropriate response of holiness and glory by the angels, and who himself appropriately responded: "Woe is me! For I am lost; for I am a man of unclean lips, and I dwell in the midst of a people of unclean lips; for my eyes have seen the King, the LORD of hosts!" (Isa 6:5). This is a night and day contrast; or better yet, ultra light and deeply heavy versions of God's glory.

But if God is immutable and unchangeable, and his glory, therefore, has not diminished, then our contemporary worship songs and service that lighten his glory is nothing short of profane. But please be assured, God's name will not be profaned and his glory will still go forth and fill the earth regardless of our pathetic attempts to turn the heavy weight of God's glory into a featherweight form of anthropocentric entertainment. We must conform our doctrines and worship and lifestyle to the majestic glory of God if we are to expect revival. And when we glorify God, only then can we enjoy him forever.

—AARON B. HEBBARD

11. Let Pastors Feed Their Flocks to Flourish Under Expository Preaching

Preach the word; be ready in season and out of season;
reprove, rebuke, and exhort, with complete patience and teaching.

—2 Timothy 4:2

We are living in days of a severe spiritual drought in which there is a famine in the land for the hearing of the word of the Lord. The prophet warned, "'Behold days are coming,' declares the Lord God, 'when I will send a famine on the land, not a famine for bread or a thirst for water, but rather for hearing the word of the Lord'" (Amos 8:11). Such days without rain or crops are now here.

Where the Scripture was once harvested by pastors in their study and fed to well-nourished souls, countless churches are now as barren as locust-stripped fields. Malnourished congregations are being served the bare husks of amusing stories, philosophical musings, and homespun religion. "Thus says the Lord" is off the menu. "It seems to me" is the daily special. Exposition has been replaced with entertainment, theology with theatrics, hermeneutics with hype, preaching with performances, and the unfolding drama of redemption with just plain drama.

If a steady diet of preaching the Word is not restored in the modern day pulpit, the church will continue to languish in its present starvation. When pastors withhold the ministry of the Word, the church is weakened and can no longer function as the true church. The shortage of biblical preaching has been the chief contributor to the weakened worship, walk, and witness of churches today. Unless biblical preaching is returned to its rightful place, this famine will only intensify.

To correct this shortfall, those who stand in pulpits must reestablish the primacy and centrality of expository preaching. Throughout the Old Testament, God sent prophets who would proclaim his Word. After four hundred years of silence, God sent a preacher, John the Baptist, to prepare the way of the Messiah. God then sent His Son, Jesus Christ, to be a preacher. The Lord Jesus himself trained and commissioned His disciples to be preachers of the Word. Throughout church history, the greatest seasons of reformation and revival have been when preachers faithfully heralded the Word. Conversely, the weakest eras of the church have been when there were few, if any, such preachers to be found. This is where we find ourselves today. The biblical preacher has become an endangered species.

If the contemporary church is to be restored to her previous strength, a return to the faithful exposition of Scripture is absolutely necessary. No church will rise any higher than the dynamics of its preaching ministry. Strong pulpits build strong churches, but weak pulpits inevitably produce weak churches. As the pulpit goes, so goes the church.

If there is to be a new reformation, the church must return to its primary duty in the preaching of the Word of God. This remains job number one. Transformed lives are principally the result of the divinely-inspired Scripture being proclaimed. The infallible Word is a sharp sword that pierces our souls (Heb 4:12), and it is a heavy hammer that shatters our self-sufficiency (Jer 23:29). It is a perfect mirror that reveals our inner self (Jas 1:23) and a living seed that germinates life (Mark 4:14). It is a shining lamp that guides our feet (Ps 119:105) and pure milk that nurtures our faith (1 Pet 2:2). Specifically, the Word of God must be preached to every person if they are going to exercise saving faith in Jesus Christ (Rom 10:14–17). Through expository preaching, worship is elevated, holiness is produced, fellowship is purified, saints are equipped, and evangelism is energized. By the preaching of the Word, every aspect of the church is put into its rightful place.

With renewed vigor, pastors must devote themselves to the disciplined study and diligent exposition of the Word. Starving souls must be fed by spiritual leaders who, themselves, are thoroughly immersed in Scripture. In turn, these Scripture-saturated ministers must faithfully expound its riches. Therefore, congregations must pray for those who stand before them in pulpits with an open Bible. They must encourage their shepherds in this sacred calling so that they not become discouraged and faint in this demanding work.

If the church is to be in a spiritually-healthy state, its spiritual leaders must return to the preaching of God's Word. May the Lord raise up a new generation of passionate expositors, men ignited by the Holy Spirit, who boldly herald the inspired text of Scripture. May these servants be sound in doctrine and powerful in delivery. May they give themselves without reserve to the ministry of the word as never before. And may we see the full harvest of truth where a famine now exists.

—Steven J. Lawson

12. Let the Church Rightly Handle the Word of Truth

Do your best to present yourself to God as one approved,
a worker who has no need to be ashamed, rightly handling the word of truth.

—2 TIMOTHY 2:15

A gain and again we emphasize that if there is going to be a reformation in our day, it must come about as a direct benefit from studying, learning, and obeying the Word of God. Reformation is far more about biblical conformity than it is about updating our methodologies. Therefore, we must become vigilant Bereans in receiving the Word with eagerness and in searching the Scriptures so that we know what is presented as the eternal truth of the Word of God (Acts 17:11) is not actually the fanciful twisted words of an eisegetical gymnast, who uses Scripture to back up his perspective of his own personal hobbyhorses. No, the true interpreter, the godly hermeneut, and the responsible exegete will expose the light of Scripture for what God has to say through his appointed human author, even when the truth is not easy to swallow. Truth must prevail, and what is truth except the Living Word of God in the person of Jesus Christ, and the Written Word of God in the breathed-out written words of the Triune God.

The first and foremost imperative is that the interpreter and reader of Scripture must understand the weightiness of the present activity, in studying, teaching, and preaching. We are handling the Word of God; we must do so with fear and trembling, knowing that we are accountable for every word we declare to be the voice of God himself. Matthew 12:33–37 presents our words that flow from our hearts as distinguishing marks between good fruit and bad fruit, good treasure and evil treasure, words of justification and words of condemnation. Which of our words are more crucially important than when we are saying, "Thus saith the Lord"? But if we misrepresent God while claiming to represent God, we are positioning ourselves for condemnation. The gospel is the power of God (Rom 1:16) but if we are speaking idle or careless words (Matt 12:36), then our speech is clearly not graciously seasoned with salt, and we are answering others out of ignorance (Col 4:6), and not in the power of the gospel. We are called to speak the Word of God into our times and culture with purity and power.

When approaching Scripture we ought to begin with prayer, knowing that the Author is fully accessible to us as readers. This accomplishes three major mindsets: 1) that there is an integral relationship between the Book and its Author (2 Tim 3:16; 2 Pet 1:20–21); 2) in this relationship the living and accessible Author continues to enliven his Word to us (Heb 4:12); and 3) He will lead and guide us in our understanding of its deep spiritual truths (John 16:13). Unlike any other book, the Bible is at once both alive and active—inasmuch as the Holy Spirit continues to apply it to our understandings and furthermore, renews our memories of it—as well being closed—inasmuch as it is not open to further written inclusions. And unlike any other book, which we do not have access to the author and his heart, mind, and meaning; we actually have the Author, the Holy Spirit, dwelling in us (John 14:17). The most important book with the most important meaning has the most accessible Author who makes the most important revelations pertaining to life and godliness (John 6:68; 2 Pet 1:3).

The primary method the Holy Spirit uses to bring us into deeper understanding of the Word is through the exposure to the simpler portions of the Word. In other words, we affirm that Scripture interprets Scripture because the Holy Spirit illumines by his own infallible and perfect light, and not the light of another. We affirm that Scripture interprets Scripture because the Holy Spirit is both Author and Interpreter.

This Holy Book was written expressly for our reading, understanding, and transformation. We must handle it with extreme care and prudence, using sound and godly principles of interpretation. Our theological conclusions must follow Scripture as it is rightly handled, and never should Scripture be used as prooftexts to support the whims and fancies of a text-manipulator. Speak loudly where the Bible speaks loudly; speak softly where the Bible speaks softly. Major on major, and minor on minors.

Let the church become expert sword wielders as we learn from the Master Swordsman, the Holy Spirit (Eph 6:17; Heb 4:12), and doing so in the likeness of Christ (Matt 4:1–11).

—Aaron B. Hebbard

13. Let the Church Prioritize Special Revelation Over General Revelation

Heaven and earth will pass away,
but my words will never pass away.

—Mark 13:31

One of my favorite rabbinic stories tells of the elderly Rabbi Johanna who was walking along the road with his younger disciple, Rabbi Hiyya. As they walked the elderly rabbi pointed out fields, then orchards, then vineyards, and then groves that he once owned but had sold them in order to study Torah. After a while the disciple stopped and cried that the rabbi had nothing left in his old age. To this the old rabbi confidently responded, "Why would I not sell what the Almighty created in only six days in order to gain what he gave in forty days?"

We do not prioritize special revelation—the Bible, the book of God's words—above general revelation—Creation, the book of God's works—because we just so happen to like the words of Moses more than the Red Sea, or Psalms of David more than music, or the wisdom of Daniel more than lions, or the epistles of Paul more than gold, silver and precious stones. We prioritize the special revelation over general revelation because Scripture prioritizes itself above Creation, though clearly both types of revelation emanate from God, and therefore, are originally flawless.[7]

Moses and David, in their own way, make this priority by implicit means.[8] Isaiah and Jesus more explicitly make special revelation of higher importance than general revelation. Isaiah states, "The grass withers and

---

7. We hold that the inerrancy of Scripture is held in the original manuscripts; and in like manner, Creation is only perfect prior to the Fall of man (Gen 1:31), after which, it too reflects the conditions of the Fall (Gen 3:17–19; Rom 8:19–22).

8. Moses associates the title of Elohim with his Creation; but YHWH, the proper name held in highest reverence, in connotation with his special relationship to Adam in Genesis 2. Moses, furthermore, paints Creation as preparatory habitation for man, who is the forethought of all of creation (Eph 1:4). David likewise associates the title Elohim with Creation in Psalm 19:1–6, but in verses 7–14, David uses YHWH in association with his law, testimony, precepts, commandments, etc., and as the personal Rock and Redeemer.

flower fades but the word of our God will stand forever" (Isa 40:8); and Jesus says, "Heaven and earth will pass away, but my words will never pass away" (Mark 13:31). The point of each verse is not to downplay general revelation, but it is to exalt special revelation.

The problem with our culture is that it disregards both forms of revelation as stemming from God. This problem with our broader culture seeps into the weakened culture of the church, and we blindly follow along in resigning special revelation to our devotional lives, while allowing godless interpreters of general revelation to dominate the disciplines. Furthermore, we have not only assigned scientists unwarranted authority in areas of bioethics, but also similar authority to philosophers with their relativistic ideas of truth and belief, to social scientists with their twisted definitions of sexuality and marriage, to historians with their godless revisioning of providential history, to psychologists with their pagan ideas of the soul and behavior, to politicians with their pragmatism of evolving law without concern for God's Law, and to educators with their supposed espousal of knowledge without any fear or acknowledgement of the Heavenly Revealer of all knowledge.

We have ignored general revelation, suppressing the truth in our unrighteousness, dishonoring the knowable God, being unthankful in our hearts, growing in foolishness with darkened hearts, and all the while we have no excuse for these thoughts before the judgment seat of God (Rom 1:18–21). But while general revelation is enough to damn the suppressor of truth, it is not enough to save him; only special revelation brings salvation (Rom 10:17). We have not only lost our way in learning from and living out special revelation but we have inverted the importance of special and general revelation to our own detriment: "Claiming to be wise, they became fools, and exchanged the glory of the immortal God for images resembling mortal man and birds, and animals and creeping things" (Rom 1:22–23).

Let us specifically address the issue of Creation. Though the physical evidences can be convincing to an extent, we ourselves would be without excuse if we see the *biblical* account of Creation as less than sufficient in itself. When we compromise in this clear and simple doctrine, we find ourselves compromising in many other areas. We don't want to seem ignorant to a world that puts a premium on scientific data. So after losing adherence to a young earth Creationism, we deny the historical Adam, then the Second Adam and his virgin birth, death and resurrection. If we are thought to be foolish for thinking of a literal seven-day Creation,[9] how much more foolish

9. Though the standard position is referred to as "Six-Day Creationism," I argue for "Seven-Day Creationism" since God did create, bless, and consecrated the Sabbath, vis-à-vis nothing, on the seventh day. Six-Day Creationism subtly falls into a physicalist

are we regarded as such for our belief in a virgin birth and resurrection from the dead? What we find at the end of the day is a Christless "Christianity."

Instead of fearing what the world may think of us in an age of science, let us fear that we are not standing for the eternal truth as Scripture has revealed it. Let us fear that we have sacrificed our fear of God for the fear of man; and that we seek the good opinion of man over pleasing the Lord.

If we hold fast to the priority of special revelation, the Word of God as the drama of redemption, and enjoy the beauty of general revelation for what it is intended to be—the theater of glory that stages the drama of God's redemption—we will have priorities that will honor and glorify God according to the Word that God has given us.

—AARON B. HEBBARD

14. Let the Church Seek God Where He Has Promised to Be Found: In the Word and Sacraments

I am the living bread that came down from heaven. If anyone eats of this bread, he will live forever. And the bread that I will give for the life of the world is my flesh.

—JOHN 6:51

Martin Luther and John Calvin called on the church to seek God where he has promised to be found: in the Word, baptism, and the Lord's Supper. Calvin explains what went wrong in the Medieval Church, as it slid into doctrinal corruption and liturgical idolatry:

> But the first vice, as it were, beginning of the evil, was, that when Christ ought to have been sought in his Word, sacraments, and

---

(philosophical materialist) trap of its own making.

spiritual graces, the world [that is, the Medieval Church] after
its custom, delighted in his garments, vests, and swaddling
clothes; and thus overlooking the principal matter, followed
only its accessory.[10]

Luther also lamented that before his Reformation breakthrough, he
had been trained to seek assurance of God's favor in relics, acts of penance,
pilgrimages, and prayers to the saints. The Medieval Church all too often
went seeking for Christ in all the wrong places instead of meeting him
where he has promised to be found.

Where is the gracious God to be found? Certainly, God is present everywhere. But God has not promised to be present *in the same way* in all
times and places. He is not present on the golf course on a Sunday morning
the same way he is present where two or three are gathered in his name at
the same hour. He is not present in a swimming pool the same way he is
present in the waters of baptism. He is not present in a Big Mac the same
way he is present in the bread and wine of the Eucharist. We must know:
Where is God present *in his grace*? Where can his forgiveness and transforming power be found? Where is he present *for us*? This is the question
Luther and Calvin wrestled with, theologically and pastorally. Calvin wrote
a rather humorous *Inventory of Relics* that zeroed in on the problem. The
issue was not simply that most relics were frauds, devised to swindle pious
but gullible souls out of their money, but that the relics actually distracted
the people from seeking Christ in the proper way. Through a trusting appropriation of the Word and sacraments, Luther and Calvin, and following
them, the Westminster divines, emphasized that God must be sought in his
appointed means. The Westminster Shorter Catechism summarizes the biblical and reformational teaching:

> What are the outward means whereby Christ communicateth to
> us the benefits of redemption? The outward and ordinary means
> whereby Christ communicateth to us the benefits of redemption
> are, his ordinances, especially the word, sacraments, and prayer;
> all of which are made effectual to the elect for salvation.

If Christ communicates his benefits to us in these means, then they
are obviously crucial. God uses paper and ink, the sound waves emanat-
ing from a preacher's voice, water, bread, and wine, to give us his salvation.
The benefits Christ purchased for us are delivered to us and applied to us

---

10. Quoted in Carlos Eire, *War Against the Idols*. Cambridge, Massachusetts: Cambridge University, 211.

through these means. Luther called these means "God's trysting places"[11] with his church. These are the places the gracious God meets us in love for union and communion; but, in many ways, the contemporary Evangelical Church has reverted to the errors that plagued the Medieval Church. In the healthiest pockets of the Evangelical Church, preaching and prayer are still emphasized, but the sacraments are largely neglected. In some quarters of the church, we have even invented new "sacraments," such as "altar calls" and "rededications," just as the Medieval Church invented the pseudo-sacrament of penance. Luther and Calvin both emphasized the sacraments as instruments through which God gives us his salvation, to be received by faith. We need to recover this emphasis, for theological, pastoral, and practical reasons.

In Calvin's *Institutes*, as he transitions from discussing baptism to the Lord's Supper, he provides this summarizing statement, emphasizing that the Word, baptism, and Lord's Supper are all divine works and divine gifts: "For as in baptism, God regenerating us, engrafts us into the society of his church and makes us his own by adoption, so we have said, that he discharges the function of a provident householder in continually supplying to us the food to sustain and preserve us in that life into which he has begotten us by his Word."

According to Calvin, God gives believers new life through baptism and the Word of promise; God then sustains that new life as we partake of Christ, "the only food for our soul," at the Lord's Table.[12] Of course, Luther had been very much on the same page about how God works in the context of the church, through the means of grace, to give himself to his people.[13]

God wraps up the gift of Christ in Word and sacrament; we take hold of the gift of faith and possess him by faith. In baptism, God particularizes the general promise of the Word; our very names are inserted into the baptismal promise so *we know with certainty* that what Christ did, he did for us. "As many of you as have been baptized into Christ have put on Christ . . . Baptism . . . now saves you" (Gal 3:27; 1 Pet 3:21). At the Lord's table, we hear those most precious words: "This is my body given *for you*. . . . This cup is my blood poured out *for you*" (Luke 22:20), and so *we know with certainty* we are feasting upon Christ and receiving his benefits as we partake of the bread and wine. The Reformers give us a theologically rich and pastorally

---

11. Trigg, Jonathan D. *Baptism in the Theology of Martin Luther*. Boston: Brill, 2001, 23.

12. Calvin, John. *Institutes of the Christian Religion*. Translated by Ford Lewis Battles. Philadelphia: Westminster, 1960, 4.17.1.

13. Quoted in Philip Lee, *Against the Protestant Gnostics*. New York: Oxford University, 1987, 59.

comforting view of the sacraments, rooted in the clear language of Scripture. In many ways, we have lost this aspect of the Reformation. If we are to carry forward the work and legacy of the Reformation in today's church, it must be recovered.

—Rich Lusk

15. Let the Church Exercise Prescribed Biblical Discipline

For what have I to do with judging outsiders?
Is it not those inside the church whom you are to judge?
God judges those outside. "Purge the evil person from among you."

—1 Corinthians 5:12–13

The true church is one that preaches the Word of God—especially in the purity of the gospel—that properly administers the biblical sacraments of baptism and the Lord's Supper, and one that exercises church discipline. A true church has all three of these functions, but discipline is the one that is most often neglected and reveals the weakness of a "true" church.

In most Bible-believing churches discipline is neither believed in nor practiced, and they do not even have a definite procedure for church discipline; and this leads us to question whether the term "Bible-believing" is apropos at all. Could the reason for such lack of church discipline in the American churches be because the American Christians are so biblical and live such holy lives? Not quite. When a church excommunicates someone for committing adultery or continual theft, or all the more, if a church member is excommunicated for homosexuality, it can become a major national news item. This is enough of a potential scandal that cowardly churches will avoid it. But properly played out in covenantal and communal solidarity under the single Head of Christ over his church, an ex-communicant should not easily or comfortably be able join another Bible-believing church having been excommunicated from another Bible-believing church, whether excommunication was for unrepentant moral failure, a spirit of divisiveness, or for promotion of heretical teaching.

God requires his leaders to exercise biblically directed discipline if church members do not live according to the pattern and standard of biblical righteousness. Church discipline is a very serious responsibility God has placed upon the church and particularly upon her leaders. The health and safety of the church demands that ecclesiastical leaders diligently carry out necessary biblical discipline, even if there may be a danger of personal loss of friends, positions, or salary. If they are unwilling to do this, they should not be in Christian leadership; and if they are pastors they should resign or take a sabbatical to rethink this whole matter, and in the process, develop enough courage to exercise church discipline as their Lord demands once they return to the pastorate.

Church discipline is a very serious matter being ignored by many Evangelical churches and entire denominations. This is our shame and to the ill-health of the Body of Christ. It is also a disservice to the world for which we are supposed to be salt and light. It is also to our own peril—for should the church lose its salting quality, as Jesus said, "It is good for nothing but to be cast out and walked upon by men" (Matt 5:13). A child left to himself, undisciplined, will bring sorrow to the entire family; likewise in Christ's church, when proper discipline is not exercised, the whole church suffers.

When the church rightfully preaches the biblical moral standard, the reality of infectious sin, the abundance and sufficiency of God's grace, the proper response of repentance, and the life of ongoing sanctification and self-crucifixion, but then when the church leadership fails to discipline those who disregard every bit of this faithful lifestyle, we in essence, show our truest colors. Detriments follow and cancer in the body takes hold. The glory of God is veiled, the beautiful Bride of Christ nurses an ugly spot, the sinful member finds no deterring motive to repent, the surrounding members are infected with similar sins or apathy or bitterness, and the world looks on with their common mantra: "Hypocrites!"

We must be doers of the Word and not hearers only; we must return to the Bible's teaching on church discipline. And we are confident the church will rise in reformation!

—JAY GRIMSTEAD

16. Let the Church Restore Restoration

Brothers, if anyone is caught in any transgression, you who are spiritual should restore him in a spirit of gentleness. Keep watch on yourself, lest you too be tempted. Bear one another's burdens, and so fulfill the law of Christ.

—Galatians 6:1–2

The church must humbly confess the presence and power of remaining sin, the power of sin to blind the sinner, and therefore, the need for the Body of Christ to be committed to an ongoing ministry of spiritual restoration. There is no such thing as a grace graduate; every believer, including this author, is in need of the essential, sanctifying, and restoring ministry of the Body of Christ. We need people in our lives who will help us to see ourselves with accuracy and lovingly encourage us toward confession and repentance. Unless the church follows the Hebrews 3:12–13 injunction to "exhort one another daily lest any one be hardened by the deceitfulness of sin," we will become a community where people live with theologically-informed brains but diseased hearts, and in our daily lives we will not be living in light of the gospel we confess to believe.

To be truly transformational in the lives of those who have drifted or fallen away, this ministry must be a ministry of restoration, and not condemnation, buying into the gospel hope of forgiveness and of fresh starts and new beginnings. Galatians 6:1–2 provides a beautiful model for the gospel ministry of restoration that all of us of need: "Brothers, if anyone is caught in any transgression, you who are spiritual should restore him in a spirit of gentleness. Keep watch on yourself, lest you too be tempted. Bear one another's burdens, and so fulfill the law of Christ." There are five words in this passage that capture the character and function of this vital ministry.

1.   *Caught:* Is the condition. Caught here doesn't mean, "Aha, I caught you." No, this word pictures someone who has been ensnared ("caught") in sin. We must humbly confess that as long as sin still remains in us, we too are vulnerable to being ensnared in thoughts, desires, words, or actions that are wrong in God's eyes, and so because all of us are susceptible, all of us need this ministry in our lives.

2. *Restore:* Is the mission. When you restore something, your goal is to return it to the original condition it was designed to be in by its maker. The goal here is not to confront people because they irritate us, but to believe in the power of divine grace to rescue, restore, and transform back to God's created intent. The mission is not to condemn and walk away, but to be willing to be a tool of that restoring grace in the lives of others.

3. *Gentleness:* Is the character of the mission. You know whether a house is being restored or condemned by the choice of the equipment being used. So it is with the ministry of restoration. Wrecking-ball responses to the sin, weakness and failure of others are seldom restorative. Truth must be spoken in love or it ceases to be truth, because it gets bent and twisted by other agendas. The gentleness of Christ-like love is what opens the hearts of the fallen to listen, consider and confess.

4. *Watch:* Is the protection of the mission. The call here is to minister to others with one eye on yourself, confessing that restorative ministry is fraught with temptation to pride, anger, impatience, fear of man, and doubt of God. It means humbly admitting that the restorer needs the same rescuing grace that he is offering to the one being restored.

5. *Bear:* Is the daily goal. Isolationist, "I will take care of myself," Christianity is not the Christianity of the New Testament. Biblical maturity doesn't move from dependence to independence, but from independence to dependence. We're all interdependent members of the Body of Christ (1 Cor 12:12–31), called to love one another as Christ has loved us (John 15:12), willing to struggle and suffer for one another's redemptive good (Rom 9:1–3).

It's only when the church once again takes up the gospel call to the mutual ministry of restoration that she will be the salt and light that God intended her to be in a corrupt and darkened world. May God give us the grace to commit ourselves to the courage of loving honesty, and with the humility of approachability; and let us all strive to be spiritual so that his ongoing work of rescue and restoration will thrive everywhere we are called to life together.

—Paul David Tripp

17. Let the Church Restore Her Eldership

This is why I left you in Crete, so that you might put what remained into order,
and appoint elders in every town as I directed you.

—TITUS 1:5

I cannot begin my article with any better words than those of the French Reformation scholar Merle d' Daubigny (1794–1872). He explains why there needs to be continual reformation in our churches: "As we advance through the centuries, light and life begin to decrease in the Church. Why? Because the torch of the Scripture begins to grow dim and because the deceitful light of human authorities begins to replace it."[14]

Because the "deceitful light of human authorities" replaced the New Testament's teaching on church eldership, this doctrine had been largely lost and remained lost for nearly fourteen centuries. Elders were replaced by priests. Church eldership was ignored until the Reformation when John Calvin (1509–1564) decried its loss and promoted its restoration. As one of the first reformers to write about the demise of New Testament eldership, Calvin quoted Ambrosiaster (ca. AD 375), a Roman author who also complained of the loss of church elders:

> Gradually this institution degenerated from its original condition, so that already in the time of Ambrose the clergy alone sat in ecclesiastical judgment. He complained about this in the following words: "The old synagogue, and afterward the church, had elders, without whose counsel nothing was done. It has fallen out of use, by what negligence I do not know, unless perhaps through the sloth, or rather, pride of the learned, wishing to appear to be important by themselves alone."[15]

Still today, many churches do not even have elders. Others make deacons into elders. Multitudes of churches still think the elders are a board of directors as in a business corporation, with the pastor as the CEO. Some

---

14. Quoted in Alfred Keen, *I Will Build My Church*. Translated by Ruby Landlady. Chicago: Moody, 1971, 27.

15. *Institutes of the Christian Religion*, ed. J.T. McNeill. Translated by F.L. Battles. Philadelphia: Westminster, 1960, 2:107.

aggressively promote women elders. Following the reformers' back-to-the-Bible example, we need to revive the apostles' explicit teachings on pastoral leadership by the plurality of elders. Both the apostles Paul and Peter charge the *elders*—and *no other individual or group*—to "shepherd the flock of God." According to the New Testament evidence, the shepherd-elders are responsible for the pastoral oversight of the local church (Acts 20:28; 1 Pet 5:1–2; 1 Tim 5:17–18).

Restoring biblical eldership to our churches provides many benefits for our leaders and greater health for our churches. A biblical eldership will give our leaders true peer accountability, something desperately needed today as many churches watch their pastors fall prey to sin. It will also provide more balanced leadership for the church and for the pastor elders themselves. It will lighten the workload, so as not to burn out the elders with an overload of pastoral responsibilities. Our Lord never intended for the local church to be pastored by one individual. The concept of the pastor as the lonely, trained professional is unscriptural, and may be a key reason why so many pastors are leaving pastoral ministry in surprising numbers.

As the reformers understood, there will always be the constant need for reformation, renewal, and revival of biblical truths. May we not be seduced by the "deceitful light of human authorities." Biblical elders are men who desire to shepherd God's flock and who are above reproach in character, knowledgeable in Scripture, sound in doctrine, and able to teach the Word, and to protect the church from false teachers. The eldership of a church is not a passive, ineffective, uninvolved committee, but a Spirit-appointed body of qualified, functioning shepherds, jointly pastoring God's flock. In biblical terms, the elders are the overseers, shepherds, stewards, teachers, and leaders of the local church. This gives new life to Paul's commendation that, "If anyone aspires to the office of overseer, he desires a noble task" (1 Tim 3:1).

—Alexander Strauch

18. Let the Church Elders Remain Biblically Qualified

He must manage his own household well . . . for if someone does not know how to manage his own household, how will he care for God's church?

—1 TIMOTHY 3:4–5

Without a doubt the only means by which an elder—or overseer, bishop, or pastor—should be gauged as being qualified for his position is the Word of God (1 Tim 3:1–7; Titus 1:5–9). Some—but sadly not all, and therefore, not enough—churches take the biblical criteria of eldership seriously before they lay hands on them as elders to shepherd and oversee the flock of Christ (1 Tim 5:22). The examining and training of such men are important endeavors knowing that all undershepherds are held accountable to their Heavenly Shepherd.

What happens too often is that once an elder or pastor passes muster on these qualifications, they have crossed the threshold into the biblical level of acceptance but then neither the church nor the pastor ever considers the standards again. The prevailing attitude is that once an elder or pastor qualifies during in his role as a simple home shepherd, and then graduates into a church shepherd, home shepherding is then allowed to take a back seat to the shepherding of the church flock. So the church puts pressure on the pastor to work obscene hours at the expense of his family. Perhaps the pastor himself is under the false impression that he alone is God's man for the task at hand and that the church needs him to be fully devoted to his ministry to the church, and again, at the expense of his family. In the meantime, his family flock suffers from an absent father and is in the process of beginning to resent the church, only later to resent Christ himself.

In this respect the irony lives large; the biblically qualified man has worked himself into biblical disqualification by doing the very work for which he was originally trained and examined. In an attempt to manage the church, he has mismanaged his own household through neglect and through a false competition between home and church. Here is a clear warning to address this situation: the church does not need a single pastor, except the one single Pastor who oversees all flocks. To you, pastor or elder:

the church does not need you, but your family does, in fact, need you. This is God's perfect design for the family.

Please do not misunderstand what I am saying: God does call the pastor who is appointed to his task "to equip the saints for the work of ministry, for building up the Body of Christ, until we all attain the unity of the faith and of the knowledge of the Son of God, to mature manhood, to the measure of the stature of the fullness of Christ, so that we may no longer be children, tossed to and fro by the waves carried about by every wind of doctrine by human cunning, by craftiness in deceitful schemes" (Eph 4:12–14). Just because you are not needed the way you think you should be, may be a blow to your ego, but such an unbiblical attitude undermines the value of the Father's master plan, the Son's supreme heavenly shepherding, and the Holy Spirit's work of building and unifying the members into one Body. Fear not for job security; look again at Ephesians 4:12–14; the church has a long journey of maturity that will never be attained until the Lord himself returns in glory.

To church congregations and fellow leaders: keep your eye on the biblical qualifications that are to be the standards throughout the life of the church. Shepherd your families for the sake of your love for God and them; and only then do you truly remain qualified to shepherd a church flock under the direction of our Heavenly Shepherd.

—Aaron B. Hebbard

19. Let the Church's Pastors Truly Shepherd Christ's Sheep

He tends his flock like a shepherd: He gathers the lambs in his arms and carries them close to his heart; he gently leads those that have young.

—ISAIAH 40:11

It has often been said that no one cares how much you know until they know how much you care. Today there are myriads of preachers who call themselves pastors, but in all actuality, we have very few caring shepherds.

Right out of the gate (no pun intended), we must note that the Lord is the one true shepherd (Ps 23; Heb 13:20; 1 Pet 5:4) and that elders are appointed by God to be Christ's undershepherds of his one true flock (John 10:16). We elders are to shepherd the sheep as God would have us to; not as we see fit, or to see Christ's flock as our flock to guide and direct—and manipulate—according to our personal agendas (1 Pet 5:2). The undershepherds are to lead the flock only to the Heavenly Shepherd with the help of the Holy Spirit. We are to feed Christ's lambs Christ's food, and to tend them lovingly as reflective of our love for Christ (John 21:15–17) with patience, compassion, mercy, gentleness, and genuine care. Undershepherds must never assume to own what explicitly belongs to the Heavenly Shepherd. Thus, in this sense, undershepherds never have the right to be jealous of each other if the Heavenly Shepherd assigns a modest flock to one undershepherd and a larger flock to another undershepherd.

In reforming the church, every preacher and so-called elder must graduate into an undershepherd, but how is this done? Can it be accomplished without mass resistance from the status quo? If we believe in the power of God that is working among us, we cannot throw up our hands in apathy or defeat as we look around us.

To begin with, shepherds should know the sheep, with whom they have been entrusted by our Heavenly Shepherd (John 10:14). They should know their names—of both children and adults alike—they should know their conversion stories, their struggles and triumphs, their professions, the educational paths of the children, their individual gifts that should be honed for their priestly services, their dynamics of discipling and being discipled, etc. This is necessarily informative so the undershepherds can personally pray for them by name, together as a session, and with them individually (Acts 6:4). Only after knowing the sheep can a good shepherd learn how to tend and care for the sheep with good conscience before the Lord. Only then can he customize his shepherding to fit the needs of the sick, the guilty, the rejected, the broken, the needy, and a myriad of intrinsic personal conditions. The undershepherds should visit their sheep in homes, enjoy their victories at celebrations, and comfort them in weaknesses in the hospitals.

This type of intimacy automatically eliminates a majority of so-called pastors, and their accountability before God with respect to their assigned sheep (Heb 13:17) is called into serious question. Yet, true shepherds have no option to make the pragmatic claim that their congregations are just too large to perform such a noble task. After all, they might justify, it was God himself who assigned such a large flock to that particular ministry; where it is expected that anonymous sheep (or wolves) wander in and out unknown and undetected. Mega-churches are *never* exempt from being biblical, though many pretend to be. Because the only solitary Shepherd we have is Christ, all undershepherds are supposed to work as a plurality in co-operative ministry. This too points back to the biblical model of a plurality of elders who together all oversee the church. Together, they must all tend the whole flock assigned to them. The Bible, however, is not void of pragmatic concerns in this respect as we consider the wisdom of Jethro when he advised Moses to break up the people into smaller groups with respective leaders, so as to avoid the grinding and exhausting solitary leadership assumed by Moses. This was wise and inspired wisdom of the Holy Spirit and is fruitful for the church today.

The other major task of the shepherds is the protection they are to provide for the sheep. This is a serious responsibility knowing that the undershepherds are to care for and protect the very same sheep for which Christ suffered and died to obtain. Through preaching, admonishing, and counseling, the sheep will receive protection from the internal sin (Acts 20:31; 2 Tim 2:24–26). Sheep that wander need shepherds who will go after them. This task is only possible if the undershepherds already know they have a specific flock accounted for (Luke 15:4). Woe to the undershepherds who lose Christ's sheep through negligence or desertion (John 10:12); though to be sure, Christ will not lose any of them (John 10:29). Undershepherds are to safeguard the sheep from wolves in sheep's clothing (Matt 7:15; Acts 20:29) as well as from other external threats like heresy, doctrines of demons, fluffy ear-tickling entertainment, and destructive philosophy (Titus 1:9; 1 Tim 4:1; 1:3; Col 2:8).

Yes, pastors are to feed the sheep with the Word of God, but there is much more about tending sheep than mere sustenance. We elders must do our shepherding assignments willingly, lovingly, joyfully, and sacrificially.

—Robert Herrmann

and

Aaron B. Hebbard

---

20. Let the Church Protect the Sheep from Abusive Hirelings

"Woe to the shepherds who destroy and scatter the sheep of my pasture!" declares the Lord.

—Jeremiah 23:1

For three years St. Paul daily warned that grievous wolves would arise out of the circle of overseers and would not spare the flock (Acts 20:26–31). Paul was guiltless of the blood of any because he had not failed to proclaim the whole counsel of God. That counsel has since been marginalized and its sanctions derailed, leading to today's world of untold misery for countless victims throttled by institutional machinery keeping restitution inaccessible.

Spiritual leaders evoke a profound trust, and the flock looks up to authority figures. When pastoral abuse arises, the victim's relationship with God can become mortally wounded. Those who expose a powerful leader often pay a high price: they grow more isolated while the leader's supporters grow in solidarity. Mind-searing, incapacitating depression, and post-traumatic stress are endemic, and suicide has been documented. The Hebrew term describing victimized sheep in Ezekiel 34:3–4 denotes "to lose one's self," anticipating twenty-first-century analyses of emotional trauma.

Various tactics are deployed against the abused to frustrate justice: denying the problem, ignoring the problem, minimizing the problem, role reversal to discredit the victims by destroying their reputation and integrity, hiding the abuse by muting all reference to it, passing the buck institutionally, and cutting deals to suppress exposure. These mechanisms aid the abuser by compounding the harm to the sheep. This "vocabulary of collusion" even fails to "heal the wound of My people slightly" (Jer 6:14 & 8:11) because such circle-the-wagon tactics constitute "the instruments of a foolish shepherd" (Zech 11:15), instruments that harm the sheep and protect perpetrators.

God's sanction against such shepherds is permanent removal from office: "Thus saith the Lord GOD; Behold, I am against the shepherds; and I will require my flock at their hand, and cause them to cease from feeding the flock; neither shall the shepherds feed themselves any more; for I will deliver my flock from their mouth, that they may not be meat for them." (Ezek 34:10) That discourse begins with God swearing an oath against Himself (Ezek 34:8), serving as "an end of all strife" (Heb 6:16–17) and placing the following declaration beyond dispute. Faussett: "AS I LIVE is the most solemn of oaths, pledging the self-existence of God for the certainty of the event." Greenhill: "Let me not be the living God, but be laid aside as some idol or false god, if I do not punish these shepherds which have dealt so with my flock."

God's sanction (Ezek 34:10) against such shepherds is clear. Matthew Henry: "They shall be deprived *officio et beneficio*—both of the work and of the wages." Gardiner: "the first act of mercy to the flock must be the removal of the unfaithful shepherds." Jacob Rapids (1655): "they are as far removed from their office as can be." Keil: "The task of keeping the sheep shall be taken from them, so that they shall feed themselves no more." Fairbairn: "Mercy to the flock imperatively required the execution of judgment upon those who had betrayed and injured them."

Deliverance may not be postponed because the text actually reads, "I require the flock at their hand"—i.e., now. Ezekiel 34:16–17 supports this because those shepherds are demoted to the same level as the flock, wherefore God now says, "Behold, I judge between sheep and sheep." Where sufficient witnesses are lacking, due process requires searching out the matter (as when Solomon adjudicated a case lacking corroboration in 1 Kings 3:16–28).

To favor institutional substitutes over God's sanction is to trample his pledging of his own life underfoot, provoking possible removal of a candlestick (Rev 2:5). By honoring God's sanction in Ezekiel 34:10, the church acknowledges that judgment begins at the house of God and so she must ensure that "they shall neither hurt nor destroy in all My holy mountain" (Isa 11:9, cf. Heb 12:22). Christ won't break the bruised reed or quench the smoking flax (Matt 12:20). When his Bride emulates this, and his shepherds feed the flock as commanded (as John 10 references Ezekiel 34), his Name will no longer be blasphemed among the Gentiles.

—Martin G. Selbrede

21. Let the Church Flock Honor Her Pastoral Leaders

Obey your leaders and submit to them, for they are keeping watch over your souls, as those who will have to give an account. Let them do this with joy and not with groaning, for that would be of no advantage to you.

—Hebrews 13:17

Having just heard the diligent and demanding responsibilities of the faithful undershepherd, and then the stern warnings against those hireling shepherds who beat the sheep, take advantage of their positions for power and greed, and exploit their leverage to cover these sins, we must now address the sheep and their responsibilities toward good and faithful undershepherd-servants.

Paul addresses the people directly "to respect those who labor among you and are over you in the Lord and admonish you, and to esteem them very highly in love because of their work" (1 Thess 5:12–13a). He does not tell the leaders of the church—in this case—to communicate this to the flock; this is the direct responsibility of the congregation and assigned by the Holy Spirit. Respect them—that is, highly esteem them in love—because of their work, even if a part of their work is admonishment, which many of us may have a temptation to resent instead of respect.

As a means of respect, the congregation is to appreciate them in their high calling as teachers of the Word, and, in their faithfulness and fruitful outcome, to imitate them (Heb 13:7; cf. 1 Cor 11:1). As a further act of respect, the sheep are to obey and submit (Heb 13:17). This sounds very dangerous today due to the exploitive hirelings and wolves posing as the Lord's undershepherds. This is one of the reasons it is so important for con-gregants to find a church where the pastor and elders are true and godly shepherds, so that congregants are in a good position to be obedient to the Word of God without fear of abuse or internal conflict of disrespect. By no means should a congregant ever be in obedience or submission to a pastor where the demands of the pastor are in conflict with the Word of God. Such discernment is also the responsibility of the flock as Bereans. But the Word is clear: obey, submit, and respect. If you need to find a church where you can be biblical in this regard, then do your due diligence in searching for such a church. So while the undershepherds must give an account for the sheep before God, the flock must also give an account to God for what the Word demands of them as well. Sheep cannot ignore this responsibility just because they do not have a respectable shepherd. This excuse will not hold water.

Another act of respect is to honor the elders who rule and teach well with financial compensation for their work (1 Tim 5:17). The "double honor" Paul speaks of in this context may speak directly of their propor-tionate compensation.[16] Paul also makes a case for financial compensation so that the ministry worker may give his undivided attention to the work he has been called to perform (1 Cor 9). Jesus said that where your treasure is, there your heart will be also (Matt 6:21). Do we really value our God-appointed leaders? Put your money where your heart is!

The last act of respect is to do all the aforementioned duties with joy. Happy and grateful sheep will make a happy and more productive shepherd. This is advantageous to the flock as they receive ministry from a joyful shep-herd; to the undershepherd as he has the privilege of serving Christ and his flock with enduring joy and not out of compulsion; and the church at large where the peace of God reigns. Conversely, a disgruntled and grumbling flock has the incredible potential to dismantle a great leader, such as Moses, to such a degrading level that he would prefer death over continuing his leadership over them (Num 11:15). And for this, the sheep will suffer the consequences from the Heavenly Shepherd.

16. This does not necessarily mean a double salary, though some would argue in this direction. It could imply an emotional and financial honor, or a monetary honor from church and a "tent-making" honor as well.

Finally, we need to be a thankful people; thankful for the pure grace that we are counted among the flock of Christ, and thankful for the man who brings the Word to the flock as sustenance, who protects the flock from external and internal dangers, and serves in a myriad of ways behind the scenes.

Sheep, you are called to love the Good Shepherd, and in so doing, you are also called to love the undershepherd the Good Shepherd has given you. So instead of praying for a new pastor, pray for the one he has already assigned to you.

—Aaron B. Hebbard

22. Let the Church Restore Her Diaconate

Therefore, brothers, pick out from among you seven men of good repute,
full of the Spirit and of wisdom, whom we will appoint to this duty.

—Acts 6:3

At the time of the sixteenth-century Reformation, the Roman Catholic Church had relegated the position of deacon to an apprenticeship for the priesthood and was largely ceremonial. But the reformers—Martin Luther, Martin Bucer, John Calvin, and Ulrich Zwingli—sought to restore the diaconate to its biblical origin which they believed to be found in Acts 6:1–7.

The reformer best known for articulating the Acts 6 biblical model of deacon was John Calvin.[17] Following Acts 6, Calvin believed that the diaconate was its own God-ordained office. He wanted the deacons to be chosen by their local church, to be set in place for their special ministry by the laying on of hands, and to be the church's official ministers of mercy. The deacons' tasks were to alleviate poverty and to assist widows and orphans.

---

17. Ibid., 2:1061, 1062, 1097, 1098.

"Calvin had high regard for the diaconal office, as he considered it to be holy, spiritual, and with integrity of its own. In this respect, the diaconal office is no less than that of a minister or a preacher."[18]

Among multitudes of contemporary churches, however, there is still considerable confusion and disagreement over the biblical identity and role of the deacons. Many churches make their deacons *the* governing board of the church, with deacons acting as quasi-elders or semi-overseers. Tragically for our churches, when deacons are made elders, and elders are made deacons, we are left with neither biblical elders nor biblical deacons.

Some churches hold that anyone regularly serving in the church in any capacity is a deacon (= servant). They make this claim on the assumption that the Greek term *deacons* can only mean *servant* and nothing more. Therefore, all who serve must be deacons, and the title is given to various people in the church for doing different kinds of service, i.e., parking ministry, audio-visual ministry, wedding coordination ministry, or the greeting and ushering ministry. The office of deacon does not appear to be specific with clear parameters one is admitted to, but rather a title given to people leading diverse ministries within the church. This view, however, is built on a faulty lexical assumption that the word *deacons* must mean *servant* and cannot mean anything else; an assumption now shown by newer research to be false.

A surprising number of churches do not even have deacons or see a need for them. As we will see, this is not only unbiblical but also detrimental to a church, and especially to her leadership.

The traditional view claims that deacons are the church's charity workers and ministers of mercy based on Acts 6:1–7. But neither Luke nor Paul ever make a clear connection between the table-serving seven of Acts 6 and Paul's deacons in 1 Timothy 3:8–12.[19] Berean Christians would not put up with such confusion. They would search the Scriptures and press on until they settled on God-given, biblical answers regarding who the elders and deacons are and what God instructs them to do (Acts 17:11). Our lack of Berean tenacity has led to our own confusion and subsequent neglect.

Clarence Agan III concludes that the term *deacons* in Philippians 1:1 and 1 Timothy 3:8–13 is used in the sense of agency,[20] and thus the deacons

18. Van Dam, Cornelius. *The Deacon: Biblical Foundations for Today's Ministry of Mercy.* Grand Rapids: Reformation Heritage, 2016, 106.

19. For more evidence and a full treatment of the word study on *Deacons,* see Alexander Strauch, *Paul's Theology of Deacons: Assisting the Elders with the Care of God's Church.* Littleton, Colorado: Lewis and Roth, 2017.

20. The third edition of *A Greek-English Lexicon of the New Testament and Other Early Christian Literature* (abbreviated as *BDAG*) gives one of the meanings of the

are the "assistants, aides" of the overseers.[21] An important key to understanding the deacons of 1 Timothy 3 is an accurate understanding of the officials with whom they are always associated, the *episcope* or overseers, described just prior in verses 1–7. "From the nature of the terms, *episcope* could operate without *diakonoi*, but *diakonoi* could not operate without some such mandating functionary as an *episkopos*."[22] As the context and the terms themselves indicate, the *diakonoi* operate under the leadership of the *episcope*, not the congregation. The *diakonoi* stand ready to carry out the delegated tasks of the overseers. They officially represent the overseers.

Using both lexical and contextual evidence, the best interpretation of the term *deacons* in 1 Timothy 3:8–13 is that the *diakonoi* are the aides of the *episcope*. Although this view does not limit the role of deacons to mercy ministries, it must still include mercy ministries within the responsibilities of deacons. Caring for the poor and needy is one of the most important areas where the overseers (= elders) would need assistance, in order for them to concentrate more fully on prayer, teaching, and leading the local church, as illustrated by Acts 6:2, 4. The main lessons and truths of Acts 6 are as relevant today to elders and deacons as they were to churches two thousand years ago.

The reformers taught us to go to God's Word, the Scriptures, for truth, correction, and reformation (2 Tim 3:16–17), so we should welcome any new light shed on the biblical identity and role of the deacons. *Sola Scriptura!*

—Alexander Strauch

Greek word *deacons* as: "one who gets something done, at the behest of a superior, assistant to someone." (*BDAG*, 230–231).

21. The entries for *deacons*, as it appears in Philippians 1:1 and 1 Timothy 3:8, 12, are "attendant, assistant, *aide*" (*BDAG*, 230–231).

22. Collins, John N. *Deacons and the Church.* Harrisburg, Pennsylvania: Morehouse, 2002, 92.

23. Let the Church Minister to Her True Widows

Honor widows who are truly widows.

—1 Timothy 5:3

I would venture to guess that the state of widows has vastly improved since the times of Moses, Elijah, Jeremiah, and Paul. Back then, as women without the protection and support of their husbands, they were subject to harsh economic environs and to the evil schemes of swindlers. Today, with better economic conditions all the way around, and with foresight of life insurance and retirement funds, we can rejoice in their less vulnerable situations. However, I think we have perhaps taken this overall improvement in their outlook to alleviate us from behaving biblically toward the widows in our midst.

Paul makes an important distinction about widows in his first letter to his son in the faith, Timothy. Paul calls Timothy—and us—to honor widows who are truly widows. Well, who are they? Paul narrows this group down by saying that if a woman whose husband is dead has living children or grandchildren, that they are primarily responsible for her welfare and that they should learn to care for her as an expression of their godliness and to be pleasing in the sight of God (1 Tim 5:4). In this case, the church is not the primary caretaker of such a widow; that is the job of her family,[23] whether male or female (1 Tim 5:16). However, if this widow is neglected by her family, the church's role is to call upon her negligent family to fulfill their godly obligations. If they refuse or remain negligent, and are professing believers, church discipline ought to be initiated by the widow with the support of the church (Matt 18:15–20; cf. 1 Cor 5; 1 Tim 5:8). And if they remain impenitent, or if the family members are not professing believers and remain negligent, the church must then consider being the primary caretaker of the widow.

Paul then further delimits the widow's condition. First, she has no support and is left all alone, putting her hope in God as she seeks him through

---

23. Kevin Swanson will later deal with elderly care in the family in the second sphere.

prayer diligently. Second, she must avoid self-indulgence. Third, she is at least sixty years old, and has been characteristically monogamous with a reputation for good works, has raised her children well, is hospitable and serving the saints, has cared for the afflicted, and continues to possess a devotion to good works. If these requirements are met, she is eligible to be placed on the church roll as one who is supported materially—and emotionally—by the church and whose services are devoted to the health and lifeblood of the church. One such benefit for the church in this respect is to have such a high-quality woman minister as a mentor to younger wives and mothers as seen in Titus 2:3–5. This would be advantageous for generations to come and would implement a revolving discipleship pattern of older and spiritually mature women training younger women to be godly wives, mothers, and homemakers, and to be worthy of being future mentors for women of the next generation.

The advantages of supporting widows should be clear enough, but we take our eyes off the ball when it comes down to the finances. Paul and the Early Church understood the struggles, but we are without excuse as we are likely to be miles ahead of them in our financial situations. The contemporary church spends her money on all kinds of unbiblical nonsense instead of what is clearly commanded here in 1 Timothy 5. The church—and especially the deacons, who should lead the efforts—should gather the church's resources and think creatively about how we might honor and care for the widows in our midst. Widows are a huge and consistent concern throughout the Bible, and just because we are thousands of years removed from those times and conditions, it does not mean that the heart of God has changed one iota in this respect.

—Aaron B. Hebbard

24. Let the Church Hallow
the Name of the Lord

"Holy, holy, holy is the LORD of hosts; the whole earth is full of his glory!"

—ISAIAH 6:3

When God gave Israel His commandments, constituted them as a nation, and created the foundation for a godly society, He included in His top ten commandments a law that regulated the use of His name: "You shall not take the name of the LORD your God in vain" (Exod 20:7a). The inclusion of this commandment in God's Old Testament law shows beyond doubt that He places a very high premium on the importance of His people recognizing His name as holy and treating it that way.

We see that same premium in the prayer that Jesus gave to His disciples—the prayer we know as the Lord's Prayer—when the disciples came to Jesus with a request: "Lord, teach us to pray." In response, Jesus said, "In this manner . . . pray," which set the stage for His teaching of a model prayer, an example of the kind of conversation and communion believers should have with God. He then gave them authority to address God in prayer as "Our Father in heaven." The next words of Jesus' model prayer are these: "Hallowed be Your name" (Matt 6:9b). We have a tendency to read these words and to conclude that they are part of the address, that they are simply an acknowledgment of an existing truth. However, this line of the Lord's Prayer is not simply an assertion that God's name is holy. Rather, it's a petition; the first petition among many that follow. These petitions are the priorities that Jesus indicated His disciples should ask for in their prayers. And the very first thing that Jesus told them to pray for was that the name of God would be regarded as holy.

What does it mean to say that God is holy? It means that He is different from anything that we experience or find in the material universe, that God the Creator differs from all creatures. The primary way in which God differs from all creatures is that He is uncreated and eternal; whereas, each of us is created and finite. We are not eternal but temporal. If nothing else separates the Creator from the creature, it is that high, transcendent element of God's own being, so marvelous, so majestic that He is worthy of the adoration of every creature. Jesus is teaching us to ask that God's name would be regarded as sacred, that it would be treated with reverence, and that it would be seen as holy. We must see this if we are to pray according to the pattern Jesus set for us.

The Lord's Prayer continues like this: "Hallowed be Your Name. Your kingdom come. Your will be done on earth as it is in heaven" (Matt 6:9b–10). First He listed "Hallowed be Your name," second was, "Your kingdom come," and third was, "Your will be done." Those petitions may be distinguished one from another, but they're so interconnected that we dare not divorce them from one another. I'm convinced that although we pray for the manifestation and the victory of the Kingdom of God, it is futile to hope for the victory of God's Kingdom on this planet until or unless the name of God is regarded as sacred, because God's Kingdom does not come to people who have no respect for Him. Likewise, we pray that the will of God will be done in this world, but God's will is not done by people who do not regard Him with reverence and with adoration. So the very beginning of godliness, the very beginning of transformation in our lives and in our society, and the beginning of any reformation today begins with our posture before the character of God.

If God in the Ten Commandments saw the need to require reverence for His name in the time of the exodus, and if Jesus saw the need to call on His disciples to pray that God's name would be regarded as holy in the Jewish culture of two thousand years ago, how much more crucial is it that we pray that the name of God would be hallowed in our own time? This petition, "Hallowed be Your name," should be on our lips every day. Before God's Kingdom can come to earth the way it has already come to heaven, and before His will can be done on earth the way it is done right now in heaven, the name of God has to be hallowed.

—R. C. Sproul

25. Let the Church Respond to Her Call to Holiness

Speak to all the congregation of the people of Israel and say to them,
"You shall be holy, for I the Lord your God am holy."

—LEVITICUS 19:2

Today in our culture—and yes, even our Evangelical culture—the concept of holiness seems antiquated. We sing it less and less in our songs and hymns, and we preach it less and less from our pulpits. If ever we do talk about holiness, we rightfully ascribe it to God; of course, it is His holiness more than any other attribute that makes Him worthy of our praise. But our holy God clearly demands that we, his people, also reflect his holiness. Therefore, we can say that holiness is an attribute of God—perhaps his primary attribute, adjectivally overarching and describing all others—but we must also admit that it is mysteriously a communicable attribute. That is to say, not only is God's attribute of holiness possible for us—after all, he commands it—but it is also necessary—again, because he commands it. "Be holy for I am holy" is both an Old and a New Testament command, but as we drift from the Word, our pursuit of holiness drifts even more rapidly.

No one can attain any degree of holiness without God working in his life, but just as surely no one will attain it without effort on his own part. God has made it possible for us to walk in holiness. But he has given to us the responsibility of doing the walking; He does not do that for us. Surely He has not commanded us to be holy without providing the means to be holy. The privilege of being holy is ours, and the decision and responsibility to be holy is ours. If we make that decision, we will experience the fullness of joy, which Christ has promised to those who walk in obedience to Him.

Holiness is not only expected; it is the promised birthright of every Christian. To be holy is to be morally blameless. It is to be separated from sin and, therefore, consecrated to God, and the conduct befitting those so separated. To live a holy life, then, is to live a life in conformity to the moral precepts of the Bible and in contrast to the sinful ways of the world. We are, through Christ, made holy in our standing before God, and called to be holy in our daily lives. If there is not at least a yearning in our hearts to live a holy life pleasing to God, we need to seriously question whether our faith in Christ is genuine. True salvation brings with it a desire to be made holy. When God saves us through Christ, He not only saves us from the penalty of sin, but also from its dominion.

We are given two tools to walk on the path of holiness: The Holy Spirit and the Word of God, as they are intricately bound together. The Spirit wrote the Scripture; we learn the Scripture; the Spirit brings to our mind what we learn; we apply what he brings to mind. This is a balance then between our wills (expressed by obedience to His Word) and our faith (expressed by our dependence upon the Holy Spirit). Every Christian who makes progress in holiness is a person who has disciplined his life so that he spends regular time in the Bible. There simply is no other way. But if we are to pursue holiness with discipline, we must do more than hear, read, study, or memorize Scripture; we must meditate on it.

God has not called us to be like those around us. He has called us to be like Himself. Holiness is nothing less than conformity to the character of God; and sin is nothing less than the lack of conformity to the character of God. If the church neglects its pursuit of holiness, what association will she assume: that with the world, or that with her God? If the church does not successfully strive for holiness, what difference will she make, and who will be able to find her as she mingles among the very world out from which she is called to flourish? As the last word, " . . . consider yourselves dead to sin and alive to God in Christ Jesus" (Rom 6:11).

—Jerry Bridges

26. Let the Church Confess One Lord, One Faith, One Baptism

There is one body and one Spirit—just as you were called to the one hope that belongs to your call—one Lord, one faith, one baptism, one God and Father of all, who is over all and through all and in all.

—Ephesians 4:4–6

Christ has willed the unity of all believers, which is especially explicit in his High Priestly Prayer: " . . . that they may all be one, just as you, Father, are in me, and I in you, that they also may be in us, so that the world may believe that you have sent me" (John 17:21). This is incredibly clear and yet so heartily—and mysteriously—resisted by so many Christians. Paul, as one who consistently brought the gospel of unity in Christ, was far more than just theoretical about this spiritual unification; gospel-living has deep religious and social ramifications in the community of faith. As a matter of common confession of faith, Paul reminds the church that we are one Body by the commonality of only one Spirit, and that we have our common Lord and faith and baptism.

The church has only one Lord. Our confession of the single Lord is not only our adherence to monotheism, in that we recognize that there is only one God, but also that we must submit to only one Master. This monotheism is unifying firstly in an intellectual sense, as we all must take every thought captive to the obedience of Christ (2 Cor 10:5). Secondly, since we only have one Lord to whom we are to submit our thinking, we also have only one Lord before whom we live out our lives according to his standards. The possibilities of thinking our own independent thoughts and behaving according to our own individual standards are reduced to nothing if we claim submission to the one Lord. We are thus all obliged to thinking God's thoughts and acting according to God's standards. There are no deviations from this directive, and the blessed result is unity both vertically with our Triune God and horizontally with fellow Followers of the Way.

The church has only one faith. Faith is a gift from God and is our instrument of union with Christ. Putting our trust in Christ alone for our salvation is the exercise of this instrument of faith. This being true, how can we speak of various "faiths" within Christianity as if we can be joined to Christ by another instrument not mentioned in the Word and not provided by God alone? I lament the usage of the term "Reformed Faith" and other such applications, whether used disparagingly against another denomination or esoterically as elitism for one's own affiliation. There is no Reformed Faith, or Arminian Faith, or Baptist Faith, or Lutheran Faith, or Anglican Faith, or anything-else-faith that truly claims the Lordship of Christ. No, to be sure, we stand on the rediscovery of the Reformers who loudly proclaimed *Sola Fide*. There is only one real faith that is put into only one real Lord.

The church has only one baptism. This may shock debaters on both sides of this issue; but we are all (lower case b) baptists. Some of us are credo-baptists while others of us are paedo-baptists.[24] While I am not advocating the abandonment of this crucial debate, I am saying that there is only one baptism, expressly the baptism into the Name of the Father, and of the Son, and of the Holy Spirit. Let the intramural debate continue as long as we are seeking the enlightenment of Scripture to guide our convictions. But regardless of which side of the debate we stand, we are spiritually interconnected by being baptized into our common spiritual family Name.

God has willed our unity; furthermore he has metaphysically bonded our spiritual unity. As we seek God's will on earth to be carried out as it is in heaven, we are given the Word to coordinate our thinking and our actions, and we are to confess our commonality in one Lord, one faith, and one baptism, "for there is no other name under heaven given among men by which we must be saved" (Acts 4:12).

—Aaron B. Hebbard

---

24. Paedo-baptists are simultaneously and equally discriminately credo-baptists with respect to new converts.

27. Let the Church Practice
Her Universal Unity in Local Contexts

*"Be of the same mind toward one another; do not be haughty in mind,
but associate with the lowly. Do not be wise in your own estimation."*

—Romans 12:16

Denominationalism has had its day. Like most everything, this has its
good and bad sides. Denominations were created in a catholic spirit.
They provided a form within which groups of Christians to maintain their
distinctive beliefs without de-churching the rest of the Christian world. It
would be a tragedy if the decline of denominations made the church less
catholic.

We take a more sanguine view. Denominational decline is part of the
boundary-bursting age in which we live, and, if the churches respond rightly,
a more catholic church will emerge from the rubble of denominationalism's
collapse. James Jordan long ago pointed to the recurring historical pattern
of creation, collapse, and re-creation. When God begins to make Israel new,
he first tears down the old Israel. When God gets ready to build a temple,
he first sends in the Philistines to rip apart the tabernacle. The disorienting
ecclesial chaos around us is a crisis, but crises open doors to the Christian
future. It's going to be confusing for quite a while, but that confusion is the
formless void over which the Spirit is hovering. In the darkness, we look for
the light of the Spirit and wait for resurrection.

Many churches have recognized the trend of larger city urbanization
and have reoriented their ministries toward cities. "White flight" has gone
into reverse, and many of these churches have begun to replicate the work
of the early church, stunningly summarized by Rodney Stark in what is one
of my favorite quotations: "Christianity revitalized life in Greco-Roman cities by providing new norms and new kinds of social relationships able to
cope with many urgent urban problems. To cities filled with the homeless
and the impoverished, Christianity offered charity as well as hope. To cities filled with newcomers and strangers, Christianity offered an immediate
basis for attachments. To cities filled with orphans and widows, Christianity provided a new and expanded sense of family. To cities torn by violent

ethnic strife, Christianity offered a new basis for social solidarity. And to cities faced with epidemics, fires, and earthquakes, Christianity offered effective nursing services."

Put these two factors together—denominational decline and urbanization—and you have the contours of a new model of church structure, a metropolitan one. Under denominationalism, Presbyterian pastors in Atlanta reserve their closest ties with Presbyterians in Macon or Minnesota than with the Methodist pastors across the street. In fact, the Presbyterians and the Methodists may never meet. In a metropolitan model, the Presbyterians and the Methodists are primarily co-laborers with the Lutherans and Pentecostals and Catholics on the next block, working together to build the city of God within the city of man.

Embodying a metropolitan model of the church won't be easy. There are many obstacles, and one of the problems is theology. Theological differences do have practical consequences. When churches work together, they often end up operating *de facto* on a minimalist theological basis, shuttling their theological differences to the closet reserved for "Unmentionable Things." So, if there is going to be deep cooperation, there has to be more theological consensus, and to reach a consensus, the churches and their leaders have to commit themselves to regular common prayer, worship, and study.

So what are the benefits of spiritual unity? There are two positive constants in the stories I hear. First, churches from different denominations minister together, and, second, churches cooperate with political leaders on projects that benefit the entire community. For innovative, visionary pastors and civic leaders, there are hundreds of realistic, locally-based, ecumenically-charged opportunities to foster experiments in Christian social and political renewal.

To be sure, and on the flipside, detrimental effects accompany the resistance to local church unity. Without recognizing the Body of Christ and its integral members that are most geographically connected to us, we consider ourselves wise in our own eyes by thinking we should be more connected to another similar body part—say the other elbow—than we are to the different one—say the radius—we are directly attached to. But we must stop and ponder the wisdom of the Head of the Body, and his divine arrangement.

—Peter J. Leithart

28. Let the Church Test Her Apologetics by Biblical Standards

. . . but in your hearts honor Christ the Lord as holy, always being prepared to make a defense to anyone who asks you for a reason for the hope that is in you; yet do it with gentleness and respect, having a good conscience, so that, when you are slandered, those who revile your good behavior in Christ may be put to shame.

—1 PETER 3:15–16

Apologetics is the attempt to present a reason for the hope that is in us (1 Pet 3:15). But too often, since the beginning of the apologetic tradition in the second century, the church has fallen to the temptation of compromising biblical principles while defending them. We have too often sought to make the agreement between biblical and non-Christian thought seem greater than it is, so that we can not only persuade others, but be intellectually respectable as well. As examples, consider Justin Martyr's claim that Scripture's doctrine of creation is the same as Plato's, Thomas Aquinas' Aristotelian doctrine of "natural reason," Schleiermacher's attempt to base the Christian faith on feeling rather than Scripture. Too often modern apologists adopt non-Christian views of knowledge (such as empiricism, rationalism, coherentism) in the vain hope that these strategies will lead to Christian conclusions. But these epistemologies regard the authority of the human mind as absolute and final. And one cannot assume the all-sufficiency of the human mind in order to prove the all-sufficiency of the biblical God.

So, although the church's apologetic may lead some to Christ, on the whole it has not been as powerful as it ought to be. Scripture says that with God's help we can "take every thought captive to obey Christ" (2 Cor 10:5). But it is inconsistent with that goal to start with the principle that the human mind is sufficient and does not need to be grounded in God's Word. Scripture itself denies that principle and calls on God to sanctify all our thinking with the truth of his Word (John 17:17). To deny that is to "suppress the truth" by our unrighteousness (Rom 1:18).

It surprises many people, indeed many Christians, to learn that Christ's lordship extends, not only to their worship and morals, but also to their thinking, to their intellectual life. But the unsanctified mind drains the power of Christian witness. The world can see the inconsistency, and they are rarely persuaded by the arguments. This is the main reason, in my judgment, why the world has such a low regard for Christian apologetics. Many people, well-educated in fields like philosophy and science, dismiss Christian apologetics—and therefore the gospel—as superstitious credulity.

So if the church fails to reform its apologetic, we should expect that there will be fewer and fewer intellectually serious Christians, in an era where their influence is needed more than ever. But if the church turns back to a biblical view of knowledge and an uncompromising apologetic built on God's supremacy in the life of the mind, we should expect great flourishing in evangelism and the growth of the Body of Christ.

So, as Luther and Calvin called the church back to a more consistently biblical view of salvation, rejecting the medieval compromises, so a new reformation will call the church to a renewal of all human thinking, based on Scripture's teaching. To bring about this intellectual reformation, we need first to pray, for only God can being about such a drastic transformation. The transformation we seek is a transformation of the heart and only God can reach into people that deeply. But God will make use of efforts on our part, as we train ourselves and others to think according to the principles of his Word. Our pulpits, Sunday schools, and seminaries should proclaim consistently that unless God is who he says he is, nothing else makes sense. Only the God of the Bible explains how the human mind can appropriate data from the world of experience, and draw from that data, reliable conclusions for human life. God is not so much a conclusion of human reasoning as its presupposition. It is God who validates human reason, not human reason that validates God.

—John M. Frame

29. Let the Church Become Great
at the Great Commission

"And Jesus came up and spoke to them, saying, 'All authority has been given to Me in heaven and on earth. Go therefore and make disciples of all the nations, baptizing them in the name of the Father and the Son and the Holy Spirit, teaching them to observe all that I commanded you; and lo, I am with you always, even to the end of the age.'"

—MATTHEW 28:18–20

The Lord Jesus Christ defined the mission of the church. This mission includes evangelism, discipleship, church planting, Christian education, world missions, world evangelization, and the Christian reconstruction of culture and society. All of this is involved in making the world's nations into Christ's disciples. The Christian reconstruction of culture requires faithfulness to the Great Commission of Matthew 28:18–20 and to the creation mandate of Genesis 1:28: "And God blessed them; and God said to them, 'Be fruitful and multiply, and fill the earth, and subdue it; and rule over the fish of the sea and over the birds of the sky, and over every living thing that moves on the earth.'"

This mandate and commission comprise a unity. They must not be set in opposition to one another. The Great Commission is Christ's restatement of the creation mandate, taking into consideration man's need of redemption. Christian reconstruction, then, is comprehensive. It is the work of rebuilding and renewing every idea, activity, relationship, motive, and institution of human society by the Word and Spirit of God, beginning with the human heart.

Christ has promised that the Great Commission will be successful. All nations will become Christ's disciples. "All the ends of the earth will remember and turn to the LORD. And all families of the nations will worship before Thee, for the kingdom is the LORD's, and He rules over the nations" (Ps 22:27–28). The Kingdom of Christ and the preaching of that Kingdom will gradually leaven the whole loaf of human society. "He spoke another parable to them, 'The kingdom of heaven is like leaven, which a woman took, and hid in three pecks of meal, until it was all leavened'" (Matt 13:33).

The church must work, pray, and hope for the day when, "The earth will be full of the knowledge of the Lord as the waters cover the seas" (Isa 11:9; cf. Hab 2:14).

Our failure to carry out the Great Commission will lead to a lack of reformation in general. We must note that these were Jesus' parting words and commandments to his disciples, and all disciples thereafter, and the import of Christ's words must not be lost. We will remain as stagnant as still water; we must advance the Kingdom by the authority of Christ to carry out his orders to us.

The church's motivation in the conquest of the world with the gospel is Christ's person. Her foundation is Christ's work. Her power is Christ's Spirit. Her pattern is Christ's humanity. Her protection is Christ's Father. Her governing authority is Christ's deity. Her strategy is Christ's Word. Her hope is Christ's victory. Her mandate is Christ's law. Her food is Christ's sacraments. Her aim is Christ's glory. With that said, how then can we fail? This is Christian reconstruction.

—Joseph Morecraft III

30. Let the Church Sing Glorious Songs of Sound Theology

Let the word of Christ dwell in you richly, teaching and admonishing one another in all wisdom, singing psalms and hymns and spiritual songs, with thankfulness in your hearts to God.

—Colossians 3:16

Music is a glorious reflection of the truth, beauty, and goodness of God. Martin Luther said, "Next to the Word of God, the noble art of music is the greatest treasure in the world." However, music and preferential

musical tastes have inappropriately taken center stage in a hotbed of controversy in the church today.

Like all other things, music is a truth we discover, not create *ex nihilo*.
This is not to say that composers do not use their talents to "create" new and
exhilarating sounds, but it is to say that the consistent order, the intrinsic
value, the soothing therapeutic quality, and edifying inspiration that accompanies music is exactly how God has ordained music to function in the life
of heaven and earth. However, we must recognize that even as an art form,
music has standards to distinguish between the base and the lofty. Among
the standards that we must apply to music in the church without exception
is one that critiques the theological truth and weight of our music. If we are
to use our music as a means for encapsulating the rich word of Christ, for
transmitting wisdom, and for teaching and admonishing one another, we
had better have music with sound theology (and yes, pun intended). Too
often we indiscriminately allow bad or vacant theology into our worship
because it is candy-coated and appealing in its musical expression. And we
have regularly mistaken an emotionally moving song as the presence and
approval of God.

Sadly, the Twenty-First-Century Church has largely produced and has
sung songs unworthy of proclaiming the person and work of Christ, and
would do nothing or very little in terms of teaching or admonishing. In
many respects—though certainly not all—composers of our day are shallow
and are dwarfed by the stature by the giants of the past generations whose
hymns were worthy of teaching and admonishing with wisdom. In past
generations the church praised God by singing songs of glorious substance;
now we sing songs about the act of praising God. And yes, there is a huge
difference. There is just as much about the self as there is about the true
object of worship, the Triune God.

The Old Testament has a rich history and practice of musical expression to reflect all of life's situations, complete with its own psalter, *the* Psalter.
While we may rightly assume the continuity between the testaments, the
New Testament has little to say about the place of music in the life of the
church; that is, until Revelation as it describes our eternal home around the
throne of God. We are led to sing about the Triune God's holiness, creativity, eternal existence, worthiness, sacrifice, Kingdom, reign, worldwide ran-
soming work, power to build and destroy, honor, justice, truth, revelation,
glory, vengeance, judgments, and joy. The main thrust of musical worship,
as Revelation would indicate, is to lead the congregation into the throne
room of God to be among the saints of old, the angels, the Four Living Creatures, and the Twenty-Four Elders in offering God the praise of which he is
more than worthy to receive.

The premiere Reformer Martin Luther led the charge in putting music back into the hands and life of the churchmen. He composed songs in the language of the people, and with other composers, a modest hymnal, and then taught them how to sing their praises through song. In the process he supplanted the medieval practice of having the congregation only silently witness the musical praise of God as performed by the experts who sang the Latin songs on their behalf.

We have, however, once again reverted back to the medieval mode of a performer/audience dichotomy in a variety of mediums. We have choirs that sing instead of the congregation; we have bands that play loud enough to drown out the optional voices of the people; we have singers and soloists that showcase their talents by hitting difficult notes and deviating from the musical lines in a way that laymen cannot follow but only listen in awe of them. And after it is all over, we are no more in awe of God than before, but we are more likely to render a "clap offering" to these choirs, bands, and soloists.

Reformation is needed in composers to write of the glories of God alone. We need musical worship leaders to usher the congregations into the very presence of God as their sincerest motivation. This is a high calling with strong biblical precedent in such musical leaders as Moses and Miriam, David, Asaph, Deborah and Barak, Jesus, Paul, and the angels above and here below, but we have taken it lightly or misdirected the call entirely. Given the importance of musical worship in Scripture, in the life of the church in heaven, and in the life of the church on earth, we can confidently conclude that a reformation of our music is integrally necessary for the reformation of the church.

—AARON B. HEBBARD

31. Let the Church Be Faithful in Tithing

Bring the full tithe into the storehouse, that there may be food in my house. And thereby put me to the test, says the LORD of hosts, if I will not open the windows of heaven for you and pour down for you a blessing until there is no more need.

—MALACHI 3:10

The church must be faithful in its adherence to the tithe as God's prescribed Kingdom-funding mechanism. Samuel warned and foretold as a sign of oppression the state taking as much as the tithe to the Lord (1 Sam 8:15, 17). Now the state takes far more, but this does not absolve the church from her obligation to tithe lest she rob God (Mal 3:8–10). The tithe is distinguished from "freewill" offerings because it was required as a minimal obligation. Only what is given beyond the tithe is a freewill offering (Duet 16:10–11; Exod 36:7; Lev 22:21). As with the seventh day, the tithe represents that all belongs to God, a portion of which man is to give back to him with the promise of its return in blessing. Jesus confirmed the obligation to tithe (Matt 23:23).

There are three distinct tithes given in Scripture. The first tithe is the Social or Levitical Tithe, because it was given by the individual to the Levites who provided many social functions, notably religious education and charity (Lev 27:30–33; Num 18:22–21). It was given to the Levites of choice by the tither. The Levites then tithed a tenth of that amount to the priests for their maintenance and that of the temple (Num 18:25–32, cf. Neh 12:44–45).

The second tithe has been called the Rejoicing or Festival Tithe (Deut 14:22–27; 16:3, 13, 16). This was a mandated expenditure of family income by the family in religious feasting. It is specifically mentioned as being used at Jerusalem for the Feast of Tabernacles. It was to be used at the discretion of the family for 'whatsoever thy soul desireth." It represented a command to rejoice before God.

The third tithe has been called the Poor Tithe. Every third year this was to be given to the "strangers" (foreigners), the "fatherless and widows" (a reference to any chronically poor), and to the Levites because they were denied any inheritance of land and were thus completely dependent on the tithes of the faithful. This Poor Tithe was to be given "within thy gates," that is, locally as a direct act of charity. Charity was therefore personal, not bureaucratic.

Collectively, the three tithes establish a sound means of social funding, because they acknowledge God's Lordship and man's stewardship in obedience. There is no penalty administered by any human agent for failure to pay the tithe. The consequences of such failure, however, are self-evident in our culture.

A tithing church would generate a tremendous amount of capital, which could fund social activity of many kinds. This is not a crass economic view of Kingdom building, but must be a call to repent of the church's failure to do what God has both empowered and commanded her to do. It is presumptuous for the church to pray that God do miraculously what she refuses to fund by withholding the tithe. The funding of social activity by the state has increased its power as Samuel warned. Nevertheless, the church's obligation is to faithfulness, without which she cannot expect relief.

—Mark R. Rushdoony

32. Let the Church Love the Lord and Our Neighbors in the Proper Order

Jesus answered, "The most important is, 'Hear, O Israel: The Lord our God, the Lord is one. And you shall love the Lord your God with all your heart and with all your soul and with all you strength.' The second is this: 'You shall love your neighbor as yourself.' There is no other commandment greater than these."

—Mark 12:29–31

One of my lifelong favorite passages has always been the Shemá of Deuteronomy 6:4–5 and the parallels in the Gospels (Matt 22:34–40; Mark 12:28–34; Luke10:25–28). Since Jesus summarized not just the 613 laws of Moses into a two-fold commandment, but included all of the prophets into the same swoop, we ought to pay extra careful attention. The timelessness of this summary is concurrently timely, as our generation seeks the quick and easy access to the lengthy and difficult versions that we consider arcane. To be sure, if we were to read with Spirit-filled understanding the Law and the Prophets, we should come to the same conclusions; Jesus did not falsely superimpose another agenda onto the entirety of the Old Testament. No, there is a consistency between what was written by Moses, the historical narrators, the poets, and the prophets, and the proper summary of all this literature by Jesus, who is in Tri-unity with the ultimate Author of all Scripture.

The problems that exist in the family, the church, and the culture are a lack of adherence to this most fundamental commandment. Firstly, we must recognize the YHWH is our God and him alone. If we could get this simple and yet profound concept burned into our consciences, our hearts, our essences so that we live our lives in complete and coherent *Coram Deo* mode—that is, in the face of God—then much of our worldview and practical compartmentalizing and hypocrisy will be defeated by our sole allegiance to the only God. Every Christian confesses one Lord and him alone, but we have so many opportunities to fail: we bow to others gods of our age that come in a variety of forms, from people to organizations to objects of affection to whatever is the passing fancy, so that we often lose sight of our sole allegiance to the Lord as our only God.

Secondly, we are called to love the Lord our God with all our hearts, souls, minds, and strengths. We must immediately notice that this holistic task is impossible for any one of us to accomplish unless we are in Christ, who alone is capable on our behalf of loving God with such thoroughness of being. We must live in such a way that our "in Christness" is consistent with our lifestyles. The power and tenacity to love the Lord with such absolute devotion comes from the Holy Spirit in and through the life of the Christian. Getting this pure and total love of God right is the solution to the proper love of our neighbor. This level of devotion takes our whole being: heart, soul, mind, and strength. As we look to the original version of this commandment in Deuteronomy 6:7, it also demands all of our time—from rising up and to going to bed and back again—and in all places—in private quarters and the public square. In short, no part of our being, at any time, at any place should not be completely devoted to a life of loving the Lord our God.

Thirdly, we are called to love our neighbor as ourselves. Who doesn't love themselves? I would dare to challenge many so-called self-loathers as to their honest commitment to hate their own selves. Scratch beneath the surface and we soon discover that, while there is truly much to hate, they actually desire something better for themselves. If they truly hated themselves, they would want the worst for themselves; the self-loather would love the company from others in hating their own selves. We are inherently committed to loving ourselves and protecting our own interests. Jesus' Golden Rule plays upon this reality; "So whatever you wish that others would do to you, do also to them, for this is the Law and the Prophets" (Matt 7:12). If we could love our neighbors half as much as we love ourselves, we would be doing well, but we would only be halfway to meeting the standard.

Another problem exists beyond our utter neglect of this foundational commandment, and that is the inverse ordering of these facets of these commandments. We often inadvertently prioritize the love of our neighbor over our love for God, and what comes out the other end is humanitarian "sloppy agape." When we place primacy of love for our fellow man over our resigned secondary love for God, our evangelistic attitudes and efforts, our church discipline—or lack thereof—our call for repentance from sin, our personal relationships, our vocations, etc., all get tweaked and distorted along the way. If we have a properly prioritized love for God between loving God with our whole being and loving our neighbor as ourselves, there would never be a competition. If there is, we have mistaken love for either God or neighbor as something other than what is actually should be.

—Aaron B. Hebbard

33. Let the Church Plant Other Churches by Biblical Principle

I have fulfilled the ministry of the gospel of Christ; and thus I make it my ambi-
tion to preach the gospel, not where Christ has already been named, lest I build
on someone else's foundation.

—ROMANS 15:19B–20

When I was in seminary, the "Church Growth Movement" was just getting its sea legs. So, of course, it was all the rage in the hallowed halls of academia—if not amongst the profs, most assuredly amongst their charges. Filled with uninformed enthusiasm, my peers tended to gobble up every fad and fancy that came down the pike: "Preach to felt needs"; "Aim at attracting seekers"; "Recast sermons into positive messages people can actually use."

It was almost as if we'd caught the spirit of the age like a virus. It seemed that a plague of terminal trendiness would sweep pale-church-planting-fogies like me into the dustbin of irrelevance. With the former ilk of churchy church-planters behind us, this new breed of cool church-planting hotshots could take centerstage.

The result is that almost a generation later the difficult vocation of what Eugene Peterson has vividly dubbed "a long obedience in the same direction" is almost entirely missing from our lives, our preaching, and our churches. Biblical illiteracy is pandemic. The ordinary means of grace have been left by the wayside in favor of the new-and-improved.

Even in Evangelical and Reformed congregations, the gospel has been squeezed into the mold of this world with amazing alacrity. According to David Wells in his must-read manifesto, *No Place for Truth*, "Even the mildest assertion of Christian truth today sounds like a thunderclap because the well-polished civility of our religious talk has kept us from hearing much of this kind of thing."

Indeed, the well-polished civility of our religious talk has all but eliminated true religion from our talk—to say nothing of our lives. Thus, recovery seems to have replaced repentance; dysfunction seems to have replaced sin; drama seems to have replaced dogma; positive thinking seems to have replaced passionate preaching; subjective experience seems to have replaced propositional truth; a practical regimen seems to have replaced a providential redemption; psychotherapy seems to have replaced discipleship; encounter groups seem to have replaced evangelistic teams; the don't-worry-be-happy jingle seems to have replaced the prepare-to-meet-thy-God refrain; the Twelve Steps seem to have replaced the One Way. These new church-goers prefer hoots and hollers over hallelujahs; comedic delivery in lieu of common doxology; high volume PA systems instead of unanimous praise; concert simulation rather than congregational singing; entertainment by an awesome pastor over experiencing the awe of God. Even the evangelistic raising of the hand has replaced the raising from the dead in sin to life in Christ; the sinner's prayer has replaced the cleansing waters of baptism; professions of faith are counted more valuable than genuine possessions of faith; and we want people to make decisions for Christ instead of wanting to make people into disciples of Christ.

Today it seems that it is far better to be witty than to be weighty. We want soft-sell. We want relevance. We want acceptance. We want an up-beat, low-key, clever, motivational, friendly, informal, hipster, and abbreviated faith. No doctrine, no dogma, no Bible-thumping; no heavy commitments; no strings attached. No muss; no fuss. We want the same salvation as in the Old Time Religion—but with half the hassle and a third less guilt.

In our haste to present the gospel in this kind of fresh, innovative, and user-friendly fashion, we have come dangerously close to denying its essentials altogether. We have made it so accessible that it is no longer biblical. When Karl Barth published his liberal manifesto *Romerbrief* in 1918, it was said that he had "exploded a bomb on the playground of theologians." But the havoc wreaked by the current spate of Evangelical compromise may well prove to be far more devastating. As Ben Patterson has observed, "Of late, Evangelicals have out-liberaled the liberals, with self-help books, positive-thinking preaching, and success gospels."

So, what are we to do in the face of all this? Well, very simply, we must plant churches that "Preach the word in season and out." We must "reprove, rebuke, and exhort, with complete patience and teaching" (2 Tim 4:2). And in order to do that, we will have to "Be watchful, stand firm in the faith, act like men, be strong and let all that we do be done in love" (1 Cor 16:13). After all, as Thomas Chalmers said so long ago, "Gospel preaching always requires great courage, both to execute and to tolerate, for it must ever needs be a running toward a lion's roar."

—GEORGE GRANT

34. Let the Church
Be the Agent of God's Grace

And I tell you, you are Peter, and on this rock I will build my church, and the gates of hell shall not prevail against it. I will give you the keys of the kingdom of heaven, and whatever you bind on earth shall be bound in heaven, and whatever you loose on earth shall be loosed in heaven.

—MATTHEW 16:18–19

God himself called the church of our Lord and Savior Jesus Christ into being. Creating it for His glory (Isa 43:7) and our good (Rom 8:28), God's purposes for the church are both broad and particular. Of a particular nature, the Lord calls His church to be a community marked by transforming growth (2 Pet 3:18), meaningful worship (Rom 12:1), and equipping for effective service (Eph 4:11–12).

God's purposes for the church also are broad, in that the expression of his glory is not limited to the church alone but extends to all creation. In addition to equipping believers, the church has a mission-driven focus of sending them out (Matt 8:28).

Dr. D. James Kennedy used a metaphor to describe this broader cultural engagement. He said that Jesus established his church like a great train running on two parallel rails—with both rails pointing in the same direction: the Kingdom of God.

The first rail is the Great Commission, in which we are commanded to take the gospel message to the ends of the earth. We see this in both the first and last commands of the Lord Jesus. When He called His first disciples, Jesus said: "Follow me and I will make you fishers of men" (Mark 1:17). And immediately before his ascension to heaven, we see the very last recorded command given by Jesus: "But you will receive power when the Holy Spirit has come upon you, and you will be my witnesses in Jerusalem and in all Judea and Samaria, and to the ends of the earth" (Acts 1:8).

This Great Commission comprises our call to preach the gospel to every creature (Mark 16:15), to make disciples of all nations (Matt 28:18), and to bear witness to the Person and the redeeming work of Jesus Christ (Acts

1:8). This is the message entrusted to the church, to be carried to the ends of the earth, offering hope and everlasting life to those who will trust in Him.

The second metaphorical rail of the church's earthly mission actually comes first in time. This is the Cultural Mandate found in Genesis chapter one.

> And God blessed them. And God said to them, 'Be fruitful and multiply and fill the earth and subdue it, and have dominion over the fish of the sea and over the birds of the heavens and over every living thing that moves on the earth.' (Genesis 1:28)

In this command God delegates his sovereign authority over creation to the creature—who rules in God's place over the entire earth. Included in it are the cultures and institutions of the Earth, for these also are under the sovereign authority of God.

Important concepts are implicit with this mandate. First is that God fashioned us with a creative impulse. Something in us desires to create, build, grow, and preserve. The Cultural Mandate, therefore, is something we desire—something God made us for. By it we minister to the world on God's behalf.

Second is that our delegated authority comes with an implied requirement: We must rule over creation, as God himself would rule. This stewardship responsibility is one for which we will give an account to God.

Third is that the Cultural Mandate still applies in the New Testament era. By commanding his followers to love their neighbors as themselves, Jesus directed the Body of Christ to bless the entire world and has given us the indwelling presence of the Holy Spirit to guide us in it.

We see the salutary effects of the Cultural Mandate at almost every turn—from education to religious freedom for all, from civil government to civil liberties, from economic development to the availability of medical care, from advancements in science to the creative arts. In every sphere of life we see an imperfect but overwhelmingly beneficial Christian influence.

This is the mission of the church on Earth—to serve as an agent of God's grace. Through both the Great Commission and Cultural Mandate, God is redeeming a particular people for himself, with those being redeemed living out their faith and showing the merciful heart of God to a lost and dying world.

—FRANK WRIGHT

35. Let the Church Confess Her Theology by the Use of Creeds and Confessions

For I delivered to you as of first importance what I also received: that Christ died for our sins in accordance with the Scriptures . . .

—1 Corinthians 15:3

One of the great contributions of the Reformation churches was the composing of creeds, confessions, and catechisms to summarize what they believed the Bible taught. Without confessions, the church falls into anarchy: "Everyone did what was right in his own eyes" (Judg 21:25). This anarchy is clearly a problem in the twenty-first century church.

Today, by far the majority of Christians, as well as congregations, reject out of hand creeds and confessions. They maintain that creeds are man-made additions to the Bible. But is this accusation true? Not at all. In fact, the Bible requires the making and using of creeds. But to be sure, they are not the Word but a witness to the Word and under the authority of the Word, as Paul clearly states.

In 2 Timothy 1:13,14, Paul established the biblical warrant for making and using creeds: "Retain the standard of sound words," and "Guard . . . the treasure which has been entrusted to you." In these two verses, Paul gives Timothy a twofold summary of his message.

First, he commanded Timothy to "retain [hold to] the standard of sound words." Sound words express the truths taught by Scripture. Paul has communicated these to Timothy in a summary that he called "standard" or "form." Paul declared that he had given to Timothy a form or pattern of apostolic doctrine. He was not referring to the entirety of his inspired corpus, but to the summary that he had entrusted to Timothy. This interpretation is reinforced in the parallel commandment in verse 14, when he added, "Guard . . . the treasure which has been entrusted to you." In other words, this form of sound doctrine was a specific summary (treasure) of apostolic truth. He referred to this stewardship in 2 Timothy 2:2 and commanded Timothy to entrust it to others.

In other texts of Scripture, Paul referred to this summary as "the traditions" (1 Cor 11:2; 2 Thess 2:15, 3:6). These traditions differ from the traditions taught later by the Roman Catholic Church. Roman Catholic traditions are not summaries of biblical doctrine, but rather teachings added to the teaching of the Bible. We learn then that the apostles gave the church summaries of apostolic doctrine. Creeds and confessions function as such summaries.

Why then does a healthy church need creeds? First, creeds serve as a standard for communion. One of the primary things a creed does for a church is to promote unity. Amos asked, "Do two men walk together unless they have made an appointment [agreement]?" (3:3). Think how useful it is for the congregation and those who visit the congregation to know what the church believes and teaches. In connection with this purpose, reformed churches have required their office-bearers to take an oath, by which they affirm that they hold to the doctrines expressed in the creed.

Moreover, since creeds summarize the teaching of the Bible, they aid the church in interpreting the Bible. Evangelical Christians believe that Scripture interprets Scripture and that the Bible does not contradict itself. Creeds give a consensus on the major truths of the Bible. Confessions are also tools for instruction. What more efficient way to give young Christians a compendium of the faith than by teaching them the catechism and confessions of the church? Furthermore, creeds and confessions serve as instruments for defending the faith. Paul commended this use in verse 14, with the term "Guard."

Many of you have experienced a visit from a Mormon or Jehovah's Witness cultist. Both would claim to believe that Jesus is the Son of God. Hence, you must clarify by asking the question: "Do you mean He is uncreated, eternally God, equal with God the Father?" Throughout church history, creeds have served this purpose. What better way to expose the error of a Mormon or Jehovah's Witness than by using question and answer 6 of the Westminster Shorter Catechism: "How many persons are there in the Godhead? There are three persons in the Godhead: the Father, the Son, and the Holy Ghost; and these three are one God, the same in substance, equal in power and glory." The use of creeds also protects the church from false teachers within (Acts 20:29, 30), by requiring that office-bearers subscribe to the church's confession of faith.

Creeds are a rich treasure entrusted to us. They make for a healthy church, by protecting the peace and the unity of the church.

—Joseph A. Pipa

36. Let the Church Re-engage the Practice of Catechism

And when your children say to you, 'What do you mean by this service?' you shall say, 'It is the sacrifice of the Lord's Passover, for he passed over the houses of the people of Israel in Egypt, when he struck the Egyptians but spared our houses.'

—EXODUS 12:26–27

I want to begin by referring to what Martin Lloyd-Jones wrote about in his wonderful book *Preaching and Preachers*. He speaks of the advantage that being old has with relation to encountering the new trends that get people all excited; fashions and vogues wax, wane, and disappear, only to be replaced by the next exciting enthusiasm. This sad state only reflects the church's condition in lacking stability and solidarity in the ever-glorious message of the Christian Church. While catechetical training is biblical and, therefore, certainly no fad, the anti-catechism culture of the contemporary Evangelical Church is so entrenched that we are in danger of losing this biblical pattern of training our children.

I will accept the burden of proof in disproving any sense of trendiness about catechism, and will cite biblical proof that catechetical training is not just a good principle, but actually a biblical mandate.

Abraham was brought into the counsel of God partly because the Lord had "chosen him, that he may command his children and his household after him to keep the way of the LORD by doing righteousness and justice, so that the LORD may bring to Abraham what he has promised him" (Gen 18:17–19).

Moses explicated the great monotheistic confession, "Hear, O Israel: The LORD our God, the LORD is one." The purpose of this statement was not just for the adults to love God and obey his commandments, but explicitly to "teach them diligently to your children, and shall talk of them when you sit in your house, and when you walk by the way, and when you lie down, and when you rise" (Deut 6:4–9).

The Psalmist is intent on passing on "dark sayings from of old, things that we have heard and known, that our fathers have told us. We will not hide them from their children, but tell to the coming generation the glorious deeds of the LORD, and his might, and the wonders that he has done. He established a testimony in Jacob and appointed a law in Israel, which he commanded our fathers to teach to their children, that the next generation might know them, the children yet unborn, and arise and tell them to their children, so that they should set their hope in God and not forget the works of God, but keep his commandments" (Ps 78:2b–7). This is multigenerational faithfulness by divine design; we are to hear the truths of the faith from our fathers, teach them to our children, and teach our children to teach them to their children, who are still unborn.

The Apostles in Acts summarized the history of redemption in a memorized format (Acts 7:1–53; 13:16–41). Timothy was trained at home in the faith by his mother and grandmother well before becoming Paul's son in the faith (2 Tim 1:5). The traditions received by Paul were faithfully communicated to his churches and disciples (1 Cor 11:2; 2 Thess 2:15, 3:6; 2 Tim 1:13–14, 2:2).

We could go on and on about the history of catechism in the Christian Faith, but it slowly got eclipsed in the late Medieval Church until it was recovered in the Reformation. We cannot pretend that there is no connection between reformation for today's church and catechism for tomorrow's church. Perhaps if we still stood in a solidly biblical tradition of catechism, the church would not need such a desperate reformation today.

While we seek to know the Bible as the Word of God, the confessions and catechisms are like maps in this journey. People have been studying the Word of God for many hundreds of years. And by now they have drawn us very accurate maps to show us what it really teaches. How foolish then to tell our children to ignore all of that and to make their own maps, on their own! No, what they need is catechetical teaching.

If we want upward trajectory in grace and knowledge, and if we truly want reformation in the church today, and stability in the church tomorrow, we must resist the counter-biblical trends of today and return to catechizing our children in the eternal truths of the faith.

—G. I. WILLIAMSON

37. Let Christians Commit Themselves to Faithful Church Attendance

. . . not neglecting to meet together, as is the habit of some, but encouraging one another, and all the more as you see the day drawing near.

—Hebrews 10:25

Statistics demonstrate that though 70.6 percent of Americans claim to be Christian, and though 46.5 percent claim to be Protestant,[25] only a fraction of those actually attend church on a regular basis.[26] The statistics for other Western nations are even more dismal.[27]

A great deal of money and study has been thrown at the problem, but an underlying theological foundation has often been missing. Most Christians are not convinced that regular church attendance is required by God. Christ has a single Bride as a complete body; not detached bridal body parts. Our heavenly shepherd has assigned his undershepherds to care for the flock, but isolated sheep are easily picked off by the wolves. Immature members need to be around mature members for the sake of their maturity.

---

25. "America's Changing Religious Landscape," Pew Research Center: Religion and Public Life, May 12, 2015.

26. Gallup reporting 41.6% (2009), Public Religion Research Institute reporting 31% (2013), Harris reporting 26%, etc., but those studies include liberals, Roman Catholics, and even Jews. And the difference between claims and actual attendance has been documented. The Hartford Institute of Religion Research reported that while 40% of people claim to attend weekly church services, actual attendance tallies show that less than 20% actually do. What about Evangelical Christians? According to the Pew Forum, 25.4% of Americans are "Evangelical Protestant." http://www.pewforum. org/religious-landscape-study/ However, only about half of those Evangelicals actually attend church once a week, with 14% being once or twice a month, 14% being a few times a year, 9% being seldom, 4% being never, and 1% refusing the answer. Two massive studies in 2004 and 2005 show that the percentage of professing Christians who attended church on any given weekend amounted to 17.7%. http://www.churchleaders. com/pastors/pastor-articles/139575-7-startling-facts-an-up-close-look-at-church-attendance-in-america.html While it is very hard to interpret surveys and their statistics, the general pattern shows a major problem with church attendance.

27. See "NCLS releases latest estimates of church attendance," National Church Life Survey, media release, February 28, 2004; "One in 10 attends church weekly," BBC News, April 3, 2007.

Sadly, some so-called mature members believe they are too good for the immature members and they withhold their attendance, which is good for neither the mature nor the immature. They commit not to attend until the church gets her act together (shall we say, "reform"?), but in so doing, they are missing the call and opportunity to be a reforming leaven so desperately needed by the church.

Here are the reasons we desperately need a reformation of our thinking on church attendance. God does not want his people to isolate themselves from other members of the Body (Heb 10:25; Jer 23:1; Ezek 34:6,12). Nor does he want sheep without shepherds (Jer 3:15; 23:4; Ezek 34:5; Acts 20:28; 1 Pet 5:2). Instead, he commands the people to "gather" (Deut 4:10; 31:12; Joel 2:16), to "assemble" (Joel 2:16; Acts 11:26; Heb 10:25), to "come together" (1 Cor 11:17, 18, 20, 33, 34; 14:26), to "call a sacred assembly" (Joel 1:14; 2:15; Num 29:35; Deut 16:8; 2 Chr 7:9), to hold "holy convocation" (Exod 12:16; Lev 22:3), and to gather in "assemblies" (Isa 1:13; 4:5; Amos 5:21; Jas 2:2). God makes note of the "meeting places of God in the land" (Ps 74:8). Nor was this weekly gathering in the synagogues simply a matter for the Old Testament (Acts 15:21) or for Christ (Luke 4:16). God expected Christians to belong to a Christian "synagogue" (Jas 2:2) and to "come together as a church" (1 Cor 11:18). And they did. Acts tells us that "all who believed were together" (Acts 2:44; cf. 2:2). In a word, God's people are to act as if they truly are a "flock" (Acts 20:28, 29; 1 Cor 9:7; 1 Pet 5:2, 3) in need of human shepherds (Acts 20:28; 1 Pet 5:2). They need the "one-another" ministry of the church. Just as the Old Testament saints needed the ministry of the synagogues "every Sabbath" (Acts 15:21), God calls us today to not forsake the assembling of ourselves together (Heb 10:25).[28]

If the church is really going to be the church, we actually have to be in church.

—Phillip G. Kayser

---

28. For a detailed examination of this subject, see Phillip G. Kayser, "Public Assembly: The Biblical Call To Faithful Attendance At Public Worship." Omaha, Nebraska: Biblical Blueprints, 2009. This is available for free download at biblicalblueprints.org.

38. Let the Church Be in the Ministry of Equipping the Family

Fathers, do not provoke your children to anger,
but bring them up in the discipline and instruction of the Lord.

—EPHESIANS 6:4

O ne of the major modern problems we face today is the inverse priority of the biblical order of discipleship in the church and the home. We need not go far to ascertain this fact with evidences of the schedule of the average church and the behavior of the average father in his home.

The Scriptures are perfectly clear: children should be trained in spiritual matters primarily by their fathers and mothers, and secondarily, by gifted brothers and sisters in the fellowship of the church. Husbands should be teaching their wives, and fathers their children. Such priority is primary because the Word of God commands parents to perform this function of teaching daily, while a church's instruction is less frequent. Fathers are commanded to teach, "when you sit in the house, when you walk by the way, when you lie down and when you rise up" (Deut 6:1–9). Scripture is clear: the father is a key component of the delivery system for the message of the Kingdom of God. Therefore, we need to face the fact that when we bypass him or replace him, we have rejected the biblical order for the church and the home. In the modern church we have reversed the biblical order of priority.

As the church has followed the world's system, she has nearly obliterated the scriptural role of the family, and especially the fathers, and denigrated it in church life. This has paralleled what the world has done in the broader culture. Progressively, and often unwittingly, the church has taken over the fathers' role and given it to preachers, youth pastors, women, Sunday school teachers, and childcare workers. I believe that until fathers take their jobs back as the primary preachers of righteousness, there will be no sustained reformation.

Instead of children receiving a breadth of teaching from their fathers (Deut. 6) *and* from gifted teachers in the church—as it should be—they normally receive little or no teaching from their fathers because the church has either given him a pass or actually scheduled him out of the deal.

The problem is clearly observable. Look where the bulk of the energy of human resource is directed in the average church. Massive amounts of energy are plunged into activities that secure short-term attendance bumps by making low entry-level slots for people to be involved, but neglect the daily long-term activity and energy investment that secures a future for many generations. This is especially true with men's ministries. The church gives men opportunities to go on four-wheel off-road treks and motorcycle runs, skeet shooting, deep sea fishing, and to join their softball league. This near-sighted outreach has long-view effects that are detrimental to the family and the church. First, the men who are already absent from the home for much of the time due to work schedules are then further tempted to leave the home even more to have self-serving fun in the name of ministry—to be ministered to and minister to other absent-from-home men. Second, their absence from the home destabilizes the family and ultimately the church, as these same men are failing to raise the next generation of biblically prioritized men by being poor examples.

What a men's ministry should rather look like is quite different. Men should be trained to lead their wives and families by equipping them with practical tools of sound biblical interpretation, with a solid theological framework, and with viable guidelines for conducting family worship. Furthermore, a men's ministry will be a place where iron sharpens iron, and where accountability for leading the family will be established.

In our postmodern, relativistic culture, it is important to understand that when it comes to the church and family, there is a right way and a wrong way. There is a way that "you ought to conduct yourself in the house of God" (1 Tim. 3:15). One of the "wrong ways" that is commonly accepted in the church is the diminished role of the father in the spiritual training of children. This has collapsed the biblical order. Fathers rarely do this work anymore. They have allowed the church to carry the load.

While we lost biblically prescribed priority, we gained programmatic Christianity where everything is packaged in a professionally run program and measured by its numerical success. I want to be clear: in saying these things, I am not diminishing the prime importance of the local church in the life of a family. The church must take center stage in a family's life, but, as it does, it should never usurp or diminish family discipleship that is prescribed in Scripture (Deut 6:1–9; Eph 6:1–4; Pss 78, 127, 128).

It is time for reformation. It is time for a return to the biblical order for the church and the home for the delivery of the message of the cross of the Lord Jesus Christ to the world, for the eternal joy of all who believe, to a thousand generations.

—Scott Thomas Brown

39. Let the Church Regain Her Organic Purity

. . . and you have been filled in him,
who is the head of all rule and authority.

—COLOSSIANS 2:20

In the sixteenth century Reformation Pope Leo X wrote concerning Martin Luther, "Arise, O Lord, and judge thy cause. A wild boar has invaded your vineyard." Of course, that wild boar was set loose by the Divine Vineyard Owner for his own purposes and for the benefit of the vineyard; but what is loose in the Lord's vineyard here today has no similarity. We must now pray, "Rise up, O Lord, and give your church the courage to excise an unholy and alien insertion from the very neck of your precious Bride."

I am going to guess that this is perhaps one of the most unpopular of these ninety-five essays because it hits below the belt of nearly every single church across America. Yet, on the other hand, it may be one of the easiest to understand and implement if we can only transcend our pragmatic concerns by adhering to the simplicity of biblical teaching on the organic structure of Christ's Church.

Simply understood, the Body of Christ is composed of every regenerated member of the church, and of this Body there is one—and only one—Head, Christ himself. The Body is directly under the leadership and authority of the Head, so to nod to any authority or any structure not organically placed there by the Holy Spirit is sheer betrayal and treason. So by definition, any artificial insertion into the Body of Christ has to be considered a cancer, and thus ought to be excised. Yet the American church has warmly welcomed and taken advantage of what should be understood as such a cancer; that is, our precious tax-exempt status. Please do not misunderstand me; by all means should every church in America have tax-exempt existence, as our American founding fathers would have expressly stated and assumed, as was the case up till 1954.[29] However, as the policy is currently framed, the IRS tax-exempt status comes with strings from and attached to Caesar. In exchange for our tax exemption, Caesar exerts some

29. http://hushmoney.org/501c3-facts.htm

degree of authority; authority to any and every degree rightfully belonging to Christ and Christ alone.

There is no biblical precedence for financial advantages from the government in exchange for our tithing. Even if we were to make the case that Malachi 3:10–11 offers financial return for our tithes and offerings, the return is from God and not from the state. Churches and Christians are now looking for a financial return from the state and not from God. In this scenario, the state has replaced God, or at least he is merely supplemental. How dare we render unto Caesar the things that are God's! Our motivation—I honestly believe—does not come from an attempt to offer voluntarily a slice of authority to Caesar when we know in our hearts that Christ alone is the sole Authority of the church. Our motivation is, rather, simply pragmatic; the church will pay less in taxes and will give our congregants who render their tithes and offerings to their churches a tax-deductible receipt for their tax returns.[30] While all of these benefits sound good, we must remember another admonition of Christ, "You cannot serve both God and Mammon." So "choose this day whom you will serve . . . " (Josh 24:15).

These biblical truths are universal and so simple to understand. The difficulty comes with gathering the courage to take the biblical position, and calculating what financial ramifications may result if we were to implement this proposal. But we must be strong and courageous. Times are coming—by providence—when the church may be forced to renounce its tax status: a sifting of wheat between true and false churches. Based upon God's impeccable track record, we must gather up our trust in God and ask ourselves about the other side of the equation: what rewards await us for our obedience to God, and for practicing our belief in the sole authority of Christ over his church? Perhaps there will be some financial diminish, but I cannot help but think that what the Lord will return will be far better. Are we to be hearers of the Word only, or will we practice what we know to be true in his Word?

—AARON B. HEBBARD

---

30. From a pragmatic approach, a parachurch organization could be perfectly suited to be the official 501(c)(3) umbrella on behalf of several churches as to promote and protect the churches' organic purity. For other advice consult Heal Our Land Ministries at hushmoney.org.

Sphere II

Reforming the Family

While the Reformation was a theological hotbed of controversy, its ramifications in the family life did not get the unfettered opportunity to blossom in full light until the inheritors of the Reformation were able to give it more serious contemplation and implementation. We see again the theme of *post tenebras lux*; after the darkness of a crippled view of the family espoused by the supposed celibate clergy who thought themselves above the base needs satisfied by a humble, almost menial life of a family, do we find the light of the gospel flood the theology and practice of a restored family elevated to its proper biblical place.

Yet again today, we have no excuses. We are not fighting the theological or apologetic battles to the extent that the Reformers were, thus affording us more mental, temporal, and financial energies to building a stronger and healthier family life. Still we do not live and exude family life the way we ought. Let us remember our Puritan forefathers who kept one eye on their dedication to the purity of the church in practice and doctrine and the other eye on their serious task of managing and running their households to the glory of God. We have a desperate need of reformation in the area of family in these critical times when the prevailing secular culture dismisses, disintegrates, and redefines the family unit.

The family was the first social unit in Creation; it is a reflection of trinitarian existence, and a prime vehicle God employs to build the covenantal community by carrying the gospel to the next generation. With this in mind we should not underestimate the importance of the family in the Kingdom. Reformation of the family is a crucial ingredient to the reformation of both the church and the culture; both of which are composed of family units. However, the church and the culture are not dependent upon the family in

93

the same sense. The church must be instrumental in the assistance of the reformation of the family, and the reformational family must necessarily be integral by adding multigenerational lifeblood to the reformation of the church. Furthermore, we can quite logically assert that the family is the indispensible link between the church and culture. The family is the incarnate unit that takes the culture of the church into the culture of society with the goal of cultural transformation and reformation.

In the case of culture, however, the family is not as dependent upon culture as culture is dependent upon the healthy family. The family may reform apart from cultural influences, though admittedly the reformational efforts are frustrated by a culture that seeks to dismantle, denigrate, and disintegrate the family at every turn. But culture will never reform until the biblically-defined family regains its prominence in cultural construction. Once the family and the church coordinate their efforts to reform culture, families will have a path of lesser resistance as families transition from surviving and into thriving as culture transitions from being family-hostile to being family-friendly.

In any case, the family that awaits culture to become family-friendly while they sit around in wishful thinking mode is on a fool's errand. The family must engage the culture war by being biblical, being active in church, and advancing the Christian culture in ostensible ways. The family must recognize themselves as agents of cultural reformation; even further, accept their commission to be cultural warrior-units in the midst of an intense culture war.

This sphere explores the various ways that the family must be biblical, and as a natural byproduct will inevitably be counter-cultural, which is the first step toward building the Kingdom-culture as the desired final outcome. Let the knowledge of the glory of the Lord fill the earth like the waters cover the seas (Hab 2:14; cf. Isa 11:9); and let the nations come to modern-day Zion's across this globe to learn from the Lord through his Word and bow humbly before the King (Isa 18:7; Micah 4:1–2).

40. Let the Church Vigilantly Defend God-Assigned Gender Roles

So God created man in his own image, in the image of God he created him;
male and female he created them.

—GENESIS 1:27

The world has gone crazy with respect to the way that our postmodern culture understands and promotes sexuality. Even without being an expert in anthropological and sociological history, I am going to guess that never before in the history of mankind have we dulled our minds so badly that we can't tell the difference between a male and a female. Never before have we had to ask the question of what we feel like in this moment in order to choose the more appropriate restroom we will enter. We in our culture think we are so intelligent and advanced beyond our past generations on all fronts, but we can't even read and respond to a restroom sign with confidence. We claim to be wise but we are foolish beyond compare (Rom 1:22).

Before we can address the dire need to turn our boys into men or our girls into women, we must face the reality that our culture has convinced itself that these definitions are loose at best. Today genders are self-determined, arbitrary, shifting continuously, emotionally based, incongruous with physical form, or just downright wrong and necessitating surgical reassignment. While Isaiah warns about those who call evil good and good evil (5:20), today we call boys girls and girls boys, as well as a whole other slew of in-between identifications based upon all sorts of unrighteous criteria. We judge such purposeful disorientations to be evil, and the world calls this gender confusion good and us evil; and as we celebrate the goodness of biblical masculinity and biblical femininity, the world repudiates these roles as repressive and evil.

Has the Lord let go of his restraints of evil in this respect (1 Thess 2:7) and handed us over to our own evil desires (Rom 1:24)? Certainly, human nature has always been the same in this desire to confuse the genders as an abomination to the Lord (Deut 22:5), but never has this abomination enjoyed such unchecked freedom and widespread acceptance in a culture that not only rejects the Written Word as God's special revelation but vehemently practices outright suppression of the truth God has revealed through nature, his general revelation (Rom 1:18).

While this giving over to debased minds might be true, God will never fail to have his voice heard through a remnant of his faithful ambassadors and courageous prophets. This is a culture war issue to be sure, but where is training for the cultural battlegrounds going to be most effective? The church must be faithful in proclamation in pulpit and practice, and must intentionally equip the family to be the cultural salt and light in the home and public square. God forbid we bow to popular cultural opinion and hide our lights under baskets. On the contrary, our lights are to shine before men, that they may see our good works and give glory to our Heavenly Father (Matt 5:13–16). So in this context what are our good works? Simply this: to model healthy and distinct gender roles to our children that they might grow up without confusion. We parents must raise our young boys to be biblically masculine men in training, and we must raise our young girls to be biblically feminine women in training.

The church and the Christian family may be the only voice of sanity left in this world gone mad. In this basic way we have the unique opportunity to be the city on the hill simply by recognizing and practicing the beautiful differences between male and female, and respecting the gender God has sovereignly assigned to us from before the foundations of the earth. Never apologize for what God has marvelously designed.

—AARON B. HEBBARD

41. Let Us Respect and Rejoice in the Single Status of the Lord's Servants

Now as a concession, not a command, I say this. I wish that all were as I myself am. But each has his own gift from God, one of one kind and one of another. To the unmarried and the widows I say that it is good for them to remain single, as I am.

—1 CORINTHIANS 7:6–8

We often talk about the gift of celibacy, but really don't mean it. We can only see having a spouse as a gift but we cannot fathom having no spouse as a gift. When I speak to young unmarried students about whether or not they think they have this gift, I simply ask the question, "Do you think remaining single for life is a gift or a curse?" Overwhelmingly, they view it as a curse, to which I say it is unlikely they have the gift of celibacy.

The gift of celibacy—unlike most gifts that God distributes—is one of those rare gifts that will only be considered a gift by the one to whom God has given it. When Jesus clarifies the three reasons why "eunuchs" remain single in this life (Matt 19:11–12), he sandwiches his explanation with the preface, "Not everyone can receive this saying, but only those to whom it is given," and with the addendum, "Let the one who is able to receive this receive it." Clearly he is addressing a minority among the multitudes.

Jesus gives three distinct cases for celibacy and uses the circumlocution eunuch (hardly a euphemism) to enlighten the scenarios. Some people are eunuchs from birth, which he means that some people may have prohibitive physical features that exclude marital life. Some people are made that way by man; in such cases their servitude to another person has restricted marriage. In the ancient world this status of eunuch would be literal and physical, but in application today there are certain situations in life that are dissuasive from marriage. But clearly the primary address in these three possible scenarios is the one that Jesus esteems: those who voluntarily remain single for the sake of the Kingdom of God.

This is exactly the heart of Paul when he states his preference for the current singles to remain single (1 Cor 7:32–35). The undivided devotion to the Lord encapsulated the lifestyle of Paul, and it was such a blessing to him that he would prefer all the singles to live lives similar to his for the sake of the Lord and his Kingdom, and for the sake of the single. The unmarried is single-minded in his/her approach in pleasing the Lord, and no other. They do not have the anxieties or divided devotion of pleasing the Lord and pleasing their spouses simultaneously. When the Lord calls these singles to do his work, they are far more ready to pick up and go with far less encumbrances. The married might look upon such individuals as living carefree lives; this is partly Paul's point, but actually their care and cause are solely aimed at pleasing the Lord alone.

Again, with Paul as our case-study, I know very few wives who would willingly allow or gladly want their husbands to do missionary work so they could be imprisoned, whipped with lashes, beaten with rods, stoned, shipwrecked in the open waters night and day, to be put in harm's way by rivers, cities, wildernesses, robbers, Jews, Gentiles, false brethren, and to go without sleep, food, drink, or adequate clothing in the cold, and to escape death by a narrow margin (2 Cor 11:23–27). That indeed would be unfair to his wife, but then again, Paul did not have to deal with this anxiety, and nor would she.

Paul concludes his preference toward singleness with words of encouragement for singles to benefit from good order and undivided devotion to the Lord; but simultaneously with a word of admonition not to use singleness as a means of a disorderly life and one that would entail a divided devotion of a worse sort: between the Lord and self. Singleness is a high calling, not an excuse for negligence or sloppiness.

Singleness is a gift from God; marriage is a gift from God. God gives all his children one of these gifts; "one of one kind and one of another." For those who have the gift of singleness, let us rejoice and respect them, and encourage them to use their God-given gifts to the greatest extent for the Kingdom.

—AARON B. HEBBARD

42. Let the Church Gladly Affirm, Defend, and Celebrate the Goodness of Marriage

He answered, "Have you not read that he who created them from the beginning made them male and female, and said, 'Therefore a man shall leave his father and his mother and hold fast to his wife, and the two shall become one flesh'?

—MATTHEW 19:4-5

W e the church must celebrate marriage as defined by Scripture and affirm that God's design for marriage is a testimony to the gospel of Jesus Christ. The sexual revolution presents a monumental challenge to the Christian church. This moral revolution challenges the very heart of Christian conviction, particularly on the issues of gender and marriage. Further, this revolution of ideas is transforming the entire moral structure of meaning and life. As such, Christians now find themselves on the so-called "wrong side of history" and the pressure to capitulate to the new reigning paradigm of sexual morality increases every day. Indeed, as the sexual revolution gains more and more traction in the court of public opinion, the church will continue to be displaced in the larger culture.

The modern secular mind assumes that our gender is ultimately up to us and that, as the new sexual theorists have been arguing for decades, gender and biology are not necessarily linked. Indeed, the modern assumption is that gender is essentially nothing more than a socially constructed concept that discriminates and oppresses rather than liberates.

The Christian worldview, however, confronts that assumption head on. Scripture clearly defines human beings as male and female, not by accident, but by divine purpose. Furthermore, this purpose, along with every other aspect of God's creation, is declared by the Creator to be "good." This means that human flourishing and happiness will take place only when the goodness of God's creation is honored as God intended.

As Scripture also makes clear, the identity of the human being as male and as female points to marriage as the context in which the man and the woman, made for each other, are to come together in a union that is holy, righteous, and absolutely necessary for human flourishing. The scriptural teachings concerning sexuality and marriage show that God made us sexual beings, gave us sexual feelings, passions, and urges in order that these would be channeled into the desire for marriage and the satisfactions of marital faithfulness.

Sex, gender, marriage, and family all come together in the very first chapters of Scripture in order to make clear that every aspect of our sexual lives is to submit to the creative purpose of God and channeled into the exclusive arena of human sexual behavior—marriage—defined clearly and exclusively as the lifelong, monogamous union of a man and a woman.

Christians guided by Scripture recognize current controversies and confusions over sex, marriage, and other issues of importance as part of what it means to live in a fallen world. This also reveals why the church in its distinctive witness must honor the good gifts God gives us, just as Scripture instructs us, in order to accomplish two great purposes. The first of these purposes is to obey God and to find true happiness and human flourishing as we obey. The second purpose is that we live out that obedience before a watching world in order that others may see the glory of God in the Christian's faithfulness in marriage and every other dimension of life so that others who need Christ may find him.

The Christian's faithfulness in marriage and faithful defense of marriage and gender is an act of Christian witness—indeed, one of the boldest acts of Christian witness in this secular age. The final chapter of Scripture reminds us that we will struggle with human brokenness and the effects of human sin until Jesus comes. Until then, we, Christ's Bride, are to be found both washed and waiting, eager for the redemption of our bodies and for the fullness of the Kingdom of the Lord Jesus Christ, our Bridegroom.

—R. ALBERT MOHLER JR.

43. Let Us Only Marry in the Lord

You shall not intermarry with them,
giving your daughters to their sons or taking their daughters for your sons.

—Deuteronomy 7:3

Marriage is a beautiful gift from the Lord. While all of God's image-bearers may enjoy heterosexual marriage, God's children are given the strict parameters that their marriages are to be exclusively "in the Lord" (1 Cor 7:39; 2 Cor 6:14). Therefore, this essay will assume the sanctity, honor, and high calling of marriage in general, and will consequently focus on "marriage in the Lord" in particular.

Closer inspection of 2 Corinthians 6:14–18 offers a full picture of the blessings of Christian marriage and the dangers of ungodly entanglements. While avoiding all unions with unbelievers is essential for the sake of retaining particularity of holiness that ought to be characteristic of God's people, an unequally-yoked marriage is a specific union that is especially disastrous. If two unlike animals are yoked together for a solitary purpose, each one will want to go it own way because the goal of each is radically divergent. For the believer, the goal ought to be to glorify God and to have the marriage glorify God in all respects. For the unbeliever, the self is usually the king and all aspects must be in service to the self. In such a yoking as this, the two must necessarily tug and pull in two extremes, leaving the marriage fruitless in any common goal or achievement.

Paul's logic continues in this passage as he pits the thesis against the antithesis with concision and clarity. What is the partnership of righteousness with lawlessness? How about light and darkness? In both cases these two entities do not belong together and cannot coexist without one doing severe damage to the other. What will this condition look like in a marriage? A peaceful coexisting marriage will evaporate, tension will rise, and inevitably the spiritual conflict will incur damage toward the other. In this the intent of marriage, and certainly the potential of a Christian picturesque marriage of Christ and his Bride, is lost entirely. God promises to be the Father to his children, but in an unequally-yoked marriage, the child of God who marries the child of the devil inherits one hell of a father-in-law (cf. Matt 23:15).

The marriage in the Lord, however, is beautifully reflective of God's intentional design of marriage and ultimately of the deeper spiritual reality of Christ the Bridegroom and the Church as the Bride. The covenant of the Lord with his people informs the covenantal marriage, and the covenantal marriage points back to our covenantal relationship to Christ reciprocally. Malachi 2:15 restates marriage as a union of male and female into one in which a portion of the Holy Spirit resides. The rabbis have wisely reiterated this, "Adam was created from the earth and Eve was created from Adam; both were created in the image of God. Neither man without woman nor woman without man, and nor the two of them without the Divine Presence of the Almighty." Marriage is therefore a three-party covenant, and we live in this cognizance at all times, and we must avoid all spiritual corruption and contamination of this blessed marital covenant.

God has called his people out of darkness and into light; out of lawlessness and into righteousness; and to keep the union of light with light and righteousness with righteousness. We have no right to dilute the spiritual purity of the marital union, to rob the church and the world of the exemplary witness of Christ and his Bride, to deny Christ's sovereignty over the very institute that he designed from the beginning, or to render fruitless what ought to be powerfully (re)productive in the Kingdom.

While I may be preaching to the choir, it is a message that the choir needs to preach from the home, from the pulpit, and from the mountaintops. So go and marry anyone you want,[1] as long as your choice of mate is in the Lord (1 Cor 7:39).

—Aaron B. Hebbard

---

1. This does not exclude God's providential choice for anyone's mate, the exact child that God has prepared for another child.

44. Let the Biblical Man Be the Model of Masculinity

When I was a child, I spoke like a child, I thought like a child,
I reasoned like a child. When I became a man, I gave up childish ways.

—1 Corinthians 13:11

The world offers numerous versions and criteria of what a "real" man really is. Some portraits are of a brutish Neanderthal who has no need of modern luxuries or any knowledge found in books. Other definitions of man lay out a threshold that he must cross in order to join the masculine club: how many chicks he has brought to his bed, how many guns he has in his artillery collection, how high the lift is on his four-wheel drive pickup truck, how many beers he can guzzle before he passes out, how narrowly he can escape death on his daredevil ventures, how many fights he has been in and how many he has emerged the victor, how many pounds he can bench, and on and on and on it goes.

Sadly, we allow the winds of culture to shift the definition of manhood from era to era, but the problem can be solved if we adhere to the eternal Word of God alone as the definer of timeless truth. The study into discovering what man is actually supposed to attain as the male image-bearer of God is not esoteric or hidden from plain sight of the reader of God's Word. Even general revelation reveals man as the male image-bearer of God, but special revelation gives us the refined path of being molded into the Image of the invisible God, Christ himself, the Second Adam (Col 1:15; 1 Cor 15:22, 45).

The road to manhood is not easy; if it were, we would witness more true men and fewer perpetual boys. The first order of business is simply understanding and accepting the call to meet the great demands of manhood as laid out by the Word of God. Once a man-in-process has crossed this barrier, he must dedicate himself to walk with God humbly (Mic 6:8) and to muster the strength to fear him alone, and no other. In so doing he will quickly come to look into the mirror of God's Word and realize his shortcomings, and in turn, repent of false masculinity, effeminacy, egalitarianism, and for abdicating his God-given roles as man in family, church, and society. And to be sure, until a man learns to be the biblical man and model of masculinity, he is useless in reformational efforts.

This act of repentance and dedication must now flesh out in taking responsibility in godly family leadership, in designing a viable personal and familial plan, and enacting it with godly wisdom, strength, meekness, gentleness, and constancy. This type of Christ-like leadership must necessarily involve servitude and self-denial as he puts the needs of his immediate and extended family, as well as the family of God, above his own. This man will provide and care for all those whom the Lord has put under his protection.

In being Christ-like in his treatment of his bride, he will lay down his very life for her, assist her in spiritual beauty, and will forsake all others for her (Eph 5:25–33). We know God will give us all good things because he spared not his own Son (Rom 8:32); but the man who says he will die for his wife but refuses to take out the trash for her is a liar and a hypocrite. No, on the contrary, he will live with her in an understanding way, and honor her as the weaker vessel and coheir of the grace of life (1 Pet 3:7).

Also in Christ-like manner, a man will take his fatherhood seriously. He will bring up his children in the nurture, admonition, discipline, and instruction (*paideia*) of the Lord (Eph 6:4). He will be Christ-like in his family role as prophet, priest, and king. He will be also be a reflection of the Trinity inasmuch as Christ is a Husband, as God is a Father, and as the Holy Spirit is a Spiritual Leader. He must model the father-heart of God and, in so doing, must lead his children directly to the heart of God. The father will make the spiritual health and welfare of his family of prime importance over any other hobby or project that may deter his focus.

The biblical man must also realize his role as dominion-taker, according to the specific assignment that God has given him in life. Dominion starts and ends in the home. The commands given to Adam and all men for working—that is, serving and cultivating—and for keeping—that is, guarding and protecting—are domestic duties first and foremost. Far too often men have selfish ambitions to take dominion out in the world while neglecting his domestic dominion as a means of putting all things—his most precious things—under the Lordship of Christ (Eph 1:22; cf. 1 Cor 15:27–28).

The church is in desperate need of these biblical men. We might even say that a lack of biblical men puts any attempt of church reformation at risk, and any attempt of family reformation at the level of near impossibility, save for the grace of God. When men began to abandon the church, a feminized version of spirituality, music, and décor became prominent. Now men don't return to church because their impression is that it is for women; or when they do return, they do so as emasculated men who are incapable of instigating necessary reformation. This vicious cycle will continue until biblical men return to be present and accountable for their families being in corporate worship. Let biblical men be the good leaven that leavens the whole lump.

—AARON B. HEBBARD

45. Let the Biblical Woman Be the Model of Femininity

"An excellent wife, who can find? She is more precious than jewels.
—PROVERBS 31:10

W ho is this excellent woman, and where is she? In today's current culture she is scarce. The woman of our time is torn, hopeless, bitter, and has lost sight of God, who alone has defined her. "In his image he created them, male and female" (Gen 1:27). Woman is equally in the image of God as her male counterpart. But our culture today has lost sight of the excellent woman. We are bombarded instead by the whore, the feminist, the lesbian, the self-absorbed, the anti-family, anti-marriage, anti-children, anti-God female. This distortion is everywhere: filling our TVs and magazines, our cities and neighborhoods, and even our churches while the precious woman of God is rapidly becoming extinct.

We must go to the Word of God to rediscover the biblical blueprint of this excellent woman to remember who woman is and all God has called her to be. In both Proverbs 31:10–31 and Titus 2:3–5, the Word of God paints a thorough picture of the excellent, noble woman of incomparable character. It is here that we see clearly the value and worth of this woman.

Wives are exhorted to love and respect their own husbands, and to submit to their leadership. We—and all Christians alike—must let go of the entitlement mentality of our culture today, and all the luxuries we think we deserve, and take on the biblical perspective of love: to endure, to hope, to believe, to never fail. Love is a choice, as my husband often says, "we choose our love, and then love our choice." And while this is not a direct biblical quotation, it is a biblical concept. Loving our husband is a choice we make to honor God; and by doing so we are blessed. Our husbands are to praise us, and esteem us above all others (Prov 31:28–29).

Loving a child, as Titus 2 exhorts women to do, is a 24/7 task. Even when breaks are few and far between, and exhaustion is a given, the rewards of motherhood are eternal. The beauty of partnering with God to do an eternal work is an unbelievable gift. Joining with the Holy Spirit in comforting, healing, nurturing, teaching, feeding the body and mind with the good things of God is a task on par with none other. Mothering is a hidden and lonely job at times, and often one neither encouraged nor supported in the world around us. The job appears trite and a waste of skilled talent and time, and counterproductive in this feminist-saturated culture. Yet viewing motherhood in its proper perspective is—even in the church—rare. This responsibility should be treasured and fiercely guarded; not tossed off to others so we are free to pursue selfish ambition. No one in all the world can take the place of a loving mother; no love so sweet, no care so pure than that of the mama. It is time for us to rally behind the mother and to esteem her highly.

Reverent, not slanderers, or slaves to much wine, teaching what is good, training younger women to love their husbands and children, to be self-controlled, pure, homemakers, kind, and submissive to their own husbands: these are the Titus 2 character traits of a godly woman. These are our high standards we strive for everyday: to conform ourselves to the Word of God and less to the world. To be diligent to the Titus list of qualities will create a woman who will stand out among the rest, will gain respect, be trusted, hold credibility, and cause the world around to stop and take notice. In doing this we will bring honor to the Word of God as opposed to allowing it to be reviled.

It is often said that man is head of the home, while the woman is the heart. The home ebbs and flows with her creativity, her joy, her gifts, and her touch. Home is where each family member finds rest, comfort, inclusion, and identity; it is where we belong. And so much of this begins and is fueled by the woman. A woman converts a house into a home. She fills it with love and care through hard work. So much of the Proverbs 31 description of the excellent woman centers around the home. She rises early to care for it, keeps the lamp burning late in it, clothes, feeds, comforts, nurses, teaches, creates, extends hospitality in and from the home. The home is the woman's handiwork and her greatest tool to do the work the Lord has given her to accomplish. From the home and in the home, she is the creative force by which lives are influenced and changed.

The woman today is being pulled from all sides away from the home, and a great void has been left in our men and children, and furthermore, in our churches and culture. When a woman leaves a career—no matter how prestigious the position—she will be replaced quickly by another. If she leaves her home, she is truly irreplaceable. Husbands are not honored, loved, nor encouraged. Children are not nurtured, comforted, fed, rocked, nor tended to. The result is that the family suffers and flounders, which ultimately impacts the health of the church. The woman's work in the home is indispensible and immensely valuable. She is truly and greatly esteemed above all others, and her worth is above all treasure. She is the woman of excellence; may we all strive to be worthy of such an esteemed calling.

—Nicole B. Hebbard

46. Let Us Not Delay in the Goodness of Marriage

Let your fountain be blessed, and rejoice in the wife of your youth.

—Proverbs 5:18

Marriage is a priority in the social fabric of all humanity, and this is especially true for the Christian Church that more fully understands and represents what bearing the image of God is all about. God made man as male and female in his own image (Gen 1:27) and brought them together to become one in marriage (Gen 2:18–25). This social and covenantal institution of marriage has been a priority to God from the very beginning; therefore, we need to recapture the heart of God by making it a priority in our lives as well.

However, like so many other blessings from God, we tend to let other pursuits occupy our time, energy, and resources that we prioritize illegitimately. The general trend in America has been to marry at an older age than in past generations,[2] and Christians tend to be only slightly younger than

2. For first time marriages: females marry at an average age of 26, males at 28. This

our secular counterparts, signaling that the church is being influenced by the culture far more than being an influential factor on it. Those who marry young get cross-eyed looks from the world, and not surprisingly, from many in the church as well.

The delay in marriage facilitates potentially damaging results and goes against God's design for us as his creatures, and especially for us as his elect. Firstly, we must recognize that there is no case in the Bible where marriage-delay is advised or considered virtuous; which is not to be confused with the noble call to celibacy, like that of Jeremiah and Paul. Secondly, often a delay in marriage is evidence of a postponement in maturity. Men, more often than women, want to hold on to their bachelor lifestyles for longer periods and avoid lifelong responsibilities. This keeps our men immature in the Lord in particular and in life in general; neither one is a virtue, and has rippling effects for the church since these young men should be in leadership training in local contexts. Paul told Timothy to be exemplary and not to let others despise him for his youth (1 Tim 4:12); but today we deal with full-grown adults who are excused for their perpetual youthful lifestyles. Thirdly, by God's design we reach sexual maturation and productivity in late teens and early twenties, and with it the energy to parent and raise the next generation of covenantal children. Yes, they need wisdom for parenting, which is promised to be granted to anyone who asks (Jas 1:5). By delaying marriage the youth are forced to struggle with their temptations over their sexual desires, and sad to report, many, if not most, admit to committing fornication. Given the choice between entering into marriage and committing sin against God, Paul clearly says that it is better to marry than to burn with lust (1 Cor 7:9). Fourthly, marriage is an undeniable instrument of sanctification, as men are to reflect Christ (Eph 5:25–33) and women are to reflect the church (Eph 5:22–24). And fifthly, the world observes them as a microcosm of the gospel.

Entering into marriage requires wisdom, but we need to use godly and biblical wisdom, and not confuse our sense of wisdom as being derived by the so-called wisdom of our social constructs, cultural sensibilities, and humanist pragmatics. Marriage is good and honorable, and God has designed it for his glory and our good. Reformation is not just for the here and the now; we must have an eye on the health of our future, and marriage is a critical component.

—Aaron B. Hebbard

is five years older than what was reported 1970. See http://www.albertmohler.com/2009/08/03/the-case-for-early-marriage/ and http://flowingdata.com/2016/03/03/marrying-age/.

47. Let the Church Reject
Chosen Childlessness

Behold, children are a heritage from the LORD, the fruit of the womb a reward.

—PSALM 127:3

We live in a day when it is becoming more apparent that men are calling good evil and evil good (Isa 5:20). This is a reality in many spheres of life, but there is a particular emphasis in relation to anything regarding God's order for the family.

Obviously, this is seen in our day when those who would advocate for marriage being between one man and one woman are considered to be hateful, perverted, and bigoted, while those who are going completely against God's original design are lauded as normal and good. As biblical Christians, we know what God says, and hopefully we are joyfully standing for marriage as he intended it. However, are there other areas in our lives and families this ideology may be impacting?

What about in the area of chosen childlessness? To be clear, sometimes God chooses not to bless a married couple with children. Barrenness in the Scripture is frequently a source of great heartache, as with Sarah, Rebekah, Rachel, Hannah, and Elizabeth. When I speak of chosen childlessness, I am speaking of something altogether different.

"Chosen childlessness," or "childfree life" as it is sometimes called, is a growing phenomenon in our culture wherein married couples are choosing to forgo having children, with some even having medical procedures to make the decision permanent. This trend, according to the August, 2013 cover story of *Time* magazine, is largely a selfish desire not to be encumbered with the burden of children, so as to have more time and resources for the life they want to live.

Though some who choose not to have children may have a more noble intention—for example a couple who feels it would be unhealthy and unsafe to bring children into the world because they are serving on the mission field in a very hostile region—the majority of people who hold to this philosophy, do so for the pursuit of their own selfishness. With a strong feeling that children would destroy their careers, houses, body image, ability to travel, and a host of other reasons they have declared themselves to remain childless. In the majority of cases, this choice speaks to a form of idolatry of a life unencumbered with children, so that individual pursuits can be all consuming in the life of the couple. Either way, chosen childlessness is wrong-headed and unbiblical.

Some Christians have tried to defend their choice of chosen childlessness, declaring that the Genesis 1 passage to be fruitful and multiply wasn't a command given specifically to marriage, but to creation in general, and because it wasn't repeated in Genesis 2, therefore, it isn't a command specific to marriage. This is not only biblically inaccurate and short-sighted, but historically irrelevant. Until the advent of the birth control pill and sterilization surgery, other methods of preventing pregnancy were largely ineffective. Scripture warns in 2 Timothy 3:3 about the end times when people would be "without natural affection" regarding family life, which I believe would be a reasonable category of definition for this current trend.

Christian couples should think very carefully their motivation in accepting a philosophy so unbiblical and unnatural regarding one of the primary reasons for marriage in Scripture, which is the procreation of children. "Be fruitful and multiply," was a command given at creation, Genesis 1:27–28; this command was repeated in Genesis 8:17; 9:1,7; with Noah and his sons and their wives and again in Genesis 28:1–3; when Isaac blesses Jacob, commanding him to be fruitful and multiply. The Psalmist David refers to the blessed wife as a fruitful vine (Ps 128); and the blessed man as a warrior, having his quiver filled with arrows, that is, children (Ps 127).

While this phenomena of chosen childlessness may fit well with our increasingly self-focused, materialistic, and image-conscious day, it is unconscionable that professing Christians would be following this devilish trend. We need a reformation in the church and family of our view of children. Instead of looking at them as an impediment to a wonderful, joy-filled life, we need to look at them as Jesus did, calling them the greatest in the Kingdom of God. Children are blessings to be enjoyed and weapons to be crafted, and one day launched to fulfill the work of the Kingdom.[3]

—CRAIG D. HOUSTON

---

3. On a further note, let us see the opportunity for the Christian population to continue to increase in number while the unbelieving community dwindles in size in coming generations. As an analogy, the number and strength of the Hebrew children overwhelmed Egypt, the greatest political machine of the ancient world, and felt greatly threatened.

48. Let Us See Our Children as God Does, as Blessings from Him

But when Jesus saw it, he was indignant and said to them, "Let the children come to me; do not hinder them, for to such belongs the kingdom of God.

—MARK 10:14

While it may be true, when it comes to gifts, that it is the thought that counts. On the other hand, we've also all received gifts that caused us to wonder about the giver, "What were they thinking?" The shocking truth is that Christians routinely have that same reaction about gifts sent by the all-knowing God of all the universe. God blesses us with children, and instead of giving thanks, we wonder what he could have been thinking. Worse still, we arm ourselves with sundry technologies to try to bar him from giving us such gifts. Secular pundits warn us about the cost of raising children, or about an already-overpopulated earth. Secular mindsets train us to see children as a curse rather than a blessing. But is this what God says on the matter?

> "Unless the LORD builds the house, they labor in vain who build it; unless the LORD guards the city, the watchman stays awake in vain. It is vain for you to rise up early, to sit up late, to eat the bread of sorrows; for so He gives His beloved sleep. Behold, children are a heritage from the LORD, the fruit of the womb is a reward. Like arrows in the hand of a warrior, so are the children of one's youth. Happy is the man who has his quiver full of them; they shall not be ashamed, but shall speak with their enemies in the gate" (Ps 127).

God also, in Isaiah 66:2, says, "But on this one will I look: on him who is poor and of a contrite spirit, who trembles at my word." How many of us, when we come face to face with God's Word on the blessing of children do not tremble, but instead argue? How many of us, even when we are given children, fail to give thanks to God for them, and in so doing, fail to tremble at his Word? How many of us believe that children do not come from God, but come from us? That is, how many of us jump from the certain truth that God acts through means, to acting as though the means are all that matters?

God opens and closes the womb. When he opens the womb of one of his own, we ought to rejoice, to give thanks. When he closes the womb of one of his own, we ought to mourn. When he closes the womb of one of his own, through the means of the decisions of one of his own, then we have a case of a failure to tremble at his Word.

If, on the other hand, we will repent, if we will believe what God says, the end result isn't some difficult and unpleasant duty. God's call here isn't to lay down our lives. Instead he invites us to blessing. Instead he promises joy. Instead he promises to give us life, and life abundant. If we repent, we receive this promise:

> "Blessed is every one who fears the LORD, who walks in His ways. When you eat the labor of your hands, you shall be happy, and it shall be well with you. Your wife shall be like a fruitful vine in the very heart of your house, your children like olive plants around your table. Behold, thus shall the man be blessed who fears the LORD. The LORD bless you out of Zion, and may you see the good of Jerusalem all the days of your life. Yes, may you see your children's children. Peace be upon Israel" (Ps 128).

—R. C. SPROUL JR.

49. Let the Christian Couple Counsel with the Lord Regarding Their Family Size

Trust in the LORD with all thine heart; and lean not unto thine own understanding. In all thy ways acknowledge him, and he shall direct thy paths.

—PROVERBS 3:5–6

My wife and I were very young, in love, and on fire for the Lord when we found out that we were expecting our second child. It was during this pregnancy that my wife asked me a sincere and penetrating question; a question that would change our lives forever. "Why," she asked me, "are we taught to trust in the Lord with our finances, with our time, with our witnessing, and every other area of our life, except with how many children we should have? What makes this one area an exception to the clear teaching of Proverbs 3:5–6?"

I would like to say that my response at the time was one of wisdom and maturity, but it wasn't. My twenty-year-old self replied, "We will have as many children as I say we are going to have!" Knowing my desire to walk in obedience to the Scripture, my wife patiently asked me to study this question out in the Word of God, to see what it had to say. I agreed, and, in turn, encouraged her to seek biblical counsel from other Christian women.

After doing a thorough study of Scripture, I became convinced that the building of our family was not the exception to Proverbs 3:5–6 that I had once presumed it to be. As a married Christian couple, we needed to seek the Lord about everything, including the building of our family. As I searched God's Word, he helped me see just how much he actually has to say about marriage and the fruit of marriage, which includes the opening of the womb to bring forth children.

I still marvel at the goodness of God. My wife had never attended any conference or seminar on the topic of the family size. She had never read any books or articles encouraging her to trust the Lord by faith with whatever children God would provide. Even the counsel she received from other women, which was, "God gives us wisdom to know just what we can handle," had more to do with their own understanding than the Word of God. It took the mighty work of the Holy Spirit, reforming the heart of my nineteen-year-old wife, to drive me to seek the teachings of Scripture in this area, as well as others.

The reality of it is that we didn't know just how many children we would have. No one really does. But we also knew that we would receive every child as a blessing from the Lord and not a curse, no matter how difficult the circumstances of life would be. My wife and I sought the counsel of the Lord and we heard Him say loud and clear through the plain teaching of Scripture, "Trust me."

My desire in this essay is not to tell you how many children to have, rather it is to encourage you to be the kind of Christian men and women who search God's Word for direction in everything. It is still a lamp to our feet and a light to our path, something desperately needed in the midst of this dark day, especially regarding issues that pertain to marriage and children.

The need for reformation in the history of the church and family has always come about because of a departure from the Word of God and its teaching regarding the Christian life. The resulting reformation was always a call to go back, not to what man had taught but what the Word of God demanded. The result is that reformations are necessarily painful as the traditions of man are torn from our hands and are replaced by trusting the timeless truth of the Word. Trusting is rarely easy; in fact, it is almost always the road less traveled by the church, but it is the only path in which the Lord's greatest blessings and most tender mercies can be experienced.

—CRAIG D. HOUSTON

50. Let Our Fathers Turn Their Hearts Toward Their Children

And he will turn the hearts of fathers to their children and the hearts of children to their fathers, lest I come and strike the land with a decree of utter destruction.
—MALACHI 4:6

This book is all about revival—a monergistic movement initiated by the Holy Spirit alone—and about reformation—our proper synergistic response to revival. Several of the topics we have addressed deal more directly with scriptural conditions for revival and reformation than others. The turning of fathers' hearts toward their children is one such topic. As the prophecy of Malachi announced and as fleshed out by the forerunner John the Baptist, turning the hearts of fathers to their children is part of the coming presence of the Lord.

Let us immediately disqualify misinterpretations about the hearts of mothers. Indeed, mothers' hearts ought to be equally turned toward their children, but what may come more naturally to mothers is less likely to come as naturally to fathers who get wrapped up in out-of-home schedules, professional aspirations, travels, hobbies, sports, and a plethora of distractions. The Holy Spirit is the ultimate Person who turns the heart of the father to his children, and this may be accomplished directly or through various other means: the pleading of the mother, the admonishment from church leaders, encouragement from grandparents, the explicit or implicit cries for attention from the children themselves, or through sermons, conferences, or books such as this one.

By God's grace I have not only experienced the Holy Spirit's work in my life in turning my heart toward my children, but I have seen it in lives of dozens of other godly men who, without the grace of the Holy Spirit, would have been perfectly content to have their children live mediocre lives of faith while they pursue their own interests, even their falsely prioritized kingdomly interests. Now these men live with intentionality; they want their children to thrive instead of just survive. They want their children to be strong and straight arrows in their quivers instead of soft, short, rounded, crooked little sticks. They are not ashamed to bring their offspring to the city gate where they encounter their enemies. These men are blessed (Ps 127).

Like all covenants of the Bible, there are blessings and curses. There is no greater blessing than to know that one's children are inheriting the true faith with godliness and wisdom (1 John 1:4). However, Malachi is just as clear to announce the curse resulting from fathers not turning their hearts toward their children: that the Lord would strike the land with a decree of utter destruction. The flipside of the blessings of seeing one's children walk in the truth can become a deep-cutting curse to watch one's own children walk away from the truth of the faith. Could this apostasy have been avoided if the father had only turned his heart toward his children? God only knows. But it is without dispute that the fatherless epidemic of our day has ravaged our land and culture. Children grow up in broken and fatherless homes, homes with "two mommies" or "two daddies," or in homes with physically or emotionally unavailable fathers who would rather retreat into their self-centered man-caves instead of being tangibly present in the heart of the home. Yes, we are under a curse due to such fathers who do not turn their hearts toward their children, and the rippling and disastrous effects are endless.

So what is the solution? The first call to action is to pray and repent from this heartless condition. Second is to make purposeful efforts to turn your heart toward your children, by any and all means. Third is to pray that the Holy Spirit will continue to turn your heart toward your children, and for your children to turn their hearts toward you. Fourth is to be an agent of cultural change by becoming a prayer warrior in praying for the hearts of other fathers to turn toward their children and children to their fathers.

Fifth, and continuing in the vein of being instrumental in cultural reformation, is to lead others demonstrably into the joys of turning their hearts toward their children. Sixth is making the generational effort to teach your children to have hearts for their future children, your future grandchildren.

Your children are a blessing, an inheritance from the Lord, and rewarding fruit of the womb. Go (now!) and enjoy them as such for the sake of our Heavenly Father, your children, your family, the church, revival and reformation, and our culture.

—AARON B. HEBBARD

51. Let Us Again Practice Family Worship

But as for me and my house, we will serve the LORD.

—JOSHUA 24:15C

In today's Evangelical Church many adolescents become nominal members with mere notional faith, or abandon Evangelical truth for unbiblical doctrines and modes of worship. I believe one major reason for this failure is the lack of stress upon family worship.

Joshua 24:14–15 says, "Now therefore, fear the LORD, serve Him in sincerity and in truth, and put away the gods which your fathers served on the other side of the River and in Egypt. Serve the LORD! And if it seems evil to you to serve the LORD, choose for yourselves this day whom you will serve, whether the gods which your fathers served that *were* on the other side of the River, or the gods of the Amorites, in whose land you dwell. But as for me and my house, we will serve the LORD." Notice three things in this text: First, Joshua did not make worship or service to the living God optional; second, Joshua re-enforces the service of God in families with his own example; and third, the word *serve* in verse 15 is an inclusive word, which is translated as *worship* many times in Scripture. Surely every God-fearing husband, father, and pastor must say with Joshua: "As for me and my household, we will serve the Lord. We will seek the Lord, worship Him, and pray to Him as a family. We will read His Word, replete with instructions, and reinforce its teachings in our family."

Given the importance of family worship as a potent force in winning untold millions to gospel truth throughout the ages, we ought not be surprised that God requires heads of households do all they can to lead their families in worshiping the living God. Our families owe their allegiance to God. He has placed us in a position of authority to guide our children in the way of the Lord. Clothed with holy authority, we owe to our children prophetical teaching, priestly intercession, and royal guidance.

Heads of households, we must implement family worship in the home. God requires that we worship Him not only privately as individuals, but publicly as members of the covenant body and community, and socially as families. Here are some suggestions to help you establish God-honoring family worship in your homes. We must direct family worship by Scripture, prayer, and song. Read from Scripture, memorize it together, provide daily personal instruction from it; confess family sins, petition for family mercies, offer thanksgiving as a family; sing heartily the Psalms and doctrinally pure hymns and songs. Remember and confess: "It is of Thy mercies that we are not consumed as a family."

Some people object to regular times of family worship. Don't indulge excuses to avoid family worship. In short, fight every enemy of family worship.

Let us remember that God often uses the restoration of family worship to usher in church revival. As goes the home, so goes the church. Family worship is a most decisive factor in how the home goes.

—JOEL R. BEEKE

52. Let the Family Discipline Their Children With a Biblical Mindset

For the Lord disciplines the one he loves, and chastises every son whom he receives.

—HEBREWS 12:6

Of all the resources that God has entrusted us to steward, our children are our most precious and treasured. Godly parents are commissioned to disciple godly children, and this discipleship requires discipline, as the two are integrally—and etymologically—connected, both having reference to teaching and learning.

Have you ever noticed that out in the animal world the babies and youth are prepared for independent life much earlier than humans? Beyond the parental protection provided by most mammals, some species go further by teaching their young to hunt and survive. But there must only be so much that is required to master in being a bear because this relationship is only a few years at the longest. Humans, however, physically, emotionally, and intellectually develop at a much slower rate, and we should respect that God's design is intended to bring decades of training and discipline to our offspring.

The simple fact is that we are all born as sinners into a fallen world, and accompanying our sinfulness is foolishness. Such foolishness is especially bound up in the hearts of children, and it is our parental duties to drive foolishness far from them with the rod, at least in their earlier ages (Prov 22:15). But our children must be able to receive our discipline as the clear beating of our hearts rather than the thundering of our voices or the swiftness of the paddle, and this too is our responsibility as parents to demonstrate to our children. As J.C. Ryle has pointed out, our children are like malleable chunks of metal, and like a skilled blacksmith who will shape the metal with small intentional blows over time, we should never expect a one-time correction.[4]

We are commanded to train up our children in the ways of the Lord so that when they are older they will not depart from this training (Prov 22:6). Let us firstly realize that God has not demanded from us anything he

4. Ryle, J.C. *The Duties of Parents.* Waverly, Pennsylvania: Lamplighter, 2001, 9.

will not give us the grace to obey. We ought not to protest that this task of raising children is too difficult; surely it is too difficult for us alone without the power and grace of God, but not too difficult with God who sovereignly arranged all details of our lives, including the number and temperaments of our children. Let us also note that this is not simply a great suggestion, but a solemn command. What is at stake but the very souls of our children; there are no higher stakes, nothing more important in life. Yet, let us think about how many things we allow to distract us and throw us off this high road. We must also keep the details aligned: the training is done by us, the learning is performed by our children, and the subject matter is the way of the Lord. Again, we often get the formula wrong; we allow others to take the lead in training our children in ways that are not (necessarily) of the Lord. We only come in later to make some "godly" tweaks to what foolishness has been imparted and practiced elsewhere.

Sometimes we parent by our own wisdom instead of in the way of the Lord, and we drift astray thinking we are more wise in our own eyes rather than leaning on the wisdom of the Lord (Prov 3:5–7). And lastly we must keep in mind that the end goal is generational faithfulness, not simply an outward compliance or spiritual façade of godliness while our children live under our roofs. For training to be effective, we must exhibit the fullness of joy and exuberant love of mature adult godliness and wisdom. Our children must admire and aspire to be the kind of adults we currently are. Like it or not, more will be caught than taught. If we are drab, slow, or lazy in our own obedience and only angry in our children's disobedience, what actually is attracting our children to the joyous life in the Lord?

Discipline must be both proactive training as well as necessary reactive correction. Preventive discipline includes training in righteousness, impartation of biblical knowledge, consistent prayer, participation in personal, family, and corporate worship, living with grace and forgiveness in the family, practicing truth, a strong work ethic, and love for one another, and having a demeanor of cheer, joy, and respect. Corrective discipline is demanded when preventive discipline failed to avert a wrong course of action or a sin-bent will and attitude. The correction here needs to befit the offense in proportion and correlation, as the law of God appropriates penalty to offence throughout the Old Testament. Lack or inconsistency of discipline— whether preventive or corrective—will lead to provoking our children to anger, confusion, and frustration (Eph 6:4). And we must remember that we parents are to discipline, not punish. We are to be intentional about breaking their sinful wills, but not their spirits; hence, we must seek God daily for more and more wisdom (Jas 1:5; 3:17).

The simple question is, do we love our children? If we love our children as a reflection of the Lord who loves his children, then we too must discipline. God has assigned us as their parents to be the primary conveyers of these crucial tasks. Let us take this seriously knowing the heaviness of stewarding God's children under our care.

—AARON B. HEBBARD

53. Let Us Educate Our Children as an Integral Means of Discipleship in Godliness and Christ-Like Character

My son, if you receive my words and treasure up my commandments with you, making your ear attentive to wisdom and inclining your heart to understanding; . . . then you will understand the fear of the LORD and find the knowledge of God.

—PROVERBS 2:1–2, 5

Standing against every secular theory of education in the world is this very important verse that has been emphasized by every great Christian leader in the history of the church, especially when it comes to the matter of education. No education principle is more important, and no Christian principle is rejected with so much fervor by the secular schools today than this one.

The fear of God is the beginning of knowledge about everything, including science, history, technology, economics, politics, and mathematics. To isolate these subjects from the fear of God in the textbooks and classroom instruction means the destruction of the Christian faith, education, and eventually culture. When it comes to education, the Christian is not so much interested in the teaching of chemistry sans the fear of God. What we want is the teaching of the fear of God *in* the chemistry laboratory.

Concerned Christians will pay close attention to church historical records on the matter of Christian education, still extant from the first two centuries of the church (prior to Constantine). Primary sources, of course, would include: The Didache, Igantius' letter to the Philadelphians, Paean's martyrdom under Rustics, Polycarp's Epistle to the Philippians, Barnabas, the Didascalia, Jerome's Letter to Damasus, and Jerome's Letter to Laeta, a homeschooling mother.

The Christian Church Fathers did not distinguish sharply between a "secular education" and a Christian discipleship. Generally, they frowned upon the use of classical, pagan literature as part of the *paideia* of a child. The Church Fathers would repudiate the modern secular form of education that forbids even a tacit mention of the fear of God or the worship of God in the classroom. A careful reading of the wisdom of the Church Fathers who struggled to nurture the faith in a thoroughly pagan world would yield the following determinant points: First, the fear of God is absolutely essential at every stage in a child's education. Second, parents are primarily responsible for the education and Christian training of their children. Third, life integration is critical, and practical application of knowledge in some form of trade must be included in their training. Fourth, faith and character is far more important that a prideful knowledge and mere academic lessons. The teachers must be focused more on this. Fifth, secular literature and art forms are extremely dangerous and must be approached with great caution (if at all).

Regarding education as a means of discipleship leads us to conclude that our teachers are not lecturers; they are disciples. And since this is the case, then the choice of teacher/discipler is of the utmost importance since "everyone when he is fully trained will be like his teacher" (Luke 6:40). We revive the old, humble "University of Jesus from Nazareth." We need more sandals and walking sticks than pin-striped suits and airy lecture halls; more love of the brethren than love of books; more Kingdom of God than empires of men; more Old Testament law than Aristotelian ethics; more prayer and parables than podiums and prose; more life-encompassing discipleship than narrow education. We are more interested in our students trembling before God in the chemistry laboratory and crying out in worship and fear, than we are in providing them a knowledge that puffs up (1 Cor 8:1). Thus, in the formation of character, it is important that the teacher know and love the student. These relationships take time to form.

Not only must we educate in the fear of the Lord, but we must do so with intentionality and fervency lest we incur a great cost in the next generation. Where there is no fear of God, there is no church, there is no true worship, there is no salvation, there is no true knowledge, there is no good culture, there is no wisdom; there is, however, apostasy.

—KEVIN SWANSON

---

54. Let the Family Prepare Sons and Daughters for Marriage

By wisdom a house is built, and by understanding it is established; by knowledge the rooms are filled with all precious and pleasant riches.

—PROVERBS 24:3–4

One of the primary jobs of parenting is to prepare children to leave the home and cleave to their spouses (Gen 2:24; Matt 19:5; Mark 10:7; Eph 5:31). Parents need to keep this end-goal in mind as they raise children up from the earliest of ages. As such we need to have a strategic plan of getting them from point A to point Z with purpose and intentionality.

In general preparation of both boys and girls for marriage, we must realize that training them begins from birth. This training primarily comes in the form of a healthy and godly marriage that is demonstrated before their eyes, day-in and day-out. We should never forget that before we offer any formal training in marital preparation, all of what they experientially know of marriage has been caught rather than taught. If we live out a sloppy and low-prioritized marriage, but then we attempt to teach them the high value and importance of marriage, we should not be surprised that our teaching doesn't stick any more than our slick hypocrisy sticks to our elusive sincerity.

To begin with, my wife has always made two wide parameters for the choice of future spouses: they must be Christians and of the opposite sex. Not rocket science but it needs to be said. Both young men and women need to be instructed in the biblical covenantal nature of marriage. Such instruction is counter-cultural in that marriage is often viewed as an unnecessary piece of paper or just an archaic institution from which to opt out conveniently. The covenant of marriage needs to be taught as binding and spiritual; and love needs to be defined as an enduring choice instead of a fleeting feeling. Indubitably, as we look around us at the quantity of young Christians, there is a shortage of quality and godly potential mates for our children to marry; but this state of affairs can—by God's grace—be turned around for the sake of family, church, and culture.

In the training of our sons, they need to be discipled to be competent spiritual and theological leaders of their future wives and children. They need to know how to love their wives with kindness and gentleness; and in the meantime, these skills should be practiced and exemplified toward their mother and sisters. The father should train them in biblical masculinity and in caring for his family through development of a solid work ethic and skills for work and home management. To practice their competence, the boys should learn by doing these tasks side-by-side with their fathers in construction, plumbing, vehicle maintenance, balancing finances, and even leading family worship. If they have been properly prepared, the likeliness of their future fathers-in-law accepting their intentions are far greater.

In the training of our daughters, we mothers must take Titus 2:3–5 as our guide for their discipleship. We assume the roles of the older women in this passage, while our daughters fall under the description of younger women. In the course of any given day, regardless of their ages, We must look for ways to teach our girls to love children, be good, practice purity, learn the art of homemaking, exercise self-control, and so on. While we must intentionally model the behaviors listed above, we must also demonstrate a genuine love and respect for our husbands in order that our daughters might see firsthand what a woman of godly character looks like; how she lives, loves, and brings beauty into every area of life. At a very young age mothers must speak into their daughters' lives all that God has for them as a wife and mother, pushing their hearts and minds forward to the most beautiful of gifts, marriage and motherhood. We talk of blessings, of hopes, and of joy to the day in which God brings the man he prepared for her before the foundations of the world. And above all, we return to the Word of God as our blueprint to guide and shape our daughters. We must transmit to our daughters the biblical truth of how a woman can be used by God to change the world by loving her husband and raising their children. Proverbs 31:10 asks the question, "an excellent woman, who can find?" Then, as now, the implied answer is that she is a rare gem. Only if we in the church take the discipleship of our daughters seriously will the answer to this question ever be: anywhere where Christ is Lord. And when she is found, her influence is great, her life is invaluable, and her reward is eternal. We disciple our daughters so that we send them out as excellent women who "surpass them all" (Prov 31:29).

One of the main tasks of parenting also becomes one of the greatest and joyous rewards; to see our children properly prepared for marriage and parenthood, to marry a godly spouse, and to carry on the legacy of God's eternal covenant to the next generation and the thousand generations to follow.

—Aaron and Nicole Hebbard

55. Let Us Return to Christ as the Center of Marital Matchmaking

He who finds a wife finds a good thing and obtains favor from the Lord.
—Proverbs 18:22

The church and the Christian family, as agents of change in broader culture, must return to Christ as the center of thinking about courtship for the marriages of our sons and daughters. How would we do such a thing? We must go to our only authoritative and blessed source of wisdom and knowledge—Scripture alone.

Preparing your children to be married and then guiding them through the selection process can be filled with cultural landmines. Our culture has served up a bad system of morality and an abandonment of basic Christian doctrines and practices, delivering us a dating system riddled by unbiblical ideas. We are saddled with Hollywood's definitions of love, sexuality, romance, emotions, the pursuit of marriage, and marriage itself. This system arises from a corrupt sexualized culture, which promotes infidelity, radical individualism, and autonomy. As we have slowly adopted the ways of the world in nearly every area of life in order to fulfill our lusts and maintain our respectability, we have nearly lost our ability to join our children in marriage properly by using biblical thinking. I pray these culturally accept-able practices will be abandoned by the church and replaced with more rational and intentionally biblical approaches.

Admittedly, neither the narrative nor the didactic portions of Scripture gives us a single way of getting married. The narratives in Scripture where marriages occur are very diverse and there is not a single biblical cookie-cutter procedure. God seems to use many means to bring people together. While there is not a clearly defined procedure for getting married, there is, however, a rich testimony of commands and principles that are guiding lights. Here are seven elements for thinking biblically about courtship.

First, the Bible teaches that the couple must honor parental authority and responsibility. We need to acknowledge that Scripture presents pictures with far more parental involvement than our current culture promotes or even allows. Consider Isaac and Rebekah (Genesis 24:1–67; 25:20), Jacob & Leah, Jacob & Rachel (Gen 28:1–2, 6–7; 29:1–35), and Caleb's daugh-ter Chas, (Josh 15:16–17; Judg 1:12–13). In most, if not all of the cases in Scripture, we see high involvement of fathers in the marriages of sons and daughters (Gen 38:6; Exod 21:9; Deut 7:3; Judg 14:3; 2 Chron 24:3; Ezra 9:2, 12; Neh 7:63; 10:30; 13:25; Jer 29:6). The Bible makes it clear that fathers are the heads of their sons and daughters (Num 30; Eph 6:1–4). This means that a couple must be able to place themselves under parental timelines and requirements. This works to avoid premature, vain relationships and mul-tiple mini-divorces before children are properly married. Further, the Bible presents the principle that men "marry"—an active verb—and women are "given in marriage"—a passive verb (Ps 78:63; Matt 22:30; Mark 12:25; Luke 17:27; 20:34–35). This means that daughters under normal circumstances should be "given" in marriage, implying consent. Suitors should not be al-lowed to relate with daughters in a way that would attempt to woo or try to win them until parents are convinced of the wisdom of moving forward.

Second, a process should be established for getting to know one an-other through natural relationship, interviewing, and screening in order to establish equal yoking, mutual affection, and compatible values (2 Cor 6:14).

Third, sexual purity must be maintained according to biblical defini-tions. Protections should be in place to assist in moral success (Col 3:5). There are certain things that are reserved only for marriage from which single people ought to refrain. For this reason, I believe that couples should refrain from the signs of marriage—such as kissing and beyond—until they are married.

Fourth, the couple should have a genuine tender love for one another and passion for the marriage, and not be forced into it (Gen 24:67). It is contrary to the gospel to think that love for one another is not necessary. Rather, Christ loves his church, and his church responds with love. Marriages should reflect mutual love and affection for one another (Eph 5:22).

Fifth, wise counselors who know the couple must be consulted and there should be a general affirmation for the marriage (Gen 24; Prov 15:22).

Sixth, we should consider the contrast between our modern practice of "engagement," and practice of "betrothal," that we see in Scripture (Exod 21:7–11; 22:16–17; Lev 19:20; Deut 20:7; 22:23–29; Hos 2:19–20), as with Mary and Joseph (Matt 1:18). Betrothal is a commitment that is binding between a young man and a young woman before the marriage ceremony.

Seventh, since marriage is a picture of the gospel, then everything that happens before marriage must be consistent with it. If marriage is designed to display Christ's love for the church and the church's desire for her husband and the purity of the bride, then courtship must be conducted for the glory of God. Christ's sacrificial life and the church's purity should be kept at the forefront of our thinking (Eph 5:22–33).

Though Scripture seems to present diversity of applications, I believe this means that God has designed flexibility in the process and he expects us to walk in a manner worthy of the Lord, using Scripture to guide our steps.

I pray that we in the church will not follow the ways of the gentiles in our pre-marital practices, but that we will glorify God with sweet courtships, betrothals, and marriages; honoring the Word of God, and dedicating our lives to Christ and his wonderful Kingdom (1 Cor 10:31). In order to do so, you must be faithful to the gospel, obedient to God's moral law, and honor your father and mother.

—SCOTT THOMAS BROWN

56. Let Us Educate Our Own Children

My son, be attentive to my wisdom;
incline your ear to my understanding.

—Proverbs 5:1

We live in the greatest apostasy in the history of the world, if the count of individual souls is the metric used. Never before has the Christian Church seen hundreds of millions (if not billions of people) exit the Christian faith and church. As of 2012, the non-affiliated churchless of the Greatest Generation (born 1913–1927) stands at only 5 percent, but the non-affiliated churchless of Millennial (born 1990–1994) stands at 34 percent, according to surveys conducted by the well-respected Pew Forum.[5] In terms of worldviews, Barn research found that only 0.5 percent of the Millenials retain some belief in absolutes, down from 14 percent in the previous generation indicating a 97 percent apostasy rate on this particular tenet of orthodoxy.[6]

As the apostasy reaches full maturity in the Western world, interested Christians are now asking, "What are the discernable human factors that pave the way for these apostasies?" While we are sure that nothing happens outside of the purview of a sovereign God, it is appropriate to identify the reasons for this apostasy and what we can do to stem such severe generational severance. Since it is the twenty-something's who are leaving the faith in droves, only a fool would ignore the "methodology" by which children are raised and educated in determining the cause for this mass exodus.

If there is no hard-and-fast line between discipleship and education in a biblical conception of knowledge, then who does the Bible see as the primary teacher who knows the child and loves the child and nurtures the child in fear and faith as he learns about history (Ps 78), science (Prov 30:19, Job 40–42), and the Scriptures (Deut 6:7–9)? Who will teach the child the fear of God? Who will teach the child to read the Scriptures? While delegation appears in the indicative passages here and there, the imperative

5. http://www.pewforum.org/2012/10/09/nones-on-the-rise/

6. https://www.barna.org/barna-update/article/21-transformation/252-barna-survey-examines-changes-in-worldview-among-christians-over-the-past-13-years#. UfwWCaw8mHs

passages are all directed toward fathers primarily and secondarily toward mothers.

We must reintroduce parents as the primary educators/disciples for their children. Churches must see their responsibility to equip and encourage to that end, particularly in an age where children have been increasingly handed off to state-educated professionals for their education and socialization. This has done untold harm toward the integrity of the family as well as the solidity of inter-generational relationships of grandparents, parents, and children.

We must obliterate the dualist distinction between sacred knowledge and philosophical knowledge, once and for all. To pretend that there can be religious neutrality in education is disingenuous at best, and can only ever be treacherous to the Christian faith.

We must teach the fear of God as the beginning of knowledge and wisdom in every classroom and in every textbook, whether public, private, or home school.

We must introduce a strong understanding of the antithesis into education—especially in the literature and liberal arts classes.

We must prioritize the thesis: God's revelation (the Bible), and literature written by committed, orthodox Christians. This is the material that must be taught first, because it is primary and basic to the education of children.

We must avoid setting our children at the feet of unbelieving authors and philosophers until they are matured in their understanding of a biblical worldview. When we teach non-Christian literary works, we must set the thesis against the antithesis in sharp contrast. This author is preparing a high school and college curriculum for the liberal arts student that will do just this.[7] As Western civilization crumbles, succeeding generations must understand the forces that contributed to its demise, as well as the ideas that will rebuild new cultures in the years to come.

We must move education toward a discipleship model that stresses the importance of nurturing faith, character, the fear of God, and life integration. Education is more than stuffing facts into the head of a student. A biblical epistemology always includes a life-integrated element (Jas 1:22–24), which demands more of a mentorship model in real-life context.

Without a dramatic shift in the way we educate, there will be no hope in salvaging other aspects of Christian faith and civilization. If Christian leaders are serious about salvaging the Christian faith in the Western

7. The material will be made available in textbook and workbook form as curriculum for home and school use, in the fall of 2013. Reference www.apologia.com and www.generations.com.

world, they must press for a major reformation in the area of education (for children, for higher education, and for seminary education). It is time for Christian leaders to engage in long and hard conversations on the form and content of education if there will be a church in AD 2100.[8]

—Kevin Swanson

---

57. Let Us Disciple Our Children to Disciple Their Children

Only take care, and keep your soul diligently, lest you forget the things that your eyes have seen, and lest they depart from your heart all the days of your life. Make them known to your children and your children's children.

—Deuteronomy 4:9

Discipleship is a major motif in the expansion of the Kingdom through the proclamation of the gospel. So often we set our minds on preaching the gospel to the ends of the earth and we spend our resources to send off evangelists and missionaries to distant lands. All of these are great advancements, but we have to remember that we are called to make disciples of the nations and not just converts. Getting converts but leaving them undiscipled in the faith is not only unbiblical but will not leave the church in a healthy state in the generations to come, and will certainly not bring about a reformation so desperately needed.

Wrong-headed and ignorant zealots (Rom 10:2) are those who are passionate about the discipleship of the nations but neglect the discipleship of their own children, or their future children by marriage, or even the friends of their children. God has placed covenantal children in our homes for the

---

8. I have produced a book on the biblical philosophy of education, titled *Upgrade: the Ten Secrets to the Best Education for Your Child*, in the hopes that this will be the beginning of a new conversation on primary, secondary, and higher education.

very purpose of discipleship, and we must begin where God has placed us and them. Making disciples is contingent upon converted disciple-recruits' willingness and desire to be discipled, and yet the children that God has placed in our homes are under our authority and have a sincere longing to be like their parents and to meet their approval. What an immense opportunity—and obligatory responsibility to disciple those with whom we live. We may, in fact, never make a convert from a distant land and disciple him/her in the faith, but at the end of life, we must say with confidence that we have discipled our own children—as many as the Lord has blessed us with—and that we have discipled our children to disciple their children, all of whom are the Lord's children assigned to us for purposes of discipleship. Perhaps we are also blessed with the opportunity to disciple our grandchildren alongside our children as a beautiful picture of the full implementation of multigenerational discipleship. We stand on the promises that God will raise up godly seed from the covenantal family and community to serve him from generation to generation (Pss 22:30–31; 45:16–17; 78:5–7; 145:4; 147:13b; 149:2).

God has brought us into relationship with himself, and the covenant is the parameters of that relationship. He alone has the authority to lay out the particular details of the covenantal parameters, and we must abide. Part of the covenant that we are to keep is to pass on the covenant to our children and our children's children (Deut 4:9). If we keep every point of the covenant but neglect to pass it on to our children and children's children, we have failed to keep the covenant in totality.

Moses left the Israelites with parting words of wisdom and instruction before they were to enter the Promised Land: "Know therefore that the Lord your God is God, the faithful God who keeps covenant and steadfast love with those who love him and keep his commandments, to a thousand generations." Whether we stand in a long line of God-loving, faithful, covenant-keeping generations, or whether we are privileged to be the first generation in a long godly line to follow, let us disciple our children, and disciple our children to disciple their children with an eye on a thousand generations of living in faithful covenant with the Lord our God (Deut 7:9).

—Aaron B. Hebbard

58. Let Us View Divorce as God Does

What therefore God has joined together, let not man separate.

—MARK 10:9

D ivorce is a deeply theological and covenantal topic, but today we simply give in to the concept that it is just an unfortunate but undeniable
fact of life in our culture. Marriage is beautiful and we celebrate it. So why
do we shrug our disingenuous shoulders at the ugliness of divorce? Our lack
of hatred for unbiblical divorce erodes our supposed love for covenantal
marriage. With one hand raised in bold affirmation of biblical marriage, we
use the other hand to sweep another unbiblical divorce under the rug. Suddenly we are caught; our cultural accommodation is showing to our own
shame. Divorce seems to be a privatized and acceptable sin in our midst; get
divorced on Friday and be present for worship on Sunday. No hypocrisy to
see here; just keep moving.

Let us be clear on several accounts. First, divorce is ugly and often
sinful, and has the capacity to destroy a family like no other force on earth.
Second, the Bible speaks against divorce in most cases but gives allowance
for it in several circumstances that we will later discuss. Third, since divorce
is the dissolution of a family unit, divorce is a matter of family values with
which we ought to be seriously concerned, especially in light of the divorce
rate in the broader culture, which thankfully is diminished slightly in the
church. Fourth, we must be strategic in our foresight to avoid the disaster of
divorce by building a strong biblical family ethic as a proactive measure to
be practiced in family life from cradle to grave. Fifth, the life of the family is
influential in the church, as the church is reciprocally influential in the life
of the family; and therefore, divorce needs to be addressed by the church
since one hurting part of the Body affects the whole Body (1 Cor 12:26).

Within conservative circles two claims for divorce are recognized as
biblically legitimate: sexual infidelity (Matt 5:32; 19:9), and abandonment
from a non-believer (1 Cor 7:15) or from an impenitent "believer" that the
church must judge and treat as a non-believer (Matt 18:17; 1 Cor 5:9–13). I
want to add another legitimate reason for divorce; neither to accommodate
culture nor to resort to pragmatism, but to be biblical. Malachi 2:16 states,
"'For the man who does not love his wife but divorces her,' says the LORD,

the God of Israel, 'covers his garment with violence,' says the LORD of hosts. 'So guard yourselves in your spirit, and do not be faithless.'" While I do not have the space required to exegete this passage fully to everyone's expectations and satisfaction, let us simply take keen notice of the negative words that the Lord employs to address husbands. The husband's lack of love is linked to divorce. The man who divorces his wife commits violence against her. The sum total of loveless husbandry, violence, and divorce is infidelity. In short, loveless husbandry is a breaking of covenant in marriage; divorce is violence against the wife; and faithlessness is breaking of covenant in marriage. If divorce is violence against the wife, physical violence against her legitimizes divorce because it reveals the husband's breaking of the marital covenant through loveless husbandry and faithlessness, which Jesus legitimizes in a sexual—and therefore physical—context in the NT. God's judgment is against the man who commits actual violence against his wife, and she makes official by divorce what he has done against her in his loveless, violent, and unfaithful husbandry in breaking of marital covenant. So while the two well accepted reasons for divorce previously mentioned show no partiality between the sexes, this passage suggests that only the woman is protected from her violent husband by means of divorce, and that the man may not file for divorce based upon a woman's violence toward him.

Marriage is beautiful and must be protected, but God's people are more precious. Jesus revealed that Moses allowed divorces because of hardness of heart, and likely the hardness of head (Matt 19:8). While the hard-hearted and hard-headed file for illegitimate and unbiblical divorce, God has also designed divorce to protect victims of the hard-hearted from having broken hearts and/or bruised bodies, and from being abandoned. While all unbiblical divorces are abominations to God, the biblical divorce gives the victim a second chance to find a suitable godly mate for life.

—AARON B. HEBBARD

59. Let the Family Care for Their Own Elderly

Honor your father and your mother,
for this is the first commandment with a promise.

—EPHESIANS 6:2

C hristian family eldercare is Faith 101. This is where the rubber hits the road when it comes to living out the Christian life. The Apostle Paul uses the strongest possible language, when discussing the importance of young men caring for their mothers and grandmothers in 1 Timothy 5:3–8. Even while suffering the agonizing death on the cross, the Lord Jesus Christ treated this as a matter of supreme importance. He took the time to ensure that his close associate John would care for His aging mother. In Matthew 15, Christ condemned the Pharisees for their system of *Corbin*, which purportedly relieved the Jews from caring for their parents in their old age, an ancient form of Social Security.

Our modern systems of eldercare as well as silence from our churches have generally failed to underscore the responsibilities of children to their elderly parents. Yet, the honor of parents as commanded in the Fifth Commandment must include this care for the elderly, according to our Lord's words in Matthew 15:4, 5. Every one of us should be asking ourselves in Jesus' words, "Is there anyplace where we have made the commandment of God of none effect, by our traditions?" (Matt 15:6).

In more ways than one, human relationships, and the opportunities for personal service and the expression of love have been displaced by professionals, bureaucrats, government-funded programs, and *quid-pro-quo* business arrangements. Billions of dollars of would-be godly inheritance to be passed on to children have been transferred to the state. And, trillions of dollars of government money is expended on eldercare. Proverbs 13:22 states, "A good man leaves an inheritance to his children's children, but the sinner's wealth is laid up for the righteous." The storehouse of God's resources seems to be flowing in the opposite direction.

The next twenty years will be the most defining years in this nation's history, as marriage rates collapse and child-bearing implodes. These will be major socio-economic changes. Socialism as a system of government cannot survive. From the beginning, it was God's intent that families take care of their own. Should a man refuse to care for his own mother or grandmother, the Apostle calls him "worse than an unbeliever" (1 Tim 5:4, 8). Could this be a bit hyperbolic? Is the Apostle a little too passionate in his imprecations? Taken at face value, these words offer one fundamental trait of the true Christian man, the responsible family man . . . the freeman from governmental systems and a slave to Christ alone. The church cannot tolerate an irresponsible man who refuses to provide for his widowed mother or grandmother. Ongoing failure to take responsibility in this area is a sin deserving the disfellowship of that person from the church (2 Thess 3:14–17). It is true that many aging parents are not interested in receiving care from their children. They may be more interested in socialist programs than the challenges in personal relationships and the restoration of the covenantal family.

Will family relationships disintegrate across the generations, or will families reintegrate the generations? Will the relationships between children, parents, and grandparents be closer or farther apart than ever? Will we find cross-denominational churches, where the eighty-year-old and the eight-year-old sit in the same pew? Now is the time to restore relationships across the generations. There is no better way to do this than by restoring home-based eldercare as the Lord leads in various families across this country and around the world.

Ask yourself these questions: Would you be willing to take a less prestigious career path that would not move you away from your aging parents so that you may obey God and honor your parents by caring for them? Would you be willing to make frequent treks to your parents' homes to check in on them? Would you be willing to reduce your standard of living by sacrificing for your parents the way they did for you in raising you? Would you be willing to build an in-law cottage on your property? Would you be willing to make room for them in your own home? Would you be willing to change their diapers as happily as they had changed yours?

There are many wonderful benefits with home-based eldercare, most of which—but not all—are on the intangible side (Eph 6:2). The world doesn't understand these intangibles. How do thousands of hours of back-breaking, sacrificial service result in blessings? Rest assured that we have a God who can supernaturally turn sacrifice into blessing.

—Kevin Swanson

Sphere III

Reforming the Culture

This section dealing with the reformation of the culture is the most difficult for several reasons. First, it is the largest sphere, and therefore, the most difficult to narrow down with respect to the areas that need addressing. Second, it is the hardest to pinpoint since it is so fluid and most resistant to categorical precision. Some, if not many, of issues addressing the larger culture may more properly belong to the sphere of church or family. Third, while the other spheres are easier to take a logical sequence in addressing, this section may have an appearance of a shotgun blast as opposed to the precision of a sniper rifle.

The reformation of the culture, on the flipside, may be the easiest to gauge. That is to say that if the culture begins to take shape in reformation, it will be most visible to those in the church, family, and even to those whose primary comfort zone is in the culture. As progress is made, we shall be encouraged as we reap the fruit of our labor, knowing we have been instruments of the Holy Spirit, while advancing the gospel and the Kingdom of God.

Without the reformation of the church and without the reformation of the family, the culture will never experience a real reformation. It may indeed experience an upward swing in morality or in financial responsibility or in returning to classical values of truth, beauty, and goodness, but without a Trinitarian, scriptural worldview that holds the gospel in its purest form like moorings, the culture will inevitably drift. These essays are not directed to secular cultural leaders; but are equally pointed to the church and the family as the two previous spheres. If the culture is the report card of the church, she must take inventory of her grades and through the Holy Spirit must rectify the areas in which she is not living up to her potential.

Francis A. Schaeffer said with clear insight, "The ignorance of the church is more dangerous for a culture than the decadence of the world." As long as I have been a student and educator, ignorance has always resulted in a dismal report card.

Cultural reformation must come in stages toward progress. The first stage comes by being counter-cultural. Many things in our culture defy God's laws and standards, and these are the very things that the church must resist and fight against in order to make room for an accurate portrait of Christ and the Kingdom of God. The second stage is taking cultural redemption seriously. In other words, we must wisely discern those things in culture that need to be destroyed as opposed to those things that need to be redeemed and brought under the Lordship of Christ. The third stage is building Christian culture proactively, and in so doing, be so strongly influential and winsome that the broader culture will desire to be a reflection of our robustly joyous Christianized culture.

The conveyer of truth that confronts culture must come from the prophetic voices of God's people. We must know the truth, love the truth, speak the truth, and live out the truth. If the church reforms and the family reforms but we do not care to see the culture reform, we have stopped short in our role of what God will do to bring forth the radiance of his glory throughout the whole earth. Let us desire to fill the earth with the knowledge of the glory of God as the waters cover the seas (Isa 11:9; Hab 2:14).

60. Let Us Begin All Our Endeavors With the Fear of God

The fear of the Lord is the beginning of knowledge:
but fools despise wisdom and instruction.

—Proverbs 1:7

We all want to be smart, or at least regarded as somewhat intelligent; we all want to be wise, or at least so in the eyes of others. As Christians we have a huge advantage if we dedicate ourselves to abiding by the Word of God. If we want true knowledge and sound wisdom, we must begin with the acknowledgement and the practice of the fear of the Lord.

So let's do a little exercise by taking our heads out of the safe sand and glancing quickly around at the foolishness that abounds. I'm sure once you've seen enough you will want to put your head back in the sand, but instead let's take this opportunity to be the salt of knowledge and the light of wisdom to the world around us. Our world is full of antithetical knowledge of God, which, by biblical definition, is foolishness. Yet, we have been given a tremendous promise; God's children are encouraged—better yet, commanded—to ask for wisdom from God who owns it all and gives it generously without reproaching us for being foolish (Jas 1:5). In fact, we may say that not admitting our need for wisdom and being wise in our own eyes are sure signs of inherent foolishness (Prov 12:15; 26:5, 12, 16; Isa 5:21). Contrarily, our admitting the need for wisdom is wisdom from above already at work. Only the wisdom as light from God can pierce the world darkened by foolishness.

I do not pretend to say that the world cannot grasp any wisdom or knowledge; in fact, people can grasp knowledge and wisdom by the very nature of being created in the image of God, whose attributes include wisdom and knowledge. But there is a radical difference between the knowledge

known and the wisdom practiced by the world and that known and practiced by the Christian. The foundation of knowledge and wisdom for the
Christian is the fear of the Lord, but the foundation of the world's knowledge and wisdom is devoid of the fear of the Lord, and hence, their foundation is nothing, and it is only a matter of time before it all collapses due to
instability at the base. By knowledge and wisdom we must conclude that
neutrality in knowledge and wisdom is impossible. To pretend to come to
know or to gain wisdom apart form the Revealer of knowledge and wisdom,
and giving him no recognition or reverential respect is to be the pottery that
ignores the potter who has created it (Jer 18). To enjoy the benefits of God's
knowledge while ignoring God himself is to become unthankful in heart
and futile in thought, and to become all the more foolish by any claim to
be wise (Rom 1:21–22). When God answers the fool according to his folly
(Prov 26:5), God's "folly" is preached unto salvation where man's "wisdom"
is impotent; God's "folly" is wiser than man's "wisdom"; God's "folly" shames
those who profess to be wise; and God's "folly" of the cross is only folly to
those who are perishing, but to us this "folly" is the power of God (1 Cor
1:18–31; cf. 1 Cor 3:19–20).

With all this said and the Scriptures so abundantly clear, how many ventures, pursuits, hobbies, and intellectual quests do we embark upon without
the proper foundations of the fear of the Lord in our lives? Let us not be wise
in our own eyes, but fear the Lord and turn away from evil (Prov 3:7).

—AARON B. HEBBARD

61. Let the Church Shape the Education of Worldview

Therefore, as you received Christ Jesus the Lord, so walk in him,
rooted and built up in him and established in the faith, just as you were taught,
abounding in thanksgiving.

—Colossians 2:6–7

Five-hundred years ago Europe, and subsequently the rest of the Western world, was reshaped by the Reformation, providing a worldview based on proper theological understanding of soteriology and ecclesiology. As a result, enormous advancements were made in nearly all major spheres of life, including science, astronomy, medicine, philosophy, economics, ethics, government, and education. When God and his Word are honored culturally, everything flourishes.

For three centuries progress was evident, but then once again, the church took her eye off the prize, a Christianized world, and withdrew from the development of a biblically-based civilization. A new "gospel" was advanced focusing simply on the salvation of souls and the psychological healing of man's nature. A worldview shift was underway and nowhere more profoundly evident than in the classrooms of youth. Gone from the lecterns and the pulpits where scriptural commands such as these resound:

> Romans 12:2: Do not be conformed to this world, but be transformed by the renewal of your mind, that by testing you may discern what is the will of God, what is good and acceptable and perfect.
>
> Colossians 2:8: See to it that no one takes you captive by philosophy and empty deceit, according to human tradition, according to the elemental spirits of the world, and not according to Christ.
>
> 2 Corinthians 10:5: We destroy arguments and every lofty opinion raised against the knowledge of God, and take every thought captive to obey Christ.

In the past 200 years America went from 85 percent church attendance to 25 percent. In the process we jettisoned fundamental principles of marriage, family, decency, self-government, and reverence for God. It is my contention that the primary sphere where we lost our way is in education. In the early 1960s we told God, "Not welcome" in the classroom. Since then, many well-meaning Christian organizations have made attempts to restore our Judeo-Christian heritage. Organizations such as Moral Majority, Eagle Forum, Focus on the Family, and Promise Keepers made valiant efforts to bring God back to America. However, their work primarily was an attempt to clean the river and thus failed to stop the filth at the fountainhead. Each passing year brought new and more filth to be removed from the stream of life.

It seemed that almost no one paid attention to the source of pollution destroying marriages, families, and reverence for God. That source, in my view, is the state-run secular public school system where academics are steadily being weakened at the altar of social engineering, especially in the "subject areas" of sex-education and multiculturalism. Education was taken further off track with its focus on environmentalism and globalism. Truly, schooling has gotten in the way of educating. This change of focus within the public schools began much earlier, a 150 years earlier, in fact.

Atheist John Dewey (1859–1952), signer of the Humanist Manifesto I, was the chief architect of a secular school system with the intent of removing the "myth" of the existence of God and an inerrant Word of God from the classroom.

The Humanist Manifesto II states: "We believe, however, that traditional dogmatic or authoritarian religions that place revelation, God, ritual, or creed above human needs and experience do a disservice to the human species. Salvationism, based on mere affirmation, still appears as harmful, diverting people with false hopes of heaven hereafter." Do we, as Christians, want our children schooled in a system with those foundations? Apparently so; 85 percent of the Christian community still uses the government school system to train up their children. John Dewey labored a lifetime in de-Christianizing America's classrooms. Unfortunately, the church was looking in another direction and now we must declare, Dewey et al. won. This is not to say that every teacher and every administrator and all curricula in public schooling are hostile to the Christian faith, but as a system, it is against Christ: "Whoever is not with me is against me" (Matt 12:30).

The problem of secular education is the single greatest threat facing the church today. If this problem is not addressed head-on by church leaders, we are simply consigning the next several generations to darkness and barbarianism. The family unit will continue to destruct as marriage is redefined. It is foolish to believe that we can continue to ask a pagan education system to prepare our youth for life and expect a Christian worldview to come out the other end.[1]

If the Church does recapture education, including the offer to provide education of youth from non-Christian homes, the shift in worldview will bring us back to a Christ-centered, God-honoring culture. We would see things such as healthy two-parent homes, honest money system, restful Sabbaths, and little crime. This is precisely what King Jesus told us: "Every healthy tree bears good fruit, but the diseased tree bears bad fruit. A healthy tree cannot bear bad fruit, nor can a diseased tree bear good fruit" (Matt 7:17–18).

—Daniel J. Smithwick

62. Let the Church's Christian Worldview Be a Cultural Agent of Reformation

Now we have received not the spirit of the world, but the Spirit who is from God, that we might understand the things freely given us by God. And we impart this in words not taught by human wisdom but taught by the Spirit, interpreting spiritual truths to those who are spiritual.

—1 Corinthians 2:12–13

One of the most serious plagues facing Christendom today is the failure to apply biblical truths to everyday circumstances. For many Christians the idea of applying the Law of God to the realities of life, and all of society's institutions, is an alien concept. Modern theology has merely become

1. While a proper diagnosis of the problem is a must, it is also a must that it be followed by a well-designed solution. To that end, we offer this to the Church: *The Worldview Course: Winning the Culture, not the Culture War.* Read about this at: www.worldviewcourse.com. For a free info pack, call 1–800–948–3101 and request the Kingdom Seminar Pastor's Kit.

an ecclesiastic exercise existing only within the confines of the individual, family and church, while rarely venturing into the other spheres of life such as politics, education, economics, law, international affairs, medicine, literature, art, science, and other like disciplines. Whenever God's Word is, in fact, introduced into the societal realm, it is usually marginalized, or compartmentalized, making it painfully ineffective. Thus, this dangerous lack of an applied biblical world-and-life-view has promoted a worldwide cultural disintegration. While the modern Evangelical Church may have an outward form of Christianity, it has all but lost its power (2 Tim 3:1–5).

Too many Christians talk of the culture war as if it were a television reality series where they can simply sit back unaffected, while eating popcorn from the security of their "Rapture-Hope" of "Get-me-out-a-here eschatology."[2] This mindset is not only unbiblical, it does not accurately represent the historic Christian faith. The covenant commission of the Sovereign Lord Jesus Christ is a commission of proactive cultural involvement utilizing biblical strategies and tactics to unseat the status quo of secular humanism and pagan ideologies.[3] To be a Christian in the scriptural sense of the word is to be responsible for the reconstruction of the culture by the application of God's Word. God's Word is not only for the self or for the family; it is a comprehensive rulebook for the entire global order. To apply the Scriptures to every area of life is what it means to advance the Kingdom of God. According to Scripture, the comprehensive establishment of God's Kingdom is to be accomplished in time and in history, and not after the world is in a blaze. We are held responsible for our culture in our lifetime.[4]

Sadly, today's Christianity has become culturally irrelevant as a result of its underlying theological assumptions of Dispensationalism and pietistic

2. The predominate mindset of the modern church is that the wickedness of the world is at critical mass and only the second coming of Christ can solve the problems of mankind. The Rapture ensures that the saints will not have to go through any trial of affliction but rather they will be whisked away into the air before any real persecution develops. This negates the fact that the Lord's Kingdom has come in both power and authority by his first advent, manifested with power in the earth at Pentecost. The Rapture philosophy negates what Christ accomplished, making it necessary for him to return.

3. Cultural involvement is commonly referred to as the Dominion Covenant, or the Dominion Mandate of Genesis 1:28. This mandate is initiated in Genesis but is repeated though Scripture in declarations such as Joshua 1 and Matthew 28, both identified as the Great Commission.

4. "Salvation increases our responsibilities because it makes us responsible men, and thereby increases our troubles. Salvation does not remove us from troubles, tribulation, or problems. Rather it thrusts us into them and at the same time gives us the assurance of victory in Jesus Christ." Rushdoony, R. J. *Salvation and Godly Rule*. Vallecito, California: Ross House, 1983, 13.

monasticism.[5] Rather than engaging the culture for its righteous recalibration, by the application of the precepts, statutes, and ordinances of God, the church has abandoned the culture by retreating from the battle in order to hide in their four-walled ghettos. Rev. Bryan Abshire observes, "Evangelical Christianity has been reduced from a comprehensive world view to a personal, spare time philosophy on the same level as stamp collecting or golf; interesting habits to be sure but nothing to becomes too fanatical about . . . Sociological studies have shown that contemporary Evangelical religion is quite simply irrelevant to modern Western Culture."[6]

If the church is to redeem herself from her apostasy and regain her much-needed societal momentum she must first begin with a re-acquaintance of her historic role as *The Church*, Militant and Triumphant. If she is unable, or unwilling to do so, a New Reformation must begin. This means that faithful men and women must abandon their apathetic churches and seek to begin new ones. Faithful pastors need to be called and trained for both the explicit exposition of God's Word and the cultural application thereof. We are experiencing today almost the same sixteenth century situations and events that staged the Reformation movement of Luther, Calvin, Zwingli, Knox, Baez, Bucer, and Viet all over again.

The culture is the report card of the church. The societal order is a direct reflection of both the church and the families that make up the church. Ethical conformity to the Word of God is critical if a long-lasting reformation is to be established. It is time to act accordingly.

—Paul Michael Raymond

---

5. Pietism, Monasticism and Two Kingdom theologies primarily teach that salvation is only for the individual and that the Christian is to only be concerned with saving souls and not the reconstruction of God's Global Order.

6. Abshire, Brian. *The Church as God's Armory*. Vallecito, California: The Chalcedon Foundation, 1998, 4.

63. Let the Church Seek God's Honor, Not this World's Acclaim

Do you not know that friendship with the world is enmity with God? Therefore whoever wishes to be a friend of the world makes himself an enemy of God.

—JAMES 4:4

Scripture forbids believers to imbibe the world's values (cf. 1 John 2:6; Rom 8:5–6; Matt 6:19–21) or set their affections on things of the earth rather than on heavenly things (cf. Col 3:2; 1 John 2:15; Matt 16:23). Christians do not belong to this world. We are not beholden to the world. We cannot legitimately court the world's admiration or approval. And it is wrong to think otherwise. Jesus told His disciples, "If you were of the world, the world would love you as its own; but because you are not of the world, but I chose you out of the world, therefore the world hates you" (John 15:9).

That truth is ignored or rejected by multitudes of twenty-first-century Evangelical Christians who wrongly believe that if the church does not first win the world's friendship and admiration, we have no hope of reaching anyone for Christ. Some of today's largest and most influential churches even take surveys to find out the desires and ambitions of unbelievers in their communities. They then plan their Sunday services accordingly, putting on a performance that caters to what people say they desire.

Popular televangelists follow a cruder version of the same strategy, promising people health, prosperity, and riches in return for money. They are today's equivalent of the medieval indulgence-sellers. These religious charlatans make their appeal blatantly and directly to "the lust of the flesh, the lust of the eyes, and the pride of life"—the same carnal cravings that 1 John 2:16 says are "not of the Father but . . . of the world."

Churches are full of people who are sinfully obsessed with the whims and entertainments of this world. They are desperate to keep up with various worldly fads and secular celebrities. They wrongly believe that if they embrace the icons of pop culture, the world will also embrace them and therefore be more open to Christ. So they wear the badges of worldly fashions; they echo the key elements of worldly wisdom; and they immerse themselves in worldly amusements. They cultivate an unhealthy appetite for attention, popularity, and worldly approval, convincing themselves that this is a valid evangelistic strategy.

Even in the highest echelons of Evangelical academia certain scholars seem driven by an unhealthy yearning for academic renown. They become so desperate to win the admiration of their counterparts in the secular academy that they willingly compromise the truth and sometimes even apostatize completely.

The wish to be noticed and admired by other people is itself a carnal, illegitimate lust. Jesus condemned the Pharisees because, "They [did] all their deeds to be seen by others" (Matt 23:5). They made a show of public piety to give the impression they were holier than anyone else.

Like the Pharisees, today's stylish Evangelicals fancy the praise and recognition of other people. But unlike the Pharisees, most of them want to be noticed for being hip, not holy.

It dishonors Christ when Christians try to fit into the fraternity of those who hate Him. Scripture is very clear about this: "Friendship with the world is enmity with God."

According to Jesus, the *only* business the Holy Spirit has with the world outside the church is to "convict [unbelievers] concerning sin and righteousness and judgment" (John 16:8). Those are precisely the themes that are typically omitted when churches become too interested in winning the world's approval.

The church must get back to preaching the gospel, remembering that the message of the cross, when faithfully preached, is *by God's own design* "a stumbling block to Jews and folly to Gentiles, but to those who are called, both Jews and Greeks, Christ the power of God and the wisdom of God" (1 Cor 1:23–24). The gospel alone is "is the power of God for salvation to everyone who believes" (Rom 1:16). Christians should not be ashamed to proclaim it.

It's true that if we are faithful, many in the world will view us with contempt as enemies—and we must be prepared for that. "Do not be surprised, brothers, that the world hates you" (1 John 3:13). The world put Christ to death, and he said, "A servant is not greater than his master. If they persecuted me, they will also persecute you" (John 15:20).

Furthermore, our Lord Himself didn't shy away in shame or retaliate in anger. Indeed, "to this you have been called, because Christ also suffered for you, leaving you an example, so that you might follow in his steps. . . . When he was reviled, he did not revile in return; when he suffered, he did not threaten, but continued entrusting himself to him who judges justly" (1 Pet 2:21–23).

—Phil Johnson

64. Let Us Learn How to Love God
With Our Whole Minds

But grow in the grace and knowledge of our Lord and Savior Jesus Christ. To him
be the glory both now and to the day of eternity. Amen.

—2 PETER 3:18

In our reaction against modernity with its scientific reductionism and
materialistic rationalism, we have become increasingly anti-intellectual.
But, ironically, the postmodern world of today has become even more anti-
intellectual, to the point of rejecting objective truth altogether. Christians
have a unique opportunity today to take up what has been cast away by
recovering and building upon their intellectual and educational heritage.
This will mean rediscovering what it means to "love the Lord your God . . .
with all your mind" (Matt 22:37).

Today's culture, it is said, has banished Christianity from the public
square. That is, it is generally considered inappropriate for the Christian
worldview and moral teaching to exercise authority and influence in the
society as a whole. Nevertheless, religion and "spirituality" are acceptable,
as long as they remain private, personal, and interior, with little to say about
the external world.

Not only does this unique and unprecedented view of religion margin-
alize Christianity, with its truth-claims and its teachings about the objective
moral law, it also drains away from society and the physical world any kind
of meaning, significance, and value. Such concerns are consigned to the subjective realm of each individual. As a result, the outer world becomes mean-
ingless and the inner world becomes detached from reality. Postmodernists
say that meaning can be "constructed," imposed on the culture through acts
of power or on the physical world through ordering paradigms. But the resulting relativism prevents any possibility of consensus or social agreement.

Though this worldview is profoundly anti-Christian, Christians have
unwittingly contributed to its formation. As Nancy Pearce has shown in
Saving Leonardo: A Call to Resist the Secular Assault on Mind, Morals, and
Meaning, Christians over the last two centuries have responded to the

pressures and arguments of modernism by retreating ever more into the private realm of the self.

Thus, contemporary Christianity is often presented solely as a matter of personal experience, subjective emotions, and private opinions. The doctrines of the faith—the creation, the incarnation, Christ's atonement for sin on the cross and his resurrection from the dead (all of which are grounded in objective reality)—are often minimized in favor of self-help psychology, therapeutic advice, and feel-good emotionalism.

As a result, non-believers, who struggle with the consequences of the loss of truth, find that churches have nothing to offer them. Young people in the churches with honest questions are sometimes sent away with no answers. Often they never come back.

Churches need to relearn Christian apologetics, showing that the false ideas of our times can be answered. They need to help their members realize that Christianity is not only good and helpful and joyful; it is also true. Knowing that Christianity is objectively true—that Christ really did bear their sins on the cross at a moment of history, that he actually rose bodily from the dead—can give Christians today a confidence in the gospel that can carry them through the times when their inner lives are filled with turmoil and when the ways of the world fail them.

To be sure, the Christian faith relies on God's Word and not human reason. Christians have always acknowledged that the mind is fallen, that the intellect has its limits; that the things of God go far beyond human understanding. But the truth of God's Word provides a foundation for all of truth—including that disclosed by reason and science—and that it all has its origin in our Creator.

Today's secularists have no such foundation for truth, and they are paying the price. For all of our progress in technology, which comes from the conservative principle of building on the discoveries of the past, our culture of relativism can lead only to conflict, triviality, and dead ends.

Christians thus have a great advantage in our increasingly anti-intellectual culture, as is already becoming evident. The failures of progressive education have become obvious to nearly everyone, with the gutting of academic content and standards, and young people knowing less and less about anything beyond the state of their own feelings.

Meanwhile, Christians are becoming more and more engaged with education, as seen in the homeschool movement and in ventures such as the new classical Christian schools. These typically are outperforming the progressive schools academically. When Christians are better educated than their secularist peers—more knowledgeable, more sophisticated, able to do more things and to do them better—they will be in a position to lead and influence the culture once again.

And as Christians learn to do as Christ commands, to "love the Lord your God . . . with *all* your mind"—which would include the analyses of reason, the far reaches of the imagination, secular-seeming learning, the ordinary musings of everyday existence—every facet of their lives will be transfigured. So let us think about God and all of his works, reclaiming the Christian intellectual heritage, adding to it, bringing it back into our civilization, and faithfully pass it on to the next generation.

—Gene Edward Veith

65. Let Our Lifestyles Build and Reflect a Culture of Worship

All the ends of the earth shall remember and turn to the Lord, *and all the families of the nations shall worship before you.*

—Psalm 22:27

All of life is worship, or at least it should be. There should not be areas of life that are not worshipful as distinct from reserved areas solely dedicated for worship. Rather, we should look upon all of life as a spectrum of worshipful interaction with God and in concert with our spiritual family in Christ.

This is the biblical pattern. Let us notice a few examples to make the point. Abraham answering the Lord's call to go to Canaan was an act of worship, including the simple act of loading camels with food and possessions, but when God appeared to him to preview the covenantal promises, Abraham pitched a tent in the place he called Bethel, the House of God, and entered into heightened worship with a proper altar dedicated to God as he called upon the name of the Lord (Gen 12:4–8). Isaiah was a prophet of

God and worshiped with his lifestyle, but when he saw the Lord high and lifted up, his interaction with the Holy, Holy, Holy Lord of Hosts became a life-changing act of worship (Isa 6). Shadrach, Meshach, and Abednego worshiped God by being God-fearing and excellent wise men in the court of King Nebuchadnezzar, but their worship intensified when they stood before the king to defy him in his demands to worship his image, and intensified again as they preferred death over false worship, and intensified again when they conversed with the theophany in the midst of the fire. Then as Nebuchadnezzar witnessed the theophany and the three men unharmed, this false worshiper would later be converted to a true worshiper (Dan 3–4).

In the New Testament Peter's obedience in letting Jesus use his boat to preach from was an act of worship, only to be followed by a deeper act of worship by obeying the Lord to push his boat out and go fishing when he had already spent a night of frustrated failure, only to be followed by an even deeper worship when he came to realize his sin in the presence of Christ's holiness (Luke 5:1–11). Paul devoted himself to worship of God with every step in his missions, with every lash from the whip, with every convert to Christ, with every moment in prison, and with every word he penned. Every word he spoke or wrote in his epistles was an act of worship, even the rebukes and the naming of those to avoid, but then there came times when he could not contain himself any longer, he broke out in doxology, in the very act of praise and worship (Rom 1:25; 9:5; 11:36; 16:25–27; Gal 1:4–5; Eph 3:20–21; Phil 4:20; 1 Tim 1:17; 6:14–16; 2 Tim 4:18). We could go on and on by examples from Moses, Joshua, Samuel, David, Jeremiah, the Samaritan woman, Thomas, John, and so many more.

The point is that whatever we do, we should do as unto the Lord (Col 3:23), and should be radically different in underlying motive than the mindset of the non-Christian. For example, both the Christian and non-Christian fill their cars with gas, but the difference in conviction is diametrically opposed in motive. The Christian should perform this mundane task as an act of worship by giving God thanks for the car, the money for the gas, and for the transportation to get to work to provide for his family, to bring the family to church, and for this vehicular impetus to praise and thank God. The outward appearance of filling the gas tank may look the same for these two, but one is an act of worship and the other is not, or may even be an act of false worship if the car turns into an idol or as a means to get to a job to feed an insatiable greed.

Let us worship God throughout our lives in all contexts, and in amplified worship in private devotion, more amplified still in family worship, and even more amplified in corporate worship as we gather with the saints on the Lord's Day, until we reach the pinnacle of ultimate worship when we assemble around the throne of God with all the people of God gathered from all nations of all generations and with the angels and creatures to offer a single voice of praise unencumbered by our sin (Rev 5:9–10; 7:4–9). Our present worship sets our minds on the heavenly court above and, in so doing, we are best equipped to fight the good fight of the faith here below.

—AARON B. HEBBARD

66. Let the Church Restore the Biblical Practice of Hospitality

Contribute to the needs of the saints and seek to show hospitality.
—ROMANS 12:13

Just as sin degrades man and makes him more beastly, so the grace of God restores man to his true humanity. The more our culture departs from biblical standards, the more beastly and individualistic it becomes. This is a denial of God's own image in man and so it is not strange to hear people long for community, sincere friendships, and meaningful relationships. And the *only* place where these can be found is in the church.

But the most common complaint about the church is that it is unfriendly. And sadly, this is often true. In large measure, we have lost the spirit of life that God expects us to have and to demonstrate in the world.

We are called to be "imitators of God" as his dear children (Eph 5:1)—imitating His grace, kindness, and generosity. We are to love one another and love our neighbors, and one of the ways we show our love is by practicing hospitality—which is why we have so many commands to do this (Rom 12:9–10,13; Heb 13:1–2; 1 Pet 4:8–9; 1 Tim 3:2; 5:9–10).

The narratives and the epistles indicate how common this trait of care for one another was in the early church—they greeted one another with a holy kiss, shared their possessions, ate together, lodged ministers, cared for the sick, the orphans, the widows who had no families, and took in those who had been scattered by persecution. The church took seriously the command to practice hospitality.

But today hospitality is largely an unstudied virtue. It happens because of personality or circumstance, but it isn't done as a matter of principled obedience. This must change.

Regarding the nature of hospitality, we begin with the meaning, literally "love to strangers." So hospitality is not so much entertaining friends as it is serving and ministering to outsiders in the name of Jesus. The object is not to impress others by culinary delights but seeking to serve and encourage others.

Hospitality is founded upon four things. First, the gracious nature of God. He is a God who is good to strangers. We were all by nature, strangers, cut off from God in our sin, helpless to provide for ourselves but God came to us and clothed and fed us. And we are to follow his example (Deut 10:17–19; Gal 6:10). God's people have always been marked as hospitable people (Gen 18:1–8; 19:1–3; Job 31:32; Acts 9:43; 28:7; Rom 16:23; 2 Tim 1:16; Palm 22; 3 John 5–8; Luke 19:5–6; Acts 16:15).

Second, hospitality is founded upon our union with one another in the Body of Christ. Christians are vitally joined together in one Body. As members of the Body, we cannot exist in isolation from one another. In order for each member to prosper, he must receive nourishment from the whole. God has not ordained that His people grow up into maturity apart from the ministry of the Body as a whole (1 Cor 12:20–21, 25; Eph 4:11–16).

Third, hospitality is founded upon the mutual love we are to have for one another. Whenever this duty is enjoined upon God's people it is in the context of our obligation to love one another (Heb 13:1–2; 1 Pet 4:8–9; Rom 12:10–13). If there is a sincere love for the brethren, there will be concern for hospitality and an earnest pursuit of it (1 John 4:6–21). John's words are nothing more than an expansion of our Savior's words in John 13:34–35. God's people are set apart from the world by their love for one another.

Fourth, hospitality is rooted in love for the world. God is love. The reality of his love means that his gracious purposes will triumph over all sin and evil. Love demands that it be so. Now that Jesus has defeated the world, the flesh, and the devil, they cannot stand against his love. Since we are called to show forth the light of his love to the world, we cannot isolate ourselves from the world. We must seek to transform it. And one of the ways in which we do this is by showing the generosity and goodness of God through hospitality.

Don't be put off by the trouble involved—love always involves sacrifice. Don't worry about the costs involved. God promises to make sure you have plenty (Luke 6:38). Trust and obey and God will bless your efforts.

It is no accident that we are told that history is moving toward a great dinner party at God's house (Matt 8:11; John 14:2–3). When Jesus describes the fullness and blessedness of salvation, he describes it as sitting down to a great banquet (Luke 14:16–24) or a wedding feast (Matt 22:1–13).

This shows us the centrality of hospitality in the church and why the absence of hospitality is a fearful thing. Where there is no concern for hospitality, there is no love for God's people, there is no desire to show the love of God to the world, and no confidence in the promises and purposes of God. In a very real sense, if there is no hospitality, there is no biblical church.

—Steve Wilkins

67. Let Christians Unite as a Form of Evangelism and Apologetics

I do not ask for these only, but also for those who will believe in me through their word, that they may all be one, just as you, Father, are in me, and I in you, that they also may be in us, so that the world may believe that you have sent me.

—John 17:20–21

There are some very serious reasons the church needs to unite. This goes for individual Christians uniting with Christians as well as local churches uniting with churches and entire denominations uniting with denominations.

The unity that Jesus prays for is extreme; that believers will be as one as the Father and the Son are one. Just because we can't understand the depth of this unity does not excuse us from seeking the type of unity that Jesus is praying for in his High Priestly prayer. Could we even imagine that the prayer of Christ would not be in the will of God and would not be answered in the fullest? By no means! We are united in Christ by the Holy Spirit. To resist unity with others in Christ is to portend falsely that Christ himself is not unified in himself. That is blasphemous and heretical. No, Christ is one in person, though two in nature. We are to be one in Christ, for this is the will of the Triune God.

Jesus distinguishes us from the rest of the world by a visible attribute, one that the world is supposed to recognize easily: our love for one another (John 13:35). Sadly, we often get our evangelistic efforts off on the wrong foot as we seek to win the world to Christ with the gospel by firstly loving those whom we are evangelizing. But this is not what Christ initially calls for. He rather states clearly that we are to love one another so that the world will know that we are Christ's disciples and that God the Father has sent his Son. This is both a pre-evangelistic effort as well as an apologetic for Christ being sent from his Father. Again, just because we doubt the effectiveness of Christ's statements does not validate our opinions. Rather it exposes our weak and futile thinking having doubted the will of Christ and the Word of God.

Bible colleges, Christian universities, and churches are filled with class offerings having to do with evangelism and apologetics. And to be sure, they can be valuable, informative, and insightful, but they are unlikely to start at a point where every Christian ought to begin; that is, the love they have for their fellow believer. Could pre-evangelism and initial apologetics really be that simple? By loving one another do we really proclaim we are Christ's disciples and defend that Jesus was sent into this world by God the Father? Yes, says Jesus! And that ought to be the end of the discussion.

I'm sure there are many who will speak of the value of their evangelistic methods and/or their apologetic acumen, but how many of these evangelists and apologists could reasonably defend the fact that Christians are guilty of infighting, of shooting their own wounded, and of assuming an air of superiority as observed by the unbeliever? Could the unbeliever dismiss the faith, the reality of Christ's coming from the Father, and that we are his followers simply by pointing out our disunity? Could the unbeliever laugh us off as a sick, hypocritical joke because we seek to disciple the nations but we can't even be civil with one another? If so, we have failed to be the witnesses, evangelists, and apologists that God calls all his children to be in our assigned contexts.

To many Christians the notion of showing preferential treatment to our fellow Christians may seem counterintuitive in our evangelistic efforts. Furthermore, it may go actually against what we've been taught about loving our neighbors, and to let this preference be obvious to the unsaved world around us may be, in our minds, a sure way to repel them from the faith. But as we learn to lean not on our own understandings or be wise in our own eyes, we need to trust in the Lord that he knows the path to Christian unity, which serves as a witness to the world around us. Simply stated, we are to do good to everyone but especially to those who belong to the household of faith (Gal 6:10). As part of our reformational efforts, do we really want to spread the knowledge of the glory of the Lord across the face of this earth? Let us begin by loving our fellow brothers and sisters in the Lord with sincere intentionality and ostentatiousness.

—Aaron B. Hebbard

68. Let God's Forgiven People Be a Forgiving People

Be kind to one another, tenderhearted, forgiving one another, as God in Christ forgave you. Therefore, be imitators of God, as beloved children.

—Ephesians 4:32—5:1

As Martin Luther approached the door of the Castle Church in Wittenberg, forgiveness of sins was very much on his mind. Many of his own townspeople had crossed the Elbe River, enticed by the promises of a papal delegate selling indulgences. Anyone who would pay the price, Johann Tetzel said, would receive "a full and perfect remission of sins," effective immediately. Luther was furious: God's forgiveness had been reduced to a market commodity.

For Luther, this was intensely personal. For years, he had exhausted every means the church offered to win God's forgiveness. Peace had eluded him. Then, as he studied Psalms and Romans, the light of the gospel began to shine in his heart. As he posted his now-famous Ninety-Five Theses, he was coming to realize that forgiveness was a gift God gave to undeserving sinners, because Christ had paid their penalty. It was not a reward for merit, but a gift received by sinners who would trust in Christ. That discovery changed Luther, and world history.

Like all the Reformers, Luther delighted that faith unites us to Christ, in whom all God's blessings become ours. "He himself bore our sins in his body on the tree (1 Pet 2:24). "In him we have redemption through his blood, the forgiveness of trespasses, according to the riches of his grace" (Eph 1:7). Because of Christ, through faith alone, sinners are fully, freely, and finally forgiven. This glorious discovery rescued the gospel, and remains indispensable in our day.

In Christ we are forgiven! But wedded to this truth is God's announcement that his forgiven people must be forgiving people: "As the Lord has forgiven you, so you must also forgive" (Col. 3:13; cf. Matt 6:14–15). "You must . . . "; forgiving others is a command, not an option. Vertical forgiveness impels us to horizontally forgive those who have sinned against us.

In this regard, the history of the Reformation is less encouraging. Sadly, those who rejoiced in the great *solas* of the gospel often engaged in bitter conflict with others who shared their basic understanding. The Reformers were, beyond question, remarkable men. But they were, like us, flawed and fallen. They nursed grievances, spoke harshly, exaggerated differences, and acted shamefully. Too often they lost sight of the main thing to focus on secondary things. They fought verbally and even physically, spilling the blood of true brothers in Christ. Reading their history makes us ask what might have been, had they been as good at practicing forgiveness as at preaching it.

That is a question we must ask ourselves today. We find ourselves in an increasingly adversarial and truth-resistant culture, and we are called to contend "for the faith that was once for all delivered to the saints" (Jude 3). But it is all too easy to become contentious, lashing back at those who misrepresent and deride us. Social media often brings out the very worst in people who imagine they are doing God's work! And the issue lies even closer to home. The Evangelical world is full of broken homes, divided churches, and shattered relationships. Professing Christians often seem to prefer being angry than being righteous, retaliating than forgiving or forbearing. Divorces, prejudices, and unChristlike behaviors infest too many of our communities. Small wonder, the world finds it easy to ignore our message of a forgiving Christ.

Christians are forgiven, but we are far from sinless. We both sin and are sinned against. That is why, as Luther declares in the first of the Ninety-Five Theses, our Lord Jesus "willed the entire life of believers to be one of repentance." Repentance deepens humility, and humility instills a forgiving spirit. But forgiveness is costly and difficult. As CS Lewis wisely said, "Everyone thinks forgiveness is a lovely idea until he has something to forgive."

My instinct is to retaliate, to hurt back, or to keep score. Still, the Lord calls me to forgive as he has forgiven me. Only time spent at the cross, reflecting on how much I need his costly forgiveness, enables me to find strength to do what my Savior commands.

True forgiveness does not mean ignoring or minimizing sin, even as the perpetrator denies or even delights in it. Biblical forgiveness is given to the repentant. We are to forgive, but to do so wisely and honestly, following the pattern set out by the Lord Jesus in Matthew 18:15–20. Our churches need to establish biblical patterns of church discipline and reconciliation. Even then, offenders will often refuse to repent or even admit wrongdoing. So, when with nowhere else to go, I entrust myself to my faithful High Priest, who knows all about such mistreatment. With his grace to help, I can go forward, knowing that he is able to both defend my cause and keep me in his care.

The only hope of our broken world is the Spirit-empowered gospel proclamation of our forgiving God. That proclamation needs to be wedded to the Spirit-empowered gospel practice of his forgiven and, therefore, forgiving people. Perhaps then, in God's gracious purpose, unbelievers "may see your good deeds and glorify God on the day of visitation" (1 Pet 2:12).

—GARY INRIG

69. Let the Church Defend the Faith
with Clarity and Charity

Walk in wisdom toward outsiders, making the best use of the time.
Let your speech always be gracious, seasoned with salt,
so that you may know how you ought to answer each person.

—Colossians 4:5–6

The church must consciously obey the command of the Apostle Peter to "set apart Christ as Lord (Yahweh) in our hearts" (1 Pet 3:15, quoting Isa 8:13). Such a radical, daily orientation of our priorities in light of the incarnation and lordship of the Messiah will have such an impact upon our behavior and our reactions that men and women will come to us to ask us for a reason for that hope that is thereby clearly displayed in our lives. And it is then that we have the God-given duty to give a reason for that hope; a clear, compelling, lived-out explanation of why as followers of Jesus we have hope in the midst of sorrow, a hope unknown to those who do not bow to him.

The ground of apologetics—the giving of a reason commanded by Peter—is found in the divine act of incarnation and in the exalted Person of Jesus. It is not found in human philosophy or wisdom, nor in the arguments of the wise. Apologetics, as such, flows from theology, and is therefore nourished by obedience to the command to "grow in the grace and knowledge of our Lord and Savior Jesus Christ" (2 Pet 3:18). Apologetics cannot and should not ever exist as an isolated, separated discipline from theology but is rather a true, deep spiritual commitment to living in light of the lordship of Jesus Christ.

Apologetics is necessary in our anti-Christian age of secularism, but it is a very dangerous field. It breeds tribalism, division, and pride in those who practice it. And when it takes on a life of its own, separated from the life of the church, it can become deeply ungracious and hostile toward any who might look, act, or think differently than its practitioners. Rather than "in essentials unity, in non-essentials liberty, in all things charity," apologists and polemicists often revel in drawing deep, dark lines that greatly alter the balance between essentials and non-essentials. Rather than focusing upon the key, life-giving truths of the faith (the Trinity; the deity of Christ; the deity and Person of the Holy Spirit; the hypostatic union; the inspiration, inerrancy, and authority of Scripture; the grand themes of the gospel, such as atonement, justification, etc.), these warriors draw myriads of unnecessary and dangerous connections between agreed-upon essentials and nonessentials, not only demanding uniformity in worship and expression, but in many areas of theology where differences of opinion and understanding have existed for centuries. As a result, charges of "heresy" can fly fast when, in fact, a small amount of life-giving grace, patience, and an acceptance of our state as fallen sinners would have maintained unity and peace.

For the glory of the gospel, the church must expend great effort to maintain a clear distinction between that which defines the faith and that which does not. This does not mean non-essentials are therefore irrelevant. There is a spectrum, and some non-essentials can have great impact upon the church's overall health. We cannot ignore our differences, but we must find the proper balance that can allow us to warn of the false teachers and wolves amongst the sheep while not limiting the fellowship of the saints to a small convention of clones. This balance must be continuously sought after; for there will always be forces pushing the church one direction or the other. And it is a task to be repeated in each generation, for we cannot become complacent and assume that our fathers' conclusions remain the necessary one in light of the speed at which society changes in our information age.

No matter what the context, the church must always seek to act in mercy and grace toward those who profess faith in Jesus Christ. However, when they openly reject apostolically-defined truths, then our commitment to honor God's truth and the gospel will compel us to act with clarity. But when we can extend mercy and grace while disagreeing within the bonds of love, God is glorified therein as well.

So keep your eye on the real target and use all your focused energy to defend the faith against the enemy; and be gracious to your fellow believer, even—or especially—in the midst of disagreement. As the Reformer Ulrich Zwingli once said to his fellow Reformer Martin Luther, with whom he had ongoing disagreement, "Let us confess our union in all things in which we agree, and as for the rest, let us remember that we are brothers."[7]

—James White

---

7. *A Memorial Service for the Four Hundredth Anniversary of the Birth of the Swiss Reformer Ulrich Zwingli*, 7. Philadelphia: Reformed Church Publication Board, 1884.

70. Let Us Take Up the Full Armor of God

"For though we walk in the flesh, we do not war after the flesh:
for the weapons of our warfare are not carnal,
but mighty through God to the pulling down of strongholds.

—2 Corinthians 10:3–4

A s Christians we are engaged in an intense spiritual warfare. *"Your ad-versary the devil, as a roaring lion, walked about, seeking whom he may devour"* (1 Pet 5:8). The devil is a shrewd enemy who has been tempting God's people for centuries, placing snares and traps in our path to distract, deviate, discourage, and defeat us. If we do not deal with sin and fortify our areas of weakness, we will continue to experience spiritual defeat.

If we harbor and nurture sin, we give the devil a foothold in our lives. Once we have surrendered ground to Satan, it is vitally important that we learn how to reclaim it, how to put on the whole spiritual armor of God, and successfully resist the tempter. The weapons that God gives us are able to tear down Satan's strongholds and replace them with fortresses of faith.

If we cultivate any known sin, we are giving Satan an opportunity to gain a foothold, a beachhead in our life. "Be angry, and do not sin; do not let the sun go down on your wrath, nor give place to the devil" (Eph 4:26–27). Satan will then use this opportunity to invade and take over other areas. It is crucial that we, in the power of God's Holy Spirit, reclaim and retake the ground that we have yielded to the enemy.

The Apostle Paul said that he did not want us to be ignorant of Satan's devices (2 Cor 2:11), but most Christians today are willfully ignorant of the tactics and strategies of the enemy. So since we are given this insight as a spiritual mandate for warfare, then we must conclude that willful ignorance of such revelation is biblical defiance. With battlefields all around us in a multitude of forms, we need the power of the Sword and its Divine Fash-ioner, the Holy Spirit, to fight valiantly and victoriously.

Christians are involved in a daily battle against "all that is in the world, the lust of the flesh, and the lust of the eyes and the pride of life" (1 John 2:16). Satan's plan is to steal, to kill and to destroy (John 10:10) while "the whole world lies under the sway of the wicked one" (1 John 5:19).

The only reason why the devil is so often winning, is that the church is so seldom fighting! "Therefore, submit to God. Resist the devil and he will flee from you" (Jas 4:7). If the devil is not fleeing from us, then either we are not submitting to God, or we are not resisting the devil, or both.

But we ought to have the greatest confidence for "He who is in us is greater than he who is in the world" (1 John 4:4), thus, "We are more than conquerors through Him who loved us" (Rom 8:37).

To fight and resist the devil, we need to be free. Ephesians 4:27 warns us: "never give place to the devil." The NIV calls this a "foothold"; the NASB, an "opportunity"; and the TEV, a "chance" to the devil. And this freedom only comes from Christ who truly sets us free (John 8:36; Rom 6:7, 18, 22; Gal 5:1).

Satan is a liar and a deceiver (John 8:44), and the accuser of the brethren (Rev 12:10). Jesus is the Way, the Truth and the Life (John 14:6). It is the truth that sets us free (John 8:32). We need to renew our minds (Rom 12:2), meditating on "whatever things are pure, whatever things are lovely, whatever things are of good report, if there is any virtue and if there is anything praiseworthy" (Phil 4:8). We need to tear down the strongholds of Satan in our lives (2 Cor 10:4). In its place, we need to build towers of truth, reprogramming our mind with the life-giving and liberating Word of God. We need to take every thought captive to the obedience of Christ (2 Cor 10:5), bringing our thoughts and lives in line with God's Word and God's Will.

—Peter Hammond

71. Let Us Understand Mankind According to Biblical Teachings

"For my thoughts are not your thoughts, neither are your ways my ways,"
declares the LORD.

—ISAIAH 55:8

Let the church promote a strictly scriptural understanding of psychology, which is the study of how and why man thinks and reacts. Psychology is thus at the heart of the biblical account of man and must be theologically understood. Modern psychology based on evolutionary suppositions is antithetical to scriptural teachings about man.

Man was created in the image of God, which Scripture identifies with knowledge, righteousness, holiness, and dominion (Col 3:10; Eph 4:24; Gen 1:26). Creaturehood under God is a part of man's nature and he cannot transcend that fact; denying this aspect of man is a futile attempt to deny man's meaning and significance.

Any view of man that neglects his two great limitations, creaturehood and sinfulness, can only develop a systematic mythology masquerading as science. Man's creaturehood is a limitation on man he must recognize, but one designed into him by God. His greatest limitation, therefore, is his sin nature, which perverted what God declared good. The historic origin of man's sin nature is recorded in Genesis 3, which is the basis for all scriptural understanding of man. Man's created nature has been perverted by the fall, but it cannot be eradicated. When man attempts to live outside the reality of his created context, he rebels against a moral certainty, a course that can only lead to frustration and failure. A host of mental, familial, relational, and social problems will necessarily follow. For instance, since man was created "male and female," all attempts to deny or blur those distinctions are a flight from reality and certain to result in the destruction of man's understanding of himself and his society. The attempt to explain man and his thinking in terms of evolutionary development falsifies the scriptural teaching of man's nature and therefore his mind and thought. Evolutionary psychology begins with a false view of man's origin and hence neglects the problem of sin, which according to Scripture is man's fundamental problem and the source of his frustration in life.

The message of Scripture is that sin itself is the aberrant and destructive element that must be addressed in order for man to have peace of heart and joy in life. The redemption of God through the atonement of Jesus Christ addresses man's sin; and man's growth in God's grace is his pathway to a life of meaning, purpose, and hope. The world is to be understood in terms of the two great divisions of mankind: the fallen man, who stands before God guilty; and the redeemed man, who stands before him justified (declared righteous) by the atonement of Jesus Christ. Fallen man is in a moral conflict with the image of God in him, which he cannot escape. This results in warfare against reality itself. The redeemed are, though still sinful, regenerated by the Holy Spirit as new creatures in Christ. This, and the Word of God, enables him to understand himself in terms of a cosmic and eternal significance, which places all else in perspective.

The church must give a clear message to man that he lives in God's world and it is only therein that he understands himself and his purpose in life. All other paths lead to frustration.

—MARK R. RUSHDOONY

72. Let the Church Be the Pillar and Buttress of Truth

I hope to come to you soon, but I am writing these things to you so that,
if I delay, you may know how one ought to behave in the household of God,
which is the church of the living God, a pillar and buttress of the truth.

—1 TIMOTHY 3:14–15

There is no doubt that truth is under attack in our postmodern culture. Because humanity is sinful by nature, we tend to bend and distort truth in such a way that it is less confrontational to our sinful shortfalls. So while truth has been reduced to a state of relativity in our postmodern culture, the attack is nothing new; all generations have sought to undermine truth in their own ways. Consider Pilate who had the height of ignorance or audacity to ask, "What is truth?" in a face-to-face conversation with Truth Incarnate (John 18:38).

Paul proclaims the church as the pillar and buttress of truth. This is an interesting analogy since in Paul's day there would not have been church buildings devoted to the sole purpose of Christian worship, and therefore, we have to conclude that it is a deeply, culturally nuanced symbol. Paul is not saying that the church is infallible in her adherence to the truth or that she is the truth, but rather that she is commissioned to be the cultural representation and protector of truth. A pillar is an architectural structure with the primary function to hold up something. A buttress is an architectural structure with primary function to bolster and resist pushes that would otherwise collapse a wall. The church must uphold truth like a pillar; the church must resist the cultural pushes against the truth like a buttress. Sadly though, today the church is seen wobbling in upholding biblical truth, and is weak in her power to resist the cultural pressure to redefine truth, which often results in the church accommodating the culture instead of being the bastion of truth. If the church cannot define and defend truth to our culture, the culture will continue to unravel beyond recognition. The church's commission is crucial.

What is this truth of which the church is supposed to be the pillar and buttress? Paul does not specify but we may rightly conclude that, within the corpus of first-century Christian knowledge, it would directly point to the person of Christ, and by extension the full mission of the gospel in redemptive history. But lest we conclude that truth refers to "religious" knowledge only, I would further define truth as reality as God has ordained it to be.

So hypothetically—or in reality—let us say that the church loses her ability to be the pillar and buttress of truth, what does that do to truth? Nothing! The truth remains just as true as it has since the foundations of the world, and back into eternity past. Christ as the Truth is still the same yesterday, today and forever (Heb 13:8). So what does the church's failure do to her commission in this respect? This is the critical issue. First, I do not believe that even if many or most churches fail to be pillars and buttresses of truth, the universal church has failed. No, God has proven time and again that he will always have his remnant. Second, the church that God the Father has predestined will be the church (Eph 1:3–6); the church that Christ gave himself for will be sanctified by the washing with his Word, be presented in splendor, without spot or wrinkle, to be holy and without blemish (Eph 5:25–27); the church whose cornerstone is Christ will be built up into a holy temple by the Holy Spirit (Eph 2:20–22).

The church will not fail because our Triune God cannot fail. But this is not to say that we have nothing to do. The church must rediscover and love true truth; she must uphold truth like a pillar in the presence of our culture; she must rely on the strength of the Holy Spirit to withstand the cultural pressures against truth. She must do all to stand firm.

—Aaron B. Hebbard

73. Let Us Be People Reflecting the Trustworthiness of God's Character

But above all, my brothers, do not swear,
either by heaven or by earth or by any other oath, but let your "yes" be yes
and your "no" be no, so that you may not fall under condemnation.

—James 5:12

Christians were once known as "People of the Book"[8] and we can legitimately apply that term to the people of God's Word. But for being the people of God's Word, we certainly have a difficult time being a people of our own word. We who bear the name of Christ and adhere to God's Word often fail to represent God as his ambassadors by lacking trustworthiness.

The idea that God would or could break his word is incomprehensible, but for our benefit God made an oath before us to become witnesses of his everlasting covenantal promises so we might see their fulfillments. God could swear by no greater entity than by his own Self (Gen 22:16; Heb 6:13), thus establishing his word in himself and for us. But furthermore, God also

8. Actually, it was in a pejorative term from the Muslims, and was also directed toward Jews. I wonder if they would accuse us of it today; it is a sad commentary if they would not.

establishes an example for us to be conformed into the image of his Son (Rom 8:29) to reflect his trustworthiness.

So here is our problem: we have a fully trustworthy God in keeping his word and promises, and we have been called to be conformed into his image, but we ourselves have been greatly negligent in the area of keeping our word and promises, and thus we fail to represent and conform to the character of our trustworthy God. So in this particular area, we are failing to be his representatives and ambassadors. In a world where trust, honor, respect, and integrity are attributes we only read about in times gone by, the church needs to reestablish herself in this biblical posture.

How many times have we waited in vain for promised phone calls to be returned? How many times have we had our employers overpromise and under-deliver to us or customers, or vice versa? How many times have we told our children, "tomorrow," but tomorrow never came? How many times were we stood up without a simple courtesy call? I could go on and on. There is wisdom in the old adage, "Say what you mean, and mean what you say."

If Jesus were to have a pet peeve, hypocrisy would be high on his list. Hypocrisy takes on several connotations. One would be to say one thing and to do another (Matt 23:3). Another example would be to act one way for the prime benefit of public display (Matt 6:2, 5, 16; hypocrite literally refers to a Greek play actor, one who wears a mask). And finally, a hypocritical version that pretends to believe the right thing but lives in a manner that refutes the belief (Titus 1:16; texts classics for practical atheism). So what is the opposite of this splintered character? Integrity refers to wholeness, of being unified as one. Therefore, what we say is one with what we mean and do. What we promise is one with what we fulfill. What we believe is one with our lifestyles. Who we are in private is one with who we are in public.

The people of God must become reliable in a world where reliability is becoming a rare commodity. In this respect, may the church of God be restored in reputation as having integrity and trustworthiness, and let us be dependable as a witness to the world that our God is the maker and keeper of his promises.

—Aaron B. Hebbard

74. Let the Church Embrace a Providential Perspective on History

Remember the days of old; consider the years of many generations;
ask your father, and he will show you, your elders, and they will tell you.

—DEUTERONOMY 32:7

Providential history is an attempt to have a God-centered interpretation of historical events that inspires hope and faith in his people. A providential historian unashamedly uses biblical presuppositions[9] as "the key to knowledge" (Luke 11:52). These presuppositions include a belief that God controls every detail of history (Eph 1:12; Dan 4:35; Rom 11:36), gives purpose and meaning to every event (Eph 1:11; Acts 4:28; Rom 8:28), is driving all of history toward a goal (Eph 1:10), and is working all things together for his glory (Rom 11:36), for the preparation and advancement of Christ's Kingdom (Eph 1:10), and for the good of his church (Rom 8:28; 9:17; Eph 3:9–11). Providential history makes history relevant to the struggles, hopes, and aspirations of modern Christians (Rom 15:4; Ps 78:1–4; Deut 32:7). It also gives the Christian the biblical worldview by which to critique the history of pagan ideas, technology, warfare, and combatant outcomes.

Sadly, modern Evangelical historians have largely abandoned this older Christian approach to writing history. In part it may be an attempt to be academically respectable in the eyes of the world. In part it may be skepticism that any uninspired person can possibly understand God's purpose in history. In part it may be because many Evangelical historians do not believe that there really is (or should be) a distinctively Christian approach to historiography.[10] In part it may be an overreaction to the way some historians have imposed a meaning on history in order to promote their agenda or cause (such as the revisionist histories put out by Marxists, Feminists, homosexuals, etc). For whatever reason, most modern Evangelical historians have sadly abandoned providential history and have opted for

---

9. For the Biblical presuppositions of historiography, see Phillip G. Kayser, *Seeing History With New Eyes*, Omaha, Nebraska: Biblical Blueprints, 2009.

10. Stafford, Tim "Whatever Happened to Christian History." *Christianity Today* 45 (2001), 42.

a so-called "neutral approach" to writing history. But it may be asked, "If Christian historians write history like everyone else, what is their value?"[11] We must not be like pagans who, "although they knew God, they did not glorify Him as God" (Rom 1:21). The Christian's passion must be that of 1 Corinthians 10:30: "whether you eat or drink, or whatever you do, do all to the glory of God." That includes history.

People criticize presenters of providential history for bringing biblical presuppositions into the study of history. But the only alternative is to bring in humanistic presuppositions. It is impossible to write history without pre-suppositions. For that matter, it is impossible to think about any subject without presuppositions. Another way of saying this is that history cannot stand alone. It is part of a worldview. And a worldview is a web of assumptions by which we interpret reality. The source of those axioms/assumptions reveals the ultimate authority for that system of thought.

The starting point for Christianity must not be the assertions of *man* but must be the assertions of *God*. The Bible does not say, "Your Word is true" (as if we can judge the truthfulness of God by some man-made criteria), but "Your Word is *truth*" (John 17:17; Ps 119:160), which means that all truth claims must be judged by the Word of God. It is *the* standard for truth.[12] Jesus also called the Bible "the key of knowledge" (Luke. 11:52). Without this key of knowledge we fail to see the true significance of events. As R. J. Rushdoony said, "Men cannot give a meaning to history that they themselves lack, nor can they honor a past which indicts them for their present failures."[13]

Providential history insists that history can never be viewed neutrally, but must give Christ "the preeminence in all things" (Col 1:18). As Cornelius van Til worded it, since God in Christ created and sustains all things (Col 1:16–17; Heb 1:3), and since all things work together for his glory (Rom 11:36), it would be "impossible to interpret any fact without a basic falsification unless it be regarded in its relation to God the Creator and to Christ the Redeemer."[14] God's instructions to all historians is that he "has made His wonderful works to be remembered" (Ps 111:4). The facts that are selected as well as our interpretation of those facts either honors or dishonors the God of history. This thesis is a call to return to the reformational

---

11. Ibid.

12. Grudem, Wayne. *Systematic Theology*. Grand Rapids: Zondervan, 1994, 83.

13. Rushdoony, R. J. *Biblical Philosophy of History*. Vallecito, California: Ross House, 1969, 135.

14. Van Til, Cornelius. *Christian Theistic Evidence*. Unpublished Syllabus at Westminster Theological Seminary, iii.

approach to historiography that calls for us to interpret reality through the lens of Scripture in faithfulness to Christ and all to the glory of God.[15]

—PHILLIP G. KAYSER

75. Let the Church Recover the Richness of Her History

Remember his covenant forever, the word that he commanded,
for a thousand generations.

—1 CHRONICLES 16:15

This is needed because the contemporary self-focus of the postmodern view of truth tends to make history irrelevant. The church is often allured by the siren calls of the culture in which she lives. Today, personal aesthetic interests are becoming normative for life. If we do not reform the church's accelerating historical amnesia and our culture's self-focus on the immediate, we are on the precipice of losing our rich heritage.

What a gigantic loss this would be considering Christianity's nearly two-thousand-year history. Millions upon millions of believers before us have lived for Christ, created Christian civilizations, and have studied, taught, and applied the Scriptures. If we forget this legacy, we become the equivalent of an uprooted tree that can easily be moved. If we forget our history, the great accomplishments of the church and her remarkable heroes will not be available to encourage the coming generations. If we squander our history, we deprive ourselves of the common believers, mighty leaders, bold martyrs, sacrificial missionaries, and gifted ministers of the past who have so much to teach us about following Christ.

15. For resources to help in this endeavor, go to BiblicalBlueprints.org or ProvidentialHistoryFestival.com.

Yet Christian history should not just be preserved merely for knowledge sake. Hebrews 13:7 says, "Remember your leaders, those who spoke to you the word of God. Consider the outcome of their way of life, and imitate their faith." This text gives us the biblical warrant to love, study, and learn church history. This means that in some sense, every believer should be a student of church history.

Let us remember that "Jesus Christ is the same yesterday and today and forever" (Heb 13:8). By pursuing our knowledge of Christ and believers from the past, we begin to reform our lives and to impact the generations that follow us. In this unbroken succession of faithful believers, we discover that every generation of the history of the church stands on the shoulders of giants who have gone before.

If we reclaim the great sweep of the glorious heritage in the church, this will help launch a revival of heroic leadership. The church's history inspires believers to impact culture, reform the church, avoid errors and heresy of the past, and to bring wisdom to the church today. It has been said that those who don't know the past are condemned to repeat it. However, it has also been well observed that those who control the past control the future.

A simple plan to begin to improve your church's knowledge of history is to assure that your church, school, or community celebrates 2017 as the five-hundredth anniversary of the Protestant Reformation. Another practical step is to read a survey of church history, especially if you've never studied the story of the church. Further, if you are a pastor, determine to use illustrations from church history from time to time to whet the appetite of your congregation to know more. Also, don't overlook the rich biographies of recent and past heroes of the faith. By reading these works a fire may be kindled in the hearts of your family, your students, your congregation, and your church to impact your community for the Lord.

The best place to start is with the Bible. Why not read again Hebrews 11, the Hall of Fame of faith? In fact, the whole Bible is concerned with history, the history of redemption. The Bible is God's great story of providential intervention in human history to accomplish the salvation of his people through his sovereign Grace. So let the church recover the richness of her history, because if she doesn't, the church may lose the greatest history book of all, the Bible itself.

—Peter A. Lillback

76. Let Us Work to Build the Kingdom as Our Means of Reformation

He put another parable before them, saying, "The kingdom of heaven is like a grain of mustard seed that a man took and sowed in his field. It is the smallest of all seeds, but when it has grown it is larger than all the garden plants and becomes a tree, so that the birds of the air come and make nests in its branches."

—MATTHEW 13:31–32

As previously stated, the culture is the report card of the church, and the societal order is a direct reflection of both the church and the families that make up the church. When these two spheres are out of step with God's covenant obligations, the nations go into a graveyard spiral under the judgment sanctions of Deuteronomy 28. If repentance and reconstruction are not forthcoming, all will be lost for this generation and possibly the next.

What America needs is a Geneva revolution. If anything marked the European Reformation it was its "drive to live a life more in harmony with stern biblical morality, and thus driven also to change society."[16] Every aspect of Reformed ideology was geared toward the reformation of the self so as to reform every aspect and institution of the culture. The Geneva revolution of the Reformation prepared the lives and attitudes of individuals to take stock in the world around them for the glory of God. The Reformation thought that structured the Christianity of Western Civilization still has the power toward establishing a society of righteousness, justice, equity, and peace. Historian W. Fred Graham makes this hopeful observation, "Jesus insisted that the wine of the gospel is ever-new requiring fresh containers. Western men drank it in the sixteenth century and changed their world."[17] We must do likewise.

Kingdom-building requires a concentration on execution. We tend to think too much in the void of academics and abstracts. Reformation begins with understanding but does not remain there. Only when the ethical and judicial aspects of God's Word is applied to real life does Reformation

---

16. Graham, W. Fred. *The Constructive Revolutionary John Calvin & His Socio-Economic Impact.* Louisville: John Knox, 1979, 21.

17. Ibid, 29.

breathe the breath of life. Only then can there be change in the culture. Successful Christian Reformation is designed to bring about specific changes, all of which are based in biblical truths. If a biblical reformation is to be successful, its strategy must focus upon, and develop, a system whereby biblical results are the goal. In order for this to happen, we must begin envisioning cultural outcomes. We must ask questions such as, "What does Scripture say about the proper justice system?" or "What does a Biblical monetary system or welfare system look like?" Biblical solutions to cultural problems often require breaking with tradition, especially when that tradition is based in man's fallible ideas and not in God's inerrant Word.

As an example of implementation, every church needs to support covenant education; not "schooling" per se but real education with Christocentric scholarship, application, and leadership as the goal.[18] Churches need to become an oasis for home educating families who have been convicted of the evils of government schools and their indoctrination agenda of anti-Christian humanism. When churches are unavailable or unwilling to assist in the deconstruction of the Roman Coliseum of government education, private flexible learning centers need to be established.[19]

Albert Einstein once said, "It's not that I am smart, it's just that I hold onto the problems longer."[20] If those who are sincerely convicted that a new reformation must commence, than they will focus on a particular cultural problem until they find the biblical solution. "Genius is the ability to hold one's vision steady until it becomes a reality."[21] If we have been blessed with biblical resolve we will hold onto a cultural vision of righteousness, justice, equity, and peace until it becomes a reality in our time and in our history.

We should embrace the understanding that the church is God's solution for reformation. The reformation of the church is the starting point for all of society's solutions. No matter what part of the culture needs to be remedied, the church holds the key.

—PAUL MICHAEL RAYMOND

18. See Illich, Ivan, *De-schooling Society*, Penguin Books, 1973.

19. See "Ivan Illich: Yet Again Revisited" by Dr Lance Box, position paper, Friday 19, 2014, Alice Springs, Australia.

20. Albert Einstein as quoted in *How To Think Like Einstein* by Scott Thorpe, Naperville, Illinois: Sourcebooks, 2002.

21. Ibid.

77. Let Us View Our Work as Divinely-Appointed Vocations

But you are a chosen race, a royal priesthood, a holy nation,
a people for his own possession, that you may proclaim the excellencies of him
who called you out of darkness into his marvelous light.

—1 PETER 2:9

One of the greatest recoveries of the Reformation was the biblical exaltation of all God-honoring vocations, which is integrally intertwined with the recovery of the biblical doctrine of the priesthood of all believers. Again, we see the theme *Post Tenebras Lux*; after the medieval darkness of the church's exaltation of the ecclesiastical call to the exclusion of all other "menial" jobs, the light of the gospel shone brightly upon the reforming church as they preached the dignity of all people who equally worked for the glory of God in their respective vocations.[22]

God is about the business of reclaiming this world as his own Kingdom. He has blessed all his people by assigning them distinct jobs for them to perform for his glory. In fact, we need to recapture and redeem the term vocation—meaning our professional callings—to describe the work we do in our jobs. To whom does God offer this call? All of God's people collectively are to be a chosen race, a royal priesthood, a holy nation, and a people belonging to our God. And what does this general calling entail? All of God's people are to proclaim the excellencies of the Lord who called us—that is, assigned us our vocations—out of darkness and into his marvelous light. In other words, we are all part of God's holy and royal nation of priests who work for a Kingdom-cause far greater than mere pragmatic survival or covetous greed generally connoted with a "non-vocational" job or profession. Few workers execute their special and official priestly duties within the church in the service of God, other priests, and indirectly toward the reclamation of the world; but most workers perform their

---

22. To be clear, I believe the Bible does support the higher calling of the official ministry, though not the higher dignity of those who are called to that office (Lev 8; Jer 1; Acts 6:2; 13:2; 1 Tim 3:1; 5:17, et al.). CH Spurgeon emphatically states, "If God calls you to be a preacher, don't stoop to be the king of England."

general priestly duties out in the world in the service of God, other priests, their neighbors, and more directly toward the reclamation of the world. Regardless of context of priestly duties, all tasks of our vocations equally have the same two criteria: to love the Lord our God with our whole heart, soul, mind, and strength, and to love our neighbor as ourselves through our various vocations.

So how are we to discover our personal callings? How are we to know God's will for our lives in this respect? Thankfully, we have traditionally held that this quest is a serious matter requiring prayer and wise, godly counsel. However, we have often inverted the importance of God's general will— what he has revealed in Scripture as applicable for all Christians—in favor of God's specific will for us individually. Only once we have understood and followed God's general will for his people are we positioned to be able to gain understanding of what God may want of us individually. But to answer this question, I offer this piece of advice: deeply contemplate how the Lord has created you with your interests, your skills, your convictions, your everything. Ask yourself what you would want to do if you had the freedom to choose; and then ask if this work will provide for your family;[23] how this interest fits into the general call to work productively as unto the Lord; how this vocation can be used to further the Kingdom; and how these convictions bring the greatest glory to God. To pursue a career without having solid answers to these questions reseats yourself as sovereign over your life instead of properly yielding sovereignty to Christ alone.

God ordains homes to be built for shelter and hospitality, banks to be managed with integrity and for prosperity, businesses to be built to provide quality products and services as well as honest profit, yards to be worked and kept as reflections of the beauty of Eden, food to be prepared for survival and celebration, crops to be grown to feed mankind and animals, and to show the cyclical miracles of creation, physicians to assist in healing a marvelously made body but flawed from infectious sin, historians to study and discover the invisible hand of providence, scientists to tinker in our Father's workshop and make discoveries for the benefit of mankind, educators to teach how we may think God's thoughts after him, engineers to design machines that reverse the curse of back-breaking work, and the millions of other jobs to be redeemed and performed.

The Kingdom of God is here and in process of being built and expanded. This is dignified and royal work, and we have dignity in accomplishing

---

23. If such an interest will not provide the financial support for your family, perhaps God is calling you to perform this task as a ministry that is supported by your paying job.

it. What a privilege that all of God's people are called and equipped to cooperate in this divine work!

—Aaron B. Hebbard

78. Let Our Work Ethic Reflect God's Sovereignty

Whatever you do, work heartily, as for the Lord and not for man.
—Colossians 3:23

Our family has a motto—a battle cry, if you will—that we say upon departure from one another: *Hos To Kyrio*; that is, "as unto the Lord." This is the way we are to live our lives at every moment of every day in any and every situation; whatever we do it should be done as unto the Lord, and not for man.

Let us narrow down this application to our area of work in order that we, as Christ's ambassadors, may represent our devotion to Christ through our work ethic. The world has given us a plethora of poor pictures of work, and we have soaked them into our hearts and minds to our demise and to God's displeasure. Some have denounced the curses of work, but what they mean is that all and any work is a curse. But we must realize that God is a worker and is even now at work, and that he blesses us by creating us, calling us, and equipping us for work. Laziness is sin, partly because we are resisting and refusing to conform to the image of God in Christ, who made us to be like him in the work he has assigned us.

Some have deemed work a necessary evil, which has thus led us to bifurcate and compartmentalize our lives by trudging through our workdays as unfulfilled beings, only to find our satisfaction in the evenings or just on weekends in home or church life. But God has made us whole beings (integrity, by definition) that we might glorify God and enjoy him in all of life, and that no matter where God places us, we are to represent him and flourish in our witness. How much of our lives would be wasted if we do not exude the joy of the Lord during our working days, weeks, years, and lives?

Some claim that work is merely a means to an end; that is, that we work in order to live and provide. But in addition to the provisions that work brings—and the provision that God grants us to have the mental and physical capacity to work—God calls us to live in an abundant way while we work, not despite our work.

Some are so devoted to their work and the monetary rewards that accompany their work that idolatry has enthroned their work and money as king of their lives. But God has given us a purpose for work that does not include building our own little empires for our own reputations, but rather that we might work in building the Kingdom for Christ. God has called us to worship him with our work lest we replace the rightful place of God with our greedy desire for money; and we cannot serve both masters (Matt 6:24). Furthermore, we are prohibited from overworking by adhering to the principle of Sabbath rest; that we might rejuvenate like Mary at the feet of Jesus (Luke 10:38–42).

Some have convinced us that work is what we must do now so that we might retire comfortably later in life. But the Word of God does not recognize the idea of retirement. If we are called to work and build the Kingdom, at what point are we supposed to retire from this task? If the Kingdom is in progress of being built, who gave permission to sit on the sidelines and watch others do the work?

Please do not misunderstand me. I am not advocating the idea that we must punch a time clock till the day we die, but by all means, we must work in building the Kingdom until the day we die. If, in your retirement days, you dreamed of playing golf, then make your foursome a strategy of intentional discipleship. If you have retired from teaching, pour your knowledge into your grandchildren and participate in their home-based education. If you are physically debilitated in your retirement, suffer well for the Lord, and become the prayer warrior you could have only dreamed of being while you were physically productive. The applications are limitless.

Let the work of the world be splintered into a trillion different areas of (counter) productivity, for a kingdom divided against itself will not stand (Mark 3:24–27). However, as we adopt a biblical, God-honoring, and healthy work ethic, and by the mighty power of the Holy Spirit through us, and as we pray, "thy kingdom come . . . on earth as it is in heaven," we will be about our Father's business and build the Kingdom to God's great glory. *Hos To Kyrio!*

—Aaron B. Hebbard

79. Let Our Economics Reflect Christocentric Principles

But thou shalt remember the Lord thy God:
for it is he that giveth thee power to get wealth, that he may establish his
covenant which he sware unto thy fathers, as it is this day.

—Deuteronomy 8:18

I n order to tackle some of the more difficult issues concerning a biblical approach to economics, we must keep Christ as our center. We must have the mind of Christ as we consider such issues as: the economic responsibilities of the individual according to Scripture; the economic role of the family as a unit; the role the government may play in job creation; the Christian reconstruction of the biblical welfare and charity system; the biblical tithe as it fits into the strategies and tactics to reform Christian economics; legitimate biblical investments; the distinction between establishing a family business and establishing a family business for the glory of God; how to earn honest money and how to begin to reorient both the institutional church and the general community into using only honest money; the sort of banking system that is biblical and how the Christian community can reconstruct the fractional reserve system; etc. As we can see, the issues that relate to economics are almost never ending.

However, in this context we cannot begin to consider some of the answers to these critical issues, so we must first understand *why* we have money and *what* God has commanded it to be used for beside supplying shelter, food, and clothing for ourselves and our families.

The majority of the Christian life is based upon stewardship. Adam was commanded to steward the garden (Gen 1:28–29). Christ was "to be about (steward) his Father's business" (Luke 2:49). The Levites were stewards of the Tabernacle and the Law (Num 1:51; Deut 17:9). Stewardship commandments are economic in nature. Christians are called to stewardship. They are to steward their time, money, skills, children, and their personal goods all for the advancement of Christ's Kingdom. Stewardship is applied economics. Jesus gives us a glimpse into the importance of stewardship: "And he said also unto his disciples, 'There was a certain rich man, which had a steward; and the same was accused unto him that he had wasted his goods. And he called him, and said unto him, "How is it that I hear this of thee? Give an account of thy stewardship; for thou mayest be no longer steward"'" (Luke 16:1–2).

Stewardship is also defined as caring for another's goods or money both to protect it from loss and invest it for gain. The word *economics* comes from the Greek *oilier-nomos*, meaning *house law*. Everyone's stewardship is structured according to some law, or philosophy, which is either self-determined or determined by another. There is no such thing as neutrality when it comes to decisions about stewardship. The stewardship law of a person's house (*oikia-nomos*) will either conform to God's Law or it will not. There is no middle ground. There is no neutrality.

According to Deuteronomy 8:18 the power to get wealth, in all of its forms, which includes money, is directly given by God. Since the ability to gain wealth is directly given by God He has the legitimate authority to command what that money is to be used for. In this regard the Law of God is clear.

Every economic problem facing the modern world today is a result of Christendom's failure to understand and obey this fundamental commandment as well as the failure to establish God's Covenant Kingdom within the culture. In cooperation and coordination with the various biblical commandments and economic case studies, not only can society's economic issues be solved, but wherever there is a biblical system of economics the state is kept within its legitimate sphere of authority. Whenever that happens the threat of statist tyranny is severely minimized.

Only an ethically sound system of economics can bring stability to society. This is true for an individual, a family, a church and a nation. Every aspect and sphere of culture concerning economics, especially here in America, is unraveling. The reason is due to the unwillingness of the institutional church to take the lead by applying the appropriate biblical principles and laws to cultural issues.

The stewardship of money is a moral issue. Attached to money and wealth is an ethical component. Consequently, the use of money is an ethical issue and it is God who tells us what money is and how it is to be used. Reformation needs to work its way down to where it hurts: our wallets! But ironically, what we think will really hurt will be abundantly blessed as we are biblically conformed through wisdom and obedience.

—Paul Michael Raymond

80. Let the Church Break the Chains of Debt

Owe no one anything, except to love each other,
for the one who loves another has fulfilled the law.

—Romans 13:8

We live in a culture of instant gratification. We come, we see, we purchase; whether or not we have the expendable money to buy the goods or not. Credit has become a way of life to most Americans, including Christians. While the Bible does not explicitly condemn debt, it certainly has much to say about good stewardship that would avoid such debt.

Stewardship is the basic core of Christian economics and relies entirely upon the truth that God owns everything (Gen 1:1; Ps 24:1–2; 50:10–12) and for his good pleasure has assigned us a particular lot to each of us to steward (1 Sam 2:7; 1 Chiron 29:12; 1 Cor 7:17). So if we lack the money to make a responsible purchase, and decide to purchase our desires anyway by going into debt, we are actually demonstrating our mistrust in the sovereignty of God. We are essentially saying that God should have assigned us more than he has, so we must take it upon ourselves to correct God's oversight in this particular area. Such foolish action, in turn, only propels God to exercise his loving discipline over our lives by handing us over to the pain of slavery to debt.

Proverbs 22:7 states, "The rich rules over the poor, and the borrower is the slave of the lender." Let us immediately respect the intention of this proverb by identifying it as being descriptive as opposed to prescriptive. In other words, this proverb is not commanding the rich to rule the poor, or the lender to enslave the debtor. Instead, it expressly describes the condition of the poor and of the debtor. In Hebraic poetry the parallelism of thought is the predominant feature of this artistry, and in this case the chiastic (ABB'A') employment puts the thematic emphasis on the poor/borrower over the rich/lender since the poor/borrower is positioned in the middle (BB'). So to be perfectly clear, this proverb is not condemning the poor to slavery, but rather is making an irrefutable connection between the act of borrowing and state of being poor in a reciprocal relationship spiraling downward. But Jesus says that we shall know the truth and the truth shall set us free (John 8:32), but lest we exclusively spiritualize this verse and conclude that it has nothing to do with freedom from the slavery of debt, we should interpret this general principle to apply to all of life, including freedom from such financial slavery.

Furthermore, Jesus states that we cannot serve two masters with loyalty and undivided hearts; we cannot serve God and money (Matt 6:24). Serving God paradoxically enslaves us to eternal life of freedom in Christ and sets us free to serve him as slaves of our own free will (Gal 5:1; 1 Pet 2:16; Rom 6:16–22). Serving money will only lead to slavery, idolatry, and all kinds of evil (Prov 12:12; 1 Tim 6:10).

Great benefits will follow our responsible stewardship in many respects. First, that we might hear the coveted words, "Well done, good and faithful servant" and enter in the joyful rest of our Heavenly Master (Matt 25:21, 23). Second, that we might be free from financial slavery to live a life unencumbered by debt in order to be a more usable vessel for financially blessing others. Ephesians 4:28 states that we should not steal but engage in honest work so that we might share with those in need. The same can be applied to those in debt; interest may be taking money away that could be used to bless others in need. Third, Proverbs 13:22 declares that "a good man leaves an inheritance to his children's children, but the sinner's wealth is laid up for the righteous." This is a double-edged sword; the righteous man should have money to leave to children and grandchildren, and that God will shift wealth from the sinner to the righteous by his divine means. How completely contrary is our practice of spending our children's inheritance on the interest we owe to the (often) godless financial institutions. Fourth, in the church's position of responsible financial stewardship, the world will take notice and come to us seeking words of wisdom, which will be a platform for expressing gospel truth and life. And finally, as we stated earlier, we practice our belief in the sovereignty of God if we live within the means God has assigned to us. And to be sure, if we are faithful in the little things, we will be assigned greater things (Matt 25:21, 23).

—Aaron B. Hebbard

81. Let the Christian Family Make Wise Choices For College

Why should a fool have money in his hand to buy wisdom when he has no sense?

—Proverbs 16:16

A career path and the proper educational training grounds are part of life's biggest decisions. In the realm of higher education, there seems to be three, or perhaps four, major choices afforded to the Christian. There are so-called Bible colleges and universities, and the numerous secular colleges and universities, which are found in abundance. Sadly, many from the first category morph—whether intentionally or negligently—into those in the second category. The colleges and universities which are explicitly Christ-centered, which prepare students to be culturally relevant in the advancement of God's Kingdom, which are sadly few and far between, ought to be the Christian's only legitimate option. Of course, there are also trade schools, which provide rich hands-on education related to a particular skill but do not necessarily fall into the category of academia. Yet, even here we must confess that if Christians are to be faithful to their professed worldview, every trade must be taught from a Christ-centered presupposition. There can be no neutrality.

Invariably, whenever decisions are made as to where a Christian young person should pursue an education, the topic of career comes to the forefront as if education and its anticipation of financial success is the determining factor as to which university the student should attend. Once lucrative financial possibilities become the dominant deciding factor in choosing a university, both parent and student are then more easily able to justify going into debt in order to pay exorbitant tuitions, which, in truth, cannot guarantee future financial prosperity. This lacks biblical wisdom and conviction about the Kingdom; we are only seeking personal peace and prosperity.

The decision to go into debt, in hopes that the education will somehow automatically result in some future financial prosperity, is a clear violation of one of the most basic principles of biblical economics. If debt is the status quo of our modern education strategy, can we expect God to bless the taking on of large debt for an education that may or may not be comprehensively biblical? Certainly he will not bless any educational motive that does not conform to his commandment to advance his Kingdom.

Let us address the irony of an expensive liberal arts education. The liberal arts education by definition has historically been intended to give students the freedom to think across the academic spectrum without restriction to one or two areas of study. In short, liberal arts education is to liberate the mind to think freely, broadly, and comprehensively instead of being shackled by a narrow perspective. So here's the irony: the pursuit of an education that is designed to free the mind comes at the cost of enslavement to a different master, a financial lender. Proverbs 22:7 brings this to light as it states that the borrower is slave to the lender. So while the Bible points out that seeking to learn godly wisdom and knowledge is well worth one's monetary investment (Prov 16:16; 17:16), it does not advocate a state of debt and bad stewardship in order to do so. We are forced to ask, is liberal arts education really liberating, or is it simply shifting servitude to another master? Having freed the mind to think, have we been shackled to a new set of chains?

While the exchange rate from one slave-master to another may be preferable, no slavery at all is the only real choice. The biblical solution is this: pursue an education that fosters the discipline and instruction in godly wisdom and knowledge at the cost of a well-calculated investment, but forbids enslavement to a financial lender.

Yet, how many Christian families are drowning in debt, or considering debt, due to outrageous tuitions? Even if one can justify spending the money on what is actually being taught by that institution, does the mere price tag of an educational institution translate into a good education that is culturally relevant to the glory of God? Not usually. So what should Christian parents and students consider when choosing higher education?

The most important criteria for choosing an educational institution must be if it glorifies God; "What college can best equip my child to advance God's Kingdom within the scope of his or her chosen area of study and within the means of our divinely assigned resources?" None of God's true saints ought to be educated for the mere sake of learning or for the sake of financial advancement. Our lives are to be invested for the glory of God. All learning must be devoted to the call of God in advancing his truth. I think the Christian community has forgotten that, and has defaulted to a secular world-and-life view concerning higher education.

This is a call to all involved. The Christian higher educational institutions need to self-evaluate what service they are really doing for the students and the Kingdom if they send out students into the world shackled and enslaved with enormous debt. And consider the disservice to a young Christian marriage of two college students who meet and marry with double the debt they now have incurred. Will they then delay marriage or children? The Christian parents need to commit to sending their children to a God-glorifying school as much as they can afford without incurring debt in their lives. And certainly they should not sell their own children as slaves to a future financial taskmaster. The Christian student ought not to take out loans to make the "college experience" full of extra-curricular fun for four years only to regret it for decades to come as the student debt is slowly and barely chipped away.[24]

—Paul Michael Raymond

and

Aaron Hebbard

---

82. Let Our Christian Colleges and Universities Retain or Regain Their Distinctive Christianity

So then, brothers, stand firm and hold to the traditions that you were taught by us, either by our spoken word or by our letter.

—2 Thessalonians 2:15

The distinctive Christian character of historically and confessionally Christian colleges and universities is increasingly threatened externally and internally in our contemporary "Christian" culture.

---

24. Both Dr. Paul Michael Raymond and Dr. Aaron Hebbard have been involved with and currently operate very affordable, God-glorifying higher educational institutions.

Externally, Christian colleges face growing pressures from constituents, academic associations, accrediting bodies, and governmental agencies to align their institutions with either liberal or conservative perspectives associated with the widening culture wars. Rarely, however, do these divergent perspectives represent the distinctive biblical antithesis between belief and unbelief. Yet significant numbers of Christian colleges bow to the left, embracing variations of secularism, egalitarianism, radical "tolerance," political correctness, sexual liberation, naturalistic materialism, philosophical and theological relativism and/or collectivism. And historically Evangelical colleges frequently muddle the historic Christian faith syncretistically with rightwing causes, conservative political positions, American Civil religion, Tea Party activism, unbridled capitalism, anti-intellectualism, rationalism, and/or individualism.

Internally, Christian colleges are increasingly prone to mission-drift. They often have more in common with the dominant modern secular state research university or vocational-technical training institutes than with their founding biblical principles. The distinctive Christian vision of integrated intellectual, cultural, and spiritual discipleship (*paideia*) that inspired and sustained Christian higher education from its founding in the late Middle Ages to the early twentieth century has been largely traded for a mess of secular vocationalism, theological heterodoxy, and/or dualistic pietism or doctrinalism. Secular and Christian colleges today are nearly indistinguishable in their degree programs, curricula, course offerings, faculty requirements and expectations, student behavioral standards, and dependence on government financial aid. The church arguably plays a lesser substantive role in Christian higher education today than in any point in post-secondary academic history.

The reformation of Christian higher education and the recovery or retention of distinctive Christianity in the academy will depend on unapologetic reaffirmation of the authority of the infallible Word of God and substantive changes in at least three key areas:

1. Christian colleges and universities must recover or strengthen a distinctively Christian mission and a biblical vision for their academic pursuits which proclaim the Lordship of Christ over all things and which stand in clear, antithetical opposition to the mission and vision of the secular academy;

2. Christian colleges and universities must resist all external pressures to confuse the gospel with or to align their institutions to the dominant liberal or conservative perspectives associated with the culture wars and, instead, honestly and faithfully affirm the distinctive biblical

antithesis between belief and unbelief applied across all aspects of creation and their related academic disciplines (and *not* between majority
or minority views politically or culturally); and

3. Christian colleges and universities must recover or strengthen internally their biblical vision of integrated intellectual, cultural, and spiritual discipleship, rooted particularly in the distinctive biblical concept
of the *paideia* of the Lord,[25] which was first expressed pedagogically and
curricularly in the *Tritium* and *Quadrivium* as a means to acculturate
students into everything it means to be an heir of the King of Kings,
and which inspired and sustained Christian higher education from its
founding in the late Middle Ages until the early twentieth century.

—ROY ATWOOD

25. Thayer's definition of *paideia* [παιδεία] (see Deut 11:2, Prov 1:1-3, 3:11-12,
6:23; Eph 6:4; Heb 12:4-11) is "1) the whole training and education of children (which
relates to the cultivation of mind and morals, and employs for this purpose now commands and admonitions, now reproof and punishment); it also includes the training
and care of the body; 2) whatever in adults also cultivates the soul, especially by cor-
recting mistakes and curbing passions; 2a) instruction which aims at increasing virtue;
and 2b) chastisement, chastening, (of the evils with which God visits men for their
amendment)." See also Werner Jaeger, *Paideia: The Ideals of Greek Culture, Vol. I: Archaic Greece, The Mind of Athens.* 3 vols.; New York: Oxford University, 1945, xiii-xxix.

83. Let the Church See the Political Realm as Subject to the Sovereign God

Then comes the end, when he delivers the kingdom to God the Father
after destroying every rule and every authority and power.

—1 Corinthians 15:24

God alone has total right and jurisdiction over every area of life. Sovereignty is a religious concept, and cannot rightly be claimed by any man or human institution. When the church speaks in terms of the authoritative revealed Word of God, it speaks with spiritual authority even when it does not have jurisdictional authority.

The powers that be are ordained of God (Rom 13), and we must be submissive to legitimate authority, but in saying this, Paul specifically included and gave priority to God and his governance. Human kings, who then claimed much more authority than do modern rulers, were told to "Kiss the Son, lest he be angry" (Ps 2:10–12). Jesus Christ is declared to be "King of Kings and Lord of Lords" (Rev 19:16). Any ruler or state that claims ultimate right usurps what can only legitimately belong to God and his Christ. All human authority is delegated from and subordinate to God. No realm is exempt from the authority of God; unbelief conveys no exemption.

God has described his rule in political language, as the Kingdom of Heaven, with Christ as its Lord. This is not an allegory, but a call to a true operative loyalty, one recognized in early Christianity by unbelievers (Acts 17:5–7). The church has a duty to repudiate any claim by the state to be the highest authority over man because it is the representative of the true transcendent order of Jesus Christ. All Christians therefore have a dual citizenship, and obedience to any human authority must be subject to the higher authority of God (Acts 5:29).

The church must declare the moral basis for liberty. Even on the human level, government must not be equated with the civic function of the state. The basic government required by God is self-government, because all men are responsible to God. Other ordained institutions also have very legitimate areas of authority, "spheres" of power or authority. These spheres certainly include family and church, but can also include vocation, school, and private associations that sometimes govern us. If the state is assumed to be preeminent and man's primary loyalty is to it, there is no room for self-government and freedom is impossible. Freedom is a moral necessity because man must be self-consciously free to obey God, and the development of liberty in the West reflected this awareness and was only made possible because of the growth and development of Christendom. A strong sense of the religious duty of man and of the larger vision of the Kingdom of God resulted in a view of man as personally responsible to God. Personal accountability necessitates personal responsibility, and this is only possible with individual liberty. Paul therefore warned against voluntarily putting oneself in a position of bondage (1 Cor 7:23; Gal 5:1).

Politics deal with the realm of the state, and every state is religious because its laws represent a morality, because they decree things to be either good and therefore to be required or encouraged, or else bad and to be forbidden or discouraged. Since the fragmentation of Christianity in the West long ago, the old debate of "church versus state" has become a misleading one, because there is no church organization that could exercise control over the civil realm. The real issue today, which the church must address, is the raging battle between different religious ideas about the basis for law and its enforcement. There is no neutral or secular realm recognized as valid in Scripture. The call of the church to its members must therefore always be, "Who is on the Lord's side?"

The claims of God must be proclaimed in the realm of politics as a witness to their truth and as a prophetic witness of the consequences of their rejection. The opportunity to speak to the civil realm is therefore more than a blessing of our political system, it is a moral responsibility. Nevertheless, the fullness of the Kingdom will not come by any political top-down means, but by the bottom-up regeneration of individuals by the power and in the time decreed by the Holy Spirit.

—Mark Rushdooney

84. Let the Church Recover
the Theology of the Beauty of God

Out of Zion, the perfection of beauty, God shines forth.

—PSALM 50:2

Whereas, the Bible begins in a beautiful garden and ends in a beautiful city; and whereas, even the somber book of Ecclesiastes reminds us that God, "makes all things beautiful in its time" (Eccl 3:11), the church needs to recapture the role of beauty in God's plan.

The New Testament shows us the beauty of the gospel to transform *all* of life. The in-breaking of the Kingdom of God through the life, death, and resurrection of Christ transforms our heart and mind (Rom 12) so that we may be whole and beautiful from within (sanctification). But that is not all. The New Testament places our hope on the future day when we will finally join Christ and eternally dwell with him in the beautiful New Jerusalem. We are encouraged to look forward to that day because we will receive beautiful, glorified bodies (Phil 3:21). *Everything* will finally be beautiful because we will be fully in the presence of our Holy God; from the very surface beauty of golden streets to the very core of our heart and soul.

As Christ taught us to pray, "on earth as it is in heaven," with beauty as an essential part of the experience of heaven, the church should naturally be the leader in celebrating the beauty of God. We are called to praise God in the beauty of his holiness (Ps 96:6), and as a nation of priests (Exod 19:6, 1 Pet 2:9) we are called to present all beauty as a picture of heaven. Furthermore, we are called to be his ambassadors and to be his hands and feet restoring beauty to the broken parts of society. We are to be the instruments of God bringing beauty from ashes (Isa 61).

From the beginning, we can see the arts and beauty have always been a part of God's economy. In fact, the first person in the Bible that is "filled with the Spirit of God" was an artist (Exod 31:1–5). It was this artist, Bezalel, who was appointed by God to build with artistic creativity the Tabernacle and everything associated with worship of this Holy God, from the Ark of the Covenant, to the priestly robes, the Tabernacle itself, and even the incense of God (Exod 31–38).

When God rescued his people from Egypt, and led them across the Red Sea, he commissioned a beautiful Tabernacle. This was to be a picture of the beautiful presence of God living among his people as *Immanuel*. The artwork was an important vehicle for transforming the mindset of his people from being slaves in Egypt to becoming His covenant people. The *visual* beauty of the Tabernacle, along with the beautiful *fragrance* of God's incense were an invitation to come "taste and see" (Ps 34:8) that the Lord is good, true, and beautiful.

We lost this understanding during the Reformation. Protestants had become repulsed by the bad theology and corrupt practices within the Catholic Church. But as they left the Catholic Church, they also left behind the great artwork. Some iconoclasts sought to justify violence against the artwork, but Calvin and Luther thoughtfully rejected those ideas.

Unfortunately, we largely abandoned the arts and a theology of beauty when we abandoned the Catholic Church. It is as if we found the artwork to be guilty by association with the Catholic Church. This error was understandable back then, but after five hundred years, it is time we redeemed this part of our theology and understanding of the Kingdom of God.

Just as God recaptured the imagination of the Israelites in a physical desert, the church is called to recapture the imagination of this generation, which is lost in our cultural desert.

For far too long the church has danced too closely to the heresies of the Ascetics and Gnostics who elevate spiritual matters, while demonizing and devaluing the physical, and thus the beauty found therein. These are not truths found in Scripture. Nor are they ideas the Israelites would have ever imagined. They worshiped a God who created the lilies of the field, and promised them a land flowing with milk and honey (Exod 3:17). God never avoided the power of beautiful language or beautiful imagery in the Bible. He used it attract us to the beauty of his holiness.

The problem is clear: if we are to reach the world today, we cannot afford to ignore the arts, the design world, or media. Our children are growing up in a world where visual media is a constant river of consumption. Beauty and creativity are too often serving the hands and hearts of those who incorporate beauty in a manner opposed to God's design. The proper response for the church today is not to abandon the arts, but to restore them. If we believe our God is a redeemer of all things, then we should not shy away from being God's hands and feet within the arts, the media, and the entertainment industry.

Every instance of beauty is simply a foretaste of the beauty of heaven and life in the presence of God. Beauty points to him, and our souls will never be satisfied until we rejoice in that complete communion with him.

It is the job of the church to see the beauty of God, to celebrate the beauty of God, and then to show the world how all beauty points to the beauty of Christ our King. Then they will be brought to their senses, they will be drawn close so that they may "taste and see" the goodness of our Lord, and they will glorify Christ himself—The Beautiful One.

—Joel Pelsue

85. Let Us Suffer Well as a Reflection of God's Sovereignty

Yet if anyone suffers as a Christian, let him not be ashamed,
but let him glorify God in that name.

—1 Peter 4:16

Suffering is an inescapable part of life. Since it is, and furthermore, since we are promised suffering by our Lord Jesus Christ (John 16:33), let us suffer well as we have been called to do (1 Pet 2:21).

We may suffer with Christ. If we are faithfully walking the path that Christ has put before us and we so much as catch a sniffle, that sniffle is a part of the journey toward Christlikeness, and our suffering is counted as blessed suffering with Christ. Such suffering can manifest itself in our relationships, family, church, finances, health, and endless ways.

We may suffer for Christ. Christ promised that we will suffer directly because of our association with him (Matt 10:22; John 15:18-1). If they hated Christ they will hate us, that is, if we are truly representing him well. This suffering can often come from those who are enemies with Christ, thus enemies of us. This in itself is a blessing, for "if God is for us, who can be against us?" (Rom 8:31b). And the humble, bold, and venerable sentiments on the lips of the physically beaten Apostles, who rejoiced that they were counted worthy to suffer dishonor for the name of Christ (Acts 5:40–42), ought to be our perspective if we are trusting in the sovereignty of God.

We may suffer from Christ. If we have done wrong, expect the suffering that comes from the loving hand of discipline from our Heavenly Father. We should actually rejoice when we suffer from the discipline of our Father because it reminds us that we are truly and legitimately his children whom he corrects out of love (Heb 12:3–11). If we do wrong and are not disciplined, that is the time to wonder fearfully about the legitimacy of our adoption. Furthermore, Peter reminds us that there is no credit for suffering as a natural consequence for sin (1 Pet 2:20). Sometimes God will even use an instrument of discipline that is even more wicked than we are, to which we are likely to object, but unjustifiably (Hab 1:13, 17).

Our suffering is not in vain. All things work together for good for those who love God and are called according to his purpose (Rom 8:28). That means all things—not most things, not some things—but all things.

There is no suffering that has not been passed through the providential counsel of God (Job 1:11–12; 2:5–6; 1 Cor 10:13). God has designed it for our good and his glory. Our present circumstances of suffering have certainly not caught God off-guard, while he scrambles to figure out what to do next. Suffering will always have a purpose, even if it is veiled from us in this life, as in the case of Job. For Joseph, his suffering was to fulfill a greater plan that included bringing him from the Promised Land of Canaan to Egypt as the second-in-command. He eventually knew the reason for his suffering but did he wonder about the length of his suffering? Job, who was not privy to the heavenly dialogue between God and Satan, did not know he was offered as proof of faithful and unflinching service to God. In fact, we know more about the reasons for Job's suffering from the Bible than did Job during his own lifetime. For Christ, he willfully, intentionally, and joyfully set his face toward Jerusalem, as he embraced his mission of suffering at the hands of both Jews and Gentiles (Luke 9:51; Heb 12:2).

Good men of the Bible generally suffer from the hand of evil men. It is not unique to us or out of the ordinary in God's economy (1 Pet 4:12). On the flipside, we often see the prosperity of the wicked, who seem to skate through life undisciplined and without much suffering at all. Mystery; it's a mystery until we can adopt the psalmist's final perspective (Ps 73, especially v.17).

God is working it toward our good in sanctification and his glory. So if we are going to suffer, let us suffer well and bring the maximum glory to God and greatest approval of ourselves that we may remain shameless. The world is watching us, which presents a unique opportunity to maximize our witness to the glory of God as we believe and live the truth that the grace of

God is sufficient (2 Cor 12:8). Let us hold fast to the ultimate reality that our present suffering of this world is weak in comparison to the glory that awaits us (Rom 8:18; 2 Cor 4:17; Jas 1:12).

—Aaron B. Hebbard

---

86. Let the Church Repent of Her Apathy with Regard to Abortion

Nevertheless, the high places were not removed.
The people still sacrificed and made offerings on the high places.

—2 Kings 15:35a

Sin is as broad as it is destructive. We need search neither long nor far to see its wake. The danger of sin's ubiquity is we become accustomed to it; its horror loses its ability to horrify. This is nowhere more evident than our now decades-long acceptance of the holocaust of the unborn. To be certain, the church has, by and large, sought to support candidates for office who at least don't support any and all abortions. We have built, financed, and staffed the good ministry of crisis pregnancy centers. When we are honest with ourselves, however, we are forced to confess not only that we have not done enough, but that we don't care enough.

Just as we are wont to miss the horror of abortion, so we are wont to miss the solution. James tells us this "Pure and undefiled religion before God and the Father is this: to visit orphans and widows in their trouble, and to keep oneself unspotted from the world" (Jas 1:27). We miss the import of this text in myriad ways. First, we reduce it down to a mere truism, hearing James say merely, "It's a good thing to visit widows and orphans in their trouble." That, however, is not what James said. Rather he said that the defining quality of our religion is doing this. Visiting widows and orphans in their trouble isn't an optional add-on, but is of the essence of our faith.

Second, we miss the defining quality of both widows and orphans. It is not, as we suspect, that a widow is someone without a husband, or an orphan is someone without parents. Rather, widowhood is being bereft of the loving protection and care of a husband. Is any woman more a widow than a woman being led to an abortion mill by a boyfriend, a father, a friend, even a husband? Orphan-hood is being bereft of the loving protection and care of parents. Is any child more an orphan than the one whose parents hire an assassin to take his or her life?

We, the church, are guilty. One in six abortions is procured by a professing Evangelical. That means on any given day there are far fewer professing Christians heralding Christ at abortion mills than there are professing Christians availing themselves of murder for hire. But they are not alone in their guilt. There is blood on all our hands, as we treat this as an "issue" rather than as it is, a horror beyond measure.

What then should we do? By all means support truly pro-life candidates, those who publicly affirm their commitment to use every power of their office to protect every unborn child. By all means continue to do and to support the good work of crisis pregnancy centers. But James calls us not to invite widows and orphans to come to us for help; rather he calls us to visit them. We must go to them. Every abortion mill in the country should be adopted by a church, or several churches. And every hour that the mill is open for the destruction of the innocent, we should be there proclaiming the gospel of Jesus Christ.

When we go to these gates of hell we come under conviction for our own sin. We no longer confuse the Kingdom of God with the United States. We witness the reality of spiritual warfare, and perhaps best of all, we witness the power of the gospel, the ministry of the Holy Spirit at work. We will see life come forth from death. We will repent and believe the gospel, which is the answer to our every problem. As we repent and believe, he forgives and blesses, all because of the finished work of Christ for us.

—R. C. SPROUL JR.

87. Let the Church Abandon Seeker-Sensitive, Church-Growth Strategies

As it is written:
"None is righteous, no, not one; no one understands; no one seeks for God.

—Romans 3:10–11

God made dogs, and he made dogs in such a way that when they are happy to see their owners, or when they receive attention, or when they are fed, they wag their tails as visible signs of their happiness. We have probably all been amused and perhaps rewarded by this phenomenon, but I doubt that any of us have ever witnessed a dog's tail wagging the dog. That is until we look at the model of church growth that metaphorically allows the tail to dictate the direction of the dog's wag.

Ecclesia. The Greek word we translate as church is composed of the prefix *ek*, meaning out, and the root verb *kale*, meaning I call. The church, therefore, is made up of those who have been called out; called out of the world, called out of slavery to sin, called out of darkness, called out of the enemy's grip, and ultimately called out from behind the gates of hell, which cannot prevail when Christ calls, and from where we were living before we heard this call (Matt 16:18). Christ is outside the gates of hell and calls to his elect from inside the gates of hell. The called-out ones will come to Christ in response and not even the gates of hell will prevail in stopping, thwarting, deterring, opposing, or withstanding their march out to Christ. Their response to his call—as well as the call itself—is, as we say, irresistible.

If we have been called out, why, therefore, do we seek assimilation with the world from which we were called? Why do we make our churches look like the coffee bars, malls, theaters, and concert venues of our culture? The answer is simple; the main motive for having churches that are less churchy is for the benefit of attracting the unchurched and to make them feel at home and at ease that we might present the gospel. Those who are seeking out the meaning of life are more likely to come to this type of place than a churchy-church. The other motive—though often hidden behind a thin mask of gospel altruism—is to bolster the numbers in attendance. More people will come to the cool happening place than to the stuffy, silver-haired, hymn-singing, pew-riding saints-with-one-foot-in-the-grave caricatured-church.

Negative consequences abound from this approach. First, the Bible is clear that no one seeks after God by means of his own sinful volition. So if we are designing churches to be sensitive for seekers of God—of which there are none—we are on a fool's errand as we build churches for *no one*. And if we are designing churches for no one, God is not being worshiped nor are the saints being equipped. There may be seekers out there, but they may be seeking the benefits of Christ but not Christ himself, and we are undiscerning in their confusion of the two.

Second, to keep things simple for the unchurched "seeker," we hold back on—if not abandon—our Christianized jargon, culture, biblical references, and theology. We have to keep it culturally relevant and make references to movies and pop-culture so that our "preaching" (that is to suggest, a more casual conversation) is more palpable. So now, not only is this church not for any seeker, but even the saints who are in attendance are not growing because they've been resigned to a milky diet at best.

Third, this model necessitates the endless striving for staying current with the cultural tide. What is here today is gone tomorrow. Thousands, tens of thousands, or more are spent on this tireless chase for cultural relevance. And yet all the while the eye is on keeping up with the culture, at the high cost of keeping the eye off the timely and timeless Word of God. In this sense, the cultural trend is the dog tail that wags the church. If our Triune God has designed and is in the process of building the church today and forever, shouldn't we look to his biblical blueprints for our cues? I can only imagine how the Lord must detest the leaders of the church who look everywhere else but to him and his Word for direction and design for *his* church. Properly understood and played out, the Bible is the dog that wags the direction of the church's tail.

Lastly, we have fallen into the fallacy of equivocation. We are constantly motivated by aspirations of church growth. But what the Bible truly calls growth is not the essence of the contemporary church's vocabulary. Biblical growth refers to the depth of the faith and knowledge of Jesus Christ (Eph 2:21; 4:15–16; Col 2:19; 2 Thess 1:3; 1 Pet 2:2; 2 Pet 3:18). What we call numerical growth, the Bible calls multiplication (Acts 6:7), and surely the Bible calls for rejoicing in multiplication. And clearly, it is God alone who causes the growth both vertically and horizontally, not our strategies (1 Cor 3:6–7). Sadly, we portray our preferences to have churches that are a mile wide and an inch deep over those with serious and biblical church growth resulting in the depth of faith and knowledge of the Son. Churches with thousands of milky Christians are esteemed higher than the humble church of one hundred, but who are on a steady diet of milk, solid food, and meat (1 Cor 3:2; Heb 5:12–13; 1 Pet 2:2).

By providing a culturally familiar atmosphere to attract uncharted seekers, the motive is to make them feel like automatic church insiders. Perhaps we need to understand better the biblical distinction between those inside the gates of hell and those outside the gates of hell (and there are no fence walkers; no neutrality here). If we make outsiders/unbelievers feel like insiders/believers, then they will never feel the need to be true insiders of the church. Our tactics need to be biblically consistent; in order to make outsiders of the church feel the need to be insiders of the church, they need to feel firstly like outsiders of the church. By biblical design a God-glorifying, Christ-exalting, and Spirit-led church is really "seeker-hostile."[26] This is not to say that we become unfriendly on a personal level to church visitors, but the church needs to worship God unflinchingly, without reserve, and speak of God from the Word of God, which is the very thing designed to apply faith to hearers of the Word (Rom 10:17).

In the contemporary seeker-friendly church, the goal is that the outsider walks away with a casual appreciation for the cool-factor. However, when the New Testament speaks of outsiders in the church, and as the prophetic Word of God is proclaimed and as secrets of their hearts are disclosed, their reaction ought to be one of falling on their faces to worship God and to declare that God is really among this church (1 Cor 14:24–25).

—Aaron B. Hebbard

---

26. Wilson, Doug. *Mother Kirk*. Moscow, Idaho: Canon, 2001, 33.

88. Let Us Reject Consumerism and Embrace Covenantal Living

So whatever you wish that others would do to you, do also to them,
for this is the Law and the Prophets.

—MATTHEW 7:12

We have all come to understand that when an *ism* is placed at the end of a perfectly benign word, the connotation often takes on a sinister alliance. In this case we would be misled to think that if we are to avoid consumerism, we must necessarily avoid being consumers. This is not only untrue, but nearly and practically impossible. No, what we need to repent of instead and turn around is our sloppy lifestyles and mentalities of consumerism.

If we are to repent of consumerism with sincerity and intentionality, a definition is in order. Consumerism is the concept that our society is willingly enslaved into an insatiable thirst for more and more material goods for the purposes of elevating social status and for making life unhealthily easier. The primary problem with consumerism does not lie with the product nor service itself nor in the economic transaction of fair exchange. The primary problem lies in the mentality that happiness is to be found in the acquisition of the latest and greatest things; keeping up with the Joneses is good, but surpassing the Joneses is better; and that he who dies with the most toys wins the game of life. Money is to buy stuff; stuff is to prove that we have money; money and stuff are for the sole purpose of making us feel and look better to ourselves and to our neighbors.

This mentality has infiltrated more areas of life than simply home economics. Specifically here, consumerism has affected the way we choose our local church and what we expect our local church to do for us. When "shopping" for a church, we have our "checklists" of desirable "features." We want our local church to have the right style of music, the right length and topics of sermons, the right version of Bible, the right starting and ending time of service, the right kind of comfortable seating, the right heating and air-conditioning systems, the right age and charisma of the pastor, the right activities for our children in Sunday School, the right kind of coffee served after service, the right location on the right side of town, and the list goes on down to the most minute detail. We want the church to serve us; it's all about us and what we get out of it. And if we like what we see, we make the purchase with our tithes and offerings, and call it ours. No wonder so many churches now have more affinities with local shopping malls, movie theaters, coffee shops, and concert venues than with true churches of the past two thousand years. These churches honestly believe they have to compete for the "business patronage" against all the other churches in their town and beyond. Sadly, some churches even work to draw in more "customers" with their newest amenities so that they can put their "competition out of business." The contemporary church largely feeds on and into cultural consumerism instead of calling for and modeling covenantal living.

We might naturally expect the opposite of consumerism to be "producerism" or "productivism," but this is not the biblical picture either. Covenantal living is the opposite of consumerism in this context for several reasons. As we are in covenant with God, we are consequently in covenant with one another by God's own design for us as an organic Body directed by the same Head; a holy temple structured around the same Chief Cornerstone; and a nation of priests led by the same High Priest. As we are called to live in covenantal community, we produce that we might earn a living, which provides for our families and avails us to share our resources with one another (1 Tim 5:8; Eph 4:28; cf. Acts 2:44; 5:1–11). We are to consume where we cannot produce, and preferably purchase from one another within the covenantal community as a sign covenantal preference in order to prosper their earnings (Gal 6:10). In this respect we are keeping God's wealth in God's Kingdom as efforts toward intentional growth. With respect to the church, we are the church, a holy nation of priests who must serve one another and be humble enough to be served. Because we have freely received, we must freely give (Matt 10:8).

Consumerism is like a bodily disease that keeps its functions isolated and shares no benefit with the rest of the Body. In covenantal living we give and receive, we pray for and are prayed for, we teach and are taught, we bless and get blessed, we encourage and get encouraged, we love and are loved.

—Aaron B. Hebbard

89. Let the Church Care for Orphans

Religion that is pure and undefiled before God the Father is this: to visit orphans and widows in their affliction, and to keep oneself unstained from the world.

—JAMES 1:27

One of the central privileges of the gospel is our adoption into the family of God. We are not children of God by nature; rather, we are by nature children of wrath (Eph 2:3). God, in his glorious grace, adopts us into his family through Jesus Christ (Eph 1:4–5). The eternal Son of God became the Son of Man and suffered and died for us, that we might become children of God, born again by the Spirit into a new family (John 1:12–13; 1 John 3:1). Now, as sons in union with the Son, the Lord Jesus Christ, we cry out "Abba" to our Heavenly Father through the work of the Holy Spirit (Rom 8:15). The Triune God has adopted us, inviting us into his shared life of love and has made a home for us in eternity (John 14:2–4). God is the Adopting God. God forms his family through adoption. We love him because he first loved us, and his initiating love took the shape of adoption. Once strangers, we are now sons, with a new status, a promised inheritance, and a family to call our own.

God's adopting love is much more than a theological reality; it is also a practical model for ministry. The church has a long tradition of imitating God's adopting love by caring for the orphan. This is how God's Word defines true religion: "to visit orphans and widows in their affliction, and to keep oneself unstained by the world" (Jas 1:27). The term "visit" here is much richer than we might suspect. Throughout Scripture when God "visits" his people, he acts powerfully to rescue them and establish them in a place of safety and peace (e.g., Exod 4:31; Luke 1:68). When we "visit" the destitute and abandoned, we must work to rescue them from their plight as well. Orphan-care is rooted in the requirements of the old covenant law (e.g., Deut 10:18, Ps 68:5–6, Isa 1:17) and has been in the church's DNA from the very beginning of the new covenant.

Infanticide was legal in the Roman Empire, but Christians regularly rescued infants from exposure. Justin Martyr and Tertullian describe Christians taking collections to care for the poor, especially orphans. The first orphanages were built by Christians, often in close proximity to cathedrals.

Martin and Katie Luther took in numerous foster children who had no place to go, providing them shelter in the Black Cloister. While George Whitefield is best known for his amazing oratory as a preacher, he considered his life's work the founding and support of an orphanage in the colony of Georgia, established in 1740 and known as Bethesda Home for Boys. In the nineteenth century, George Müller famously ran an orphanage on a shoestring and a prayer (quite literally); over eight thousand children were cared for and educated thanks to his vision and labors. Charles Spurgeon was committed to the care of orphans, and joined forces with believers from other branches of the church in his day in an effort to alleviate the suffering of the destitute and fatherless in the rapidly industrializing city of London.

Today, Christians are on the forefront of foster care, ministry to women with crisis pregnancies, and the adoption of orphans in America and from abroad. These acts of mercy toward orphans should be encouraged as tangible applications of the gospel and manifestations of the Kingdom from a variety of angles.

But we must also provide some needed cautions, particularly with regard to international adoption, checking the motives and methods involved. While there is certainly a global orphan crisis, international adoption has become a burgeoning industry, rife with corruption. Before pursuing adoption, we ought to ask in any given case if it is wiser to "adopt" a family; that is, would monetary resources earmarked for adopting a child be better spent preserving the child's natural family, enabling the child's parents to feed and educate him themselves? There are many parents around the world who have given up their children not because they do not want them but because they cannot provide for them adequately. If we are going to "help without hurting" (to use a now-common phrase), we must do so wisely, looking at the problem of orphaned children from multiple angles. We should resist the adoption mythology that has become so prevalent in our day, which assumes that a child will always be better off in middle-class America with an adopting family than they could be with their own biological family, properly resourced, in a poorer country.

While we must work through these complexities, we must not give up on our calling to come to the rescue of children in need. Oftentimes, a child's only hope will be the welcoming love of a family willing to adopt. Millions of children around the globe are in need of adoption at this very moment. When children are adopted, Christian parents may rest assured that God's covenant promises extend to the child who has been brought into their family from the outside. The administration of the covenant of grace has never been based on bloodlines, but has always been structured by God's promises made to entire households (cf. Gen 17:12–13, Exod 12:43–51).

Thus, Charles Hodge argued that children in Christian orphanages could be baptized because they were going to be discipled as believers. What does this mean for adoptive parents? The adopted child should be nurtured in the Christian faith and brought into the life of the church, as part of a covenant household. Having been adopted by a Christian family, the child has been brought within the sphere of God's covenant mercies. In this way, adoption becomes a glorious mirror of our Heavenly Father's adopting love.

—Rich Lusk

90. Let Us Respect the Antithesis Between Saint and Sinner

For the eyes of the Lord are on the righteous, and his ears are open to their prayer. But the face of the Lord is against those who do evil.

—1 Peter 3:12

There are two kinds of people in the world: those who divide the world into two kinds of people and those who do not. Among the former set of folks, many varieties of divisions abound: male and female; married and single; givers and takers; etc. The Bible also divides this world into two kinds of people: saints and sinners, children of light and children of darkness, those who practice the truth and those who suppress it, those whose sins are forgiven and those who stand condemned for their sin, those who are in Christ and those who are not, those who see the light of the gospel and those who are blind and perishing, those who will dwell with God eternally and those who will be separated from God forever. There is no neutral middle ground in these respects.

As we reflect upon one of the memorable statements of the Reformer Martin Luther, *simul iustus et peccator*, we have to reconsider if we can be both righteous and sinner simultaneously. While Martin Luther was certainly not infallible—as only the Bible is—we do have to recognize his influence and give attention to his teachings. Of course, this statement is not mere double-talk or blatant contradiction; it is an attempt to explain our simultaneous sinful nature and our justified position before God. However, even in this respect this assertion does not conform to the biblical position of the believer. As Peter Leithart points out, our status as sinner can only be in relation to the Law of God, but since we are not under the Law but under grace (Rom 6:14), there is no latitude to be considered a *peccator*, a sinner.[27] We must submit our understanding of reality according to the truth as God has ordained it; and he says we are saints, not sinners.[28]

While we were once sinners, we have been redeemed and are now the children of God, saints, priests, and the collective Body and Bride of Christ. We are new creations and the old natures are rendered dead (2 Cor 5:17). Romans 5:19 clearly states we were made sinners by one man, the First Adam, and we are made righteous by another man, the Second Adam. It does not allow both *statuses* simultaneously.

Of course we are still sinful, even as saints. If we were not sinful, probably half the content of Paul's letters to the churches would be unnecessary to consult and would be superfluous for daily life. We saints still sin, but we are not sinners before God, whose declarations alone define truth. Luther's Latin phrase, however, still remains intact since *peccator* can—and should—be translated as "sinful" instead of "sinner" (i.e. Luke 5:8, Vulgate). Biblically, we can more confidently say that we are simultaneously righteous and *sinful*, but not retain the label of *sinner*, lest we undermine the transformation that our Triune God has done on our behalf.

Ultimately though, we need to address the cultural implications of this distinction between saint and sinner. We have likewise pushed another envelope further with our own inaccurate motto: "Love the sinner, hate the sin."

Without a doubt, Christ spent calculated leisure time with sinners and showed love for them in such a way that brought conviction to their lives, turning sinners into saints (Matt 10:9–13; Luke 19:1–10). Christ's love for them was perfect enough not to tolerate their sin, but rather to lead them to repentance and salvation. Even as Paul says that God demonstrated his love for us while we were sinners, the point is that we can only see this in a position having been redeemed (Rom 5:8).

27. https://www.firstthings.com/blogs/leithart/2017/01/iustus-et-peccator

28. Far too many verses to list, but be a Berea and do a NT word search on "saint" and "sinner."

This distinction between sin and sinner is unsupported biblically. Keep in mind that God judges and condemns sinners, not just sin, to hell (Matt 5:22, 29–30; 10:28). God hates sinners and is angry with them every day (Ps 5:5; 7:11; 11:5; cf. 26:5; 139:21–22). If God did not hate sinners and sin, we could rightfully question his claims to holiness and as one who cannot be in the presence of sin (Ps 5:4; Hab 1:13). When dealing with life in Christ and community, we as his saints are all called to purge sin from among us. But with those who refuse to repent of sin, we are not to treat them as saints with sin problems, but rather as sinners with sin problems, and to excise them from Christ's Body; meanwhile hoping and praying for their repentance (1 Cor 5:2, 5, 13; Matt 18:17).

The true distinction between saint and sinner, and the false dichotomy between sinner and sin, can be clarified with the biblical distinction between punishment and discipline. God *punishes* sinners for their sin (Isa 13:11; Prov 11:21; Matt 25:46; 2 Thess 1:9; Eph 5:6; Luke 12:5; Rev 21:8); but God *disciplines* his children for their sin (Job 5:17; Ps 94:12–13; 96:13). In fact, God's discipline of his children legitimizes our status as children (Heb 12:6; Rev 3:19); and God's punishment of evil-doers confirms their status as enemies of God (Isa 13:11; 26:21; Eph 5:6; Col 3:6). Both sinners and saints sin, and that is the common factor, but the *status* of the one who sins is vastly distinguishing. Christ's blood covers the saints' sins (1 John 1:7), but God's wrath abides on sinners (John 3:36). So take heart, God hates the sin but loves the saint!

The confusion of false dichotomies does not serve our witness well. We, as saints, must point out the damning status of sinners and take evangelistic opportunities to preach—and live—the gospel and the redemptive narrative of God with the climax of the cross, resurrection, ascension, and return of Christ.

—AARON B. HEBBARD

91. Let Us Submit To and Live Under the Absolute Sovereignty of Christ Alone

but in every nation anyone who fears him and does what is right
is acceptable to him. As for the word that he sent to Israel,
preaching good news of peace through Jesus Christ (he is Lord of all) . . .

—ACTS 10:35–36

Henotheism is an ancient religious mentality whereby a nation or tribe would hold allegiance and loyalty to their one god while simultaneously recognizing that their god competed against the gods of other nations or tribes. While this religious ideology may seem primitive to our post/modern, scientific, and post-Christian culture, I suspect that even our Christian culture has slumped into a modernized version of henotheism today.

Ask the basic Evangelical if s/he believes that God is absolutely sovereign and the answer will be overwhelmingly in the affirmative. Then ask if God's sovereignty applies to all of life, and again the answer will be generally positive. But then as we begin to scratch this thin veneer, we witness a crumbling of conviction before our very eyes. Suddenly, the ancient religious practice of henotheism begins to rear its ugly head.

Christ claimed to be Lord of the Sabbath (Mark 2:28), and we quickly agree. Then comes Monday, Tuesday, Wednesday, et al., and the practical pressures of daily life demand the type of shrewdness that Christlike integrity can't afford. Sadly, though no one would admit they bend the knee to other gods, they live a life throughout the remainder of the week reflective of honoring the false gods who are given their equal place with the Lord of the Sabbath.

Christ is the Lord of all true worship. Christ in his humanity leads us in the worship of God (Matt 4:10; 6:9–10; John 4); Christ in his divine Trinity receives our worship (Matt 14:33; 28:9; John 20:28; Rev 14; 19:1–8). But we have geared our worship services to please and attract people instead of God. We welcome the people to church rather than God. We promise a good time for folks instead of offering pure worship to the Lord. Sadly, today's worship is about man as well as God, and thus we continue to dismantle *Solis Deo Gloria*, and we revere God along with ourselves.

Christ is the Lord of the harvest (Matt 9:38). Sometimes we believe we are in control of the crop as we pluck along the fields by our own methods instead of taking our direction from our Master. Perhaps we fail miserably by not working at harvesting the field at all, or furthermore, we neglect to pray for more laborers.

Christ is the Lord of truth (John 14:6; 18:37). We tend to follow in Pilate's footsteps by looking into the face of Truth Incarnate and have the audacity to ask, "What is Truth?" (John 18:38). We do not know truth nor do we seek it as it is from the Lord. To our demise, we let all sorts of versions and distortions of the truth compete against the true Truth, and we even entertain the question of whether we can actually know truth or not, which only betrays our ambivalence of truly knowing Christ, the Incarnate Truth.

Christ is the Lord of creation, of heaven and earth (Luke 10:21), whose invisible attributes are clearly perceived (Rom 1:20), but we listen to scientists who set about proclaiming an existence of heaven and earth built upon unfathomable attributes of randomness, illogical fallacies, unproven theories, falsified data, and unrepeatable progression.

Christ is the Lord of our finances (Luke 19:16). We are convinced that he can be Lord over our 10 percent but not over our 90 percent. Why do we not recognize that the Lord owns the whole earth (Ps 50:10; 24:1) and has assigned us our lot to steward? Instead of thinking of the 10 percent of our finances that we offer to the Lord, we ought to orient our thinking that the Lord allows us to keep 90 percent of his resources that he assigned to us.

Christ is the Lord of life (John 1:4; 10:10) but we tolerate a culture of death through our apathy toward abortion and euthanasia. We leave the sex slaves, the poor, and oppressed—image-bearers of God—to suffer an undignified standard of living.

Christ is the Lord of marriage (Mark 10:9), but we have abused divorce clauses, ignored or abandoned marriage entirely, and have radically redefined it beyond any recognition.

Christ is the Lord not only of all things spiritual, but he is also the Lord over all things at all times in all places. He is not only Lord of our Bible classes but of our studies of physics, economics, history, biology, literature, psychology, government, math, along with an expanding host of lesser known subjects.

If we truly believe and are committed to the Lordship of Christ over all, then we cannot utter the oxymoronic "No, Lord" without being a forked-tongued hypocrite. Peter uttered such sinful nonsense on several occasions as he confessed Jesus as Christ then rebuked Jesus for declaring his imminent death (Mark 8:32–33); and when the Lord told Peter to kill and eat "unclean" animals, he refused (Acts 10:14). Today we may not verbally utter this oxymoron but our actions scream them out loud when we say with our hypocritical and henotheistic voices that Christ reigns over some things but not all things. If henotheism is our theological conclusion, then we will never attempt to change the way things are by proclaiming the total Lordship of our King. What would be the point?

Let us rather concur with Abraham Kuyper who stated, "There is not a square inch in the whole domain of our human existence over which Christ, who is Sovereign over all, does not cry, Mine!" We must be as consistent as Charles Spurgeon in his comment: "I believe that every mote of dust that dances in the sunbeam does not move an atom more or less than God wishes . . . "

Christ is Lord of all. Until we recognize this truth, until we make his invisible reign visible in the church, in the family, in the marketplace, in the academy, in the government, in the culture, and throughout the entire world, reformation cannot happen. We should be confident Christ is Lord because "God has highly exalted him and bestowed on him the name that is above every name, so that at the name of Jesus *every* knee should bow, in *heaven* and on *earth* and *under* the earth, and *every* tongue confess that Jesus Christ is *Lord*, to the glory of God the Father (Phil 2:9–10).

—AARON B. HEBBARD

92. Let Us Rejoice in the Lord

Shout for joy in the LORD,
O you righteous! Praise befits the upright.

—PSALM 33:1

Godly sorrow leads to repentance, and with it life and joy. While solemn repentance ought to be a way of life, so is the consequent joy of a

Christian's heart that is set free from eternal condemnation of God's wrath and is now at peace with God in Christ. We are forgiven people but we, with David, need to cry out for the Lord to restore unto us the joy of our salvation (Ps 51:12).

Joy is a deeply theological issue. Jesus endured the cross because "of the joy that was set before him" (Heb 12:2). Christ exchanges our burdens for his (Matt 11:28–30). Christ took our heavy burdens—the cross—and gave us a light burden—living joyously for God in the knowledge of his glory. If we are to reflect heaven on earth as Jesus taught us to pray (Matt 6:10), then we ought to have fullness of joy and pleasures forevermore because of the presence of the Lord in our life (Ps 16:11).

The theological reality that we have been saved from the eternal wrath of God and into his eternal joy, pleasure, and presence ought to turn the worst depression into deep flowing rivers of blissful delight. There is not a problem in this world that should dampen our outlook on eternal security. Our doctrines of salvation not only reveal how our souls are saved, but they should actually save us from our depression, and our witness of these doctrines ought to flow freely from a heart of gratitude and joy.

Negligence of joy is deeply misrepresentative of gospel living. Joy—true joy—is fruit of the Spirit. The absence of joy may betray the absence of the Spirit and of the eternal truths that dwell within the true believer. Joy—and not merely fleeting happiness—is a distinguishing mark of the Spirit-filled believer. Can we conclude that a lack of joy is a lack of the Spirit, and therefore a lack of joy in salvation because there is no salvation? Well, we are to be known by our fruit, or lack thereof, and that is a convicting conclusion if we do not bear such joyous fruit.

If we are not exemplifying the joy of the Lord, we are attempting to perform in our own strengths instead of relying on the strength that we draw from the Lord's joy (Neh 8:10), thus marginalizing the Spirit's absolute reign in our lives. And to be sure, reliance on our own strength will lead to disaster (Ps 118:8; Prov 3:5; Jer 17:5; Zech 4:6; John 6:63; 15:4–5). Furthermore, having no joy is failing to be Christ's ambassadors, who should be characterized as joyous representatives of the Kingdom (Rom 14:17). Christ, from the very moment of his birth, came to give us joy (Luke 2:10; cf. Matt 2:10). There is an obvious disconnect—and may we dare say, hypocrisy—between clinging to Christ and lacking the joy that accompanies life in Christ. Situations, conditions, and events that can rob us of our joy are abundant in this world, but there is no escape clause from living in joy, for Jesus solemnly promised, "In the world you will have tribulation. But take heart; I have overcome the world" (John 16:33; cf. 1 John 4:4; 5:4, 5).

We must reform our personal habits of joy, as the Bible clearly calls for us to do. Our previous weeping in the night must give way to joy in the morning (Ps 30:5). Our weeping shall be turned to laughter (Luke 6:21). Our previous laughter of foolishness (Eccl 7:6) and disbelief (Mark 5:40) shall be turned into laughter of confidence (Ps 52:6; 126:2). So often we let the hardships in life overshadow the joys, but we must be vigilant to make Christ our chief joy. Joy is not a feeling but a choice to see God's gift of life from an eternal perspective. Joy is a spiritual discipline, and often not an easy one to keep, but the Holy Spirit is faithful to us.

So in the words of Paul, who wrote these words from prison and had every carnal reason for abandoning joy, "Rejoice in the Lord always; again, I will say, rejoice" (Phil 4:4).

—AARON B. HEBBARD

93. Let Us Celebrate in the Lord

Go your way. Eat the fat and drink sweet wine and send portions to anyone who has nothing ready, for this day is holy to our Lord. And do not be grieved, for the joy of the LORD is your strength.

—NEHEMIAH 8:10

Celebration is commanded in the Bible; it really is that simple. Celebration isn't optional; it is mandatory and obligatory! Perhaps our celebratory negligence is due to our tendency to forget the goodness of the Lord and the goodness of the life he has given us. Thanksgiving for God's goodness should lead us into a constant mode of celebration. Think of the multiple times that God commands his people to remember the Lord and all that he has done for them. What does such recall lead to except thanksgiving and celebration? In fact, we should remember the Lord's daily faithfulness as our reminder and impetus to celebrate. In addition to the goodness of God toward our biblical forefathers, we ought to keep our own journals of

God's faithfulness; read entries daily and make regular entries for the sake of remembrance and posterity.

The Word of God sets the pattern for prescribed celebration. When we consider the feasts of Passover, Booths, Trumpets, Pentecost, Unleavened Bread, Day of Atonement on the annual calendar, with several of them lasting a week each, we can easily calculate that we are to "tithe" our time in celebration. Then when we consider other biblical and intertestamental celebrations like Purim and Dedication of Lights, and then weekly Sabbaths and monthly New Moon festivals, our times of celebration are pushed well beyond our tithing of time.

With our new relationship to our Father through Christ as facilitated by the indwelt Holy Spirit, our Bridegroom is present, which also lends itself to feasting over fasting (Mark 2:19). Certainly there is a place for fasting. While the presence of God is the reason to feast, there are times when the absence of God is felt, when his omnipresence is veiled, when his will is unclear; these are the times we ought to fast in order to rediscover God's presence and pleasure. Fasting must then end in God's good timing and give way to feasting.

Celebration is spiritual discipline. Jesus turned the water into wine for the purposes of keeping a celebration going, to honor the bride and groom, his own mother, and the wedding host. If celebration was not a motive, the miracle—his first miracle—becomes frivolous and can only be seen as a warm-up exercise to more significant miracles.

Jesus was accused of being a drunkard and a glutton. Christ was neither a drunkard nor a glutton, but due to their jealousy his enemies mistook his healthy habits of daily celebration as an undisciplined lifestyle. Let us practice the same joy by which Christ lived. Let the world look upon us and be jealous of our joy and our sincere reason for celebration. Let us live reflectively of the pleasures of God and be a witness to the world that our Savior is the only true source of peace and joy. Much is at stake here; so live it up. Take celebration seriously and let their jealous accusations fly!

Both pagans and Christians celebrate, but let's distinguish their respective motives. Life without resurrection or an afterlife leads to nihilism, and so they say, "Let us eat, drink, [and be merry,] for tomorrow we die" (1 Cor 15:32; Luke 12:19). The Christian should likewise say, "Let us eat, drink, and be merry, and if tomorrow we die, our lives are hidden in him, and the heavenly celebration gets kicked up a million notches."[29] We celebrate in God's good pleasure, and it is God's good pleasure to pour out his goodness on his people (Luke 12:32; Phil 2:13). So while God has poured out his

---

29. By no means am I suggesting reckless living as a way of testing God (Matt 4:7).

goodness on all people in the forms of sun, rain, flowers, trees, good food, sweet wine, loving relationships, health, and laughter, the Christian turns to God in thanksgiving but the unbeliever is not thankful and the wrath of God is being stored up against him (Rom 1:21; 2:5).

Righteous irony reveals that our proper understanding of celebration is the reason to suspend the *theory* of celebration—and frequently—to leave plenty of room for the *practice* of celebration. Celebrate with vivacity all new covenantal marriages, the births of covenantal children—and the procreative attempts of conceiving such children—baptisms, meals, drinks, music, fellowship, holidays, and even the deaths of saints who have lived well. Furthermore, the Lord's Day ought to be celebrated as the best day of the week, and our children should look forward to it all week long as a day when music is sung more joyously, the wisdom of the Word is on our lips, food is at its best, good drink flows freely, fellowship is unrestrained by time, and rest is truly rejuvenating. We are to love the Lord by celebrating our God with our whole heart, soul, mind, and strength.

God did not have to make life pleasurable but he did. "Glorify God and enjoy him forever!" and glorify God by enjoying him forever!

—Aaron B. Hebbard

---

94. Let the Church Repent

The time is fulfilled, and the kingdom of God is at hand;
repent and believe the gospel.

—Mark 1:15

Our Lord and Master, Jesus Christ, commanded us to: "Repent, for the kingdom of Heaven is near" (Matt 4:17). The whole life of a believer must be one of repentance. This cannot be interpreted as a token gesture of commitment, nor a technical salvation that is all theory and no experience. Biblical repentance involves conviction: a change of mind; contrition:

a change of heart; and conversion: a change of life. It is not enough to confess our sin, we also need to reject sin, to loathe it, and to forsake it. "Now, therefore, says the Lord, turn to me with all your heart, with fasting, with weeping, and with mourning. So rend your heart and not your garments; return to the Lord your God, for He is gracious and merciful, slow to anger and of great kindness . . . " (Joel 2:12–13). There are explicit and implicit connections between Joel and the message of the Apostle Peter on the Day of Pentecost: "Repent, and let every one of you be baptized in the Name of Jesus Christ for the remission of sins; and you will receive the gift of the Holy Spirit" (Acts 2:38). This was the message of the Early Church: "Repent therefore and be converted, that your sins may be blotted out, so the times of refreshing may come from the presence of the Lord" (Acts 3:19).

Before he returned to heaven, our Lord Jesus Christ commanded his followers: "But repentance and remission of sins should be preached in his name to all nations . . . " (Luke 24:47). This is our obligatory duty in preaching the gospel, and not merely friendly advice. Salvation is by the grace of God alone, received by faith alone, on the basis of Christ's blood atonement on the cross of Calvary alone. Biblical salvation always involves a change of behavior. "Let the wicked forsake his way, and the unrighteous man his thoughts; let him return to the LORD and He will have mercy on him; and to our God, for He will abundantly pardon" (Isa 55:7).

Those who teach that as long as you believe you are saved, regardless of how you behave, are false teachers. The Scripture makes clear that just as repentance without faith is not true repentance, so faith without repentance is not true faith. For repentance and faith are two sides of the same coin. Belief always affects behavior. "Thus also faith by itself, if it does not have works is dead. But someone will say, you have faith, and I have works. Show me your faith without your works and I will show you my faith by my works . . . for as the body without the spirit is dead, so faith without works is dead also" (Jas 2:17–26). They preach no Christian doctrine who teach that repentance is not necessary for those who seek to be right with God. The truly repentant earnestly desires to undertake full restitution, to repair, replace and restore what fails to align with God's character. In the Bible sin is specific and personal. Our repentance, therefore, must be equally specific and personal, not vague and general.

Sin is serious. Yet we are far too tolerant of sin. Sin is more defiling than filth, more dangerous than an unexploded bomb, more life threatening than a deadly disease, more insidious than a virus. The more the world celebrates sin, the more the church tolerates sin. Soon enough, the church trails behind to a point of full participation. Yes, we all need the gift of repentance.

"God now commands all men everywhere to repent" (Acts 17:30). "Seek the Lord while He may be found, call upon Him while He is near" (Isa 55:6).

When we truly repent of our personal guilt in violating God's commands, the result is forgiveness, freedom, healing, and restoration. Not only must we live lives evident of repentance, but we must also believe that our repentance has led to forgiveness, and that God's forgiveness of us leads us to the glorious and unmentionable blessings of the gospel and eternal life. The formula is easy: no repentance, no transformation; no transformation, no reformation.

And after having repented and been forgiven, justified, and adopted as his children by God, we are naturally led to our final thesis: we must therefore, be strong and courageous, for "If God is for us, who can be against us?" (Rom 8:31b).

— PETER HAMMOND

95. Let the Church Be Strong and Courageous

Only be strong and very courageous, being careful to do according to all the law that Moses my servant commanded you. Do not turn from it to the right hand or to the left, that you may have good success wherever you go.

— JOSHUA 1:7

Joshua is told repeatedly to be strong and courageous (Deut 31:7, 23; Josh 1:6, 7, 9, 18). Let us think about his situation as it relates to our own. He had the full promise of God's presence (Josh 1:5, 9); we have the full promise of God's presence in Christ and the Holy Spirit (Matt 28:20; John 14:15–30). Joshua was promised victory over enemies in taking the Promised Land (Josh 1:2–9); we are promised victory over our enemies in proclaiming the gospel, even unto death (Matt 24:14; John 16:33; Heb 12:28; 1 John 2:13–14,

4:4, 5:4–5). Joshua was to go forth and conquer (Josh 1:2–5); we are to go forth and conquer (Rom 8:37; Rev 2:7, 11, 17, 26; 3:5, 12, 21). Scripture was Joshua's guiding light (Josh 1:7–8); we also are to be guided by the light of Scripture (John 14:21, 23, 26; 15:10).

The world is the Lord's and everything therein (Ps 24:1; cf. Acts 17:24; 1 Cor 10:36), and we are his messengers to proclaim his lordship over all. This worldwide proclamation of the King's good news is a greater task of conquest than what lay before Joshua in the conquest of the Promised Land. That being true, how much more do we need to be stronger and even more courageous than he? And to be sure, "it is not by might, nor by power, but by my Spirit, says the LORD of hosts" (Zech 4:6).

Simply put, if we do not have Christ, we do not have his Spirit (John 16:7). If we do not have the Spirit, we do not have the Spirit's ministry to us to fortify us to be strong and courageous (Zech 4:6; John 14:17; 16:13). If we are not strong and courageous as he has commanded, we fail to trust God in taking him at his Word. If we fail to take God at his Word, our faith is failing at everything and we are so debilitated that we can do nothing apart from him (John 15:5). But we do have Christ, and therefore, we have no excuses.

Today, however, even with a mass population claiming to be disciples of Christ, can we even find seven thousand who do not bend the knee to the Baals of our day (1 Kgs 19:18)? True enough, many are willing in the spirit but weak in the flesh, but where are the strong and courageous? Who will stand in the gap? Who will stand up against those within the Christian community who reduce the Bible's authority and who resign it to the corners of church for a Sunday morning gratuitous nod? Who will fight to keep the doctrines of the atonement, God's omniscience, God's aseity, the Trinity, church discipline, God's supreme sovereignty, and all core teachings as biblically orthodox? We see many who hold these truths but ultimately fear man more than God when it comes to confrontational conflict. The church, both in leadership and laity, is populated with cowards who will bend the knee to our cultural Baals and fail to bend the knee to Christ as Lord, but who believe they can do both. Such conflation of allegiance is impossible but it is a lie that has deceived many a well-intentioned believer. We may even fear that we will be dismissed as ignorant backward bumpkins if hold to the faith once delivered and all that this entails.

Then as we venture into the broader and increasingly post-Christian culture, we find even fewer prophets. Where are those who protest the evils of the millions of murders of the unborn, the sacrilege of redefined marriage, the acceptance of intentional ambiguities of sexuality, the pseudo tolerance of cults and competing religions, the invasion of paganism into our culture, the outright dismissal of God's rightful place as King in our culture, the suppression of truth in exchange for such lies as evolution? And the list goes on and on. We idly stand by while truth is slain in the streets.

Let us be strong and courageous for the witness of Christ on this earth, and for the sake of the church that she may grow in strength and courage by the presence of the few. The tasks will not be easy; if it were, what is the necessity of strength and courage? We must count the cost, but if we do so with spiritual clarity and honesty, we should conclude that any cost is worth it (Luke 14:25–33). I close these ninety-five theses with this theme because if we intellectually agree with everything in this book, but we lack the strength and courage to put our hands to the plow, it is all for nothing. In fact, our newly gained knowledge will make us more accountable to God and bring a stricter judgment upon ourselves (Jas 3:1).

Peter Hammond states poignantly: "If I profess with the loudest voice and clearest exposition, every portion of the truth of God's Word, except precisely that point which the world and the devil are at that moment attacking, then I am not confessing Christ, however boldly I may be professing him. Where the battle rages, there the loyalty of the soldier is proved." We can be confident of entering the Kingdom of Heaven through many tribulations (Acts 14:22), rather than through delusions of comfort and complacency.[30] We cannot compromise where God is clear; we cannot cower where God demands courage. We should not fear man when we must fear God alone (Deut 1:17; Isa 51:12–13; Acts 4:19–20; 5:29). We are not called to be popular, we are called to be faithful. When we seek to please God, man's opinion of us doesn't matter; but if we seek to please man, God's opinion of us won't matter.

These are trying times that demand courageous men, not cautious men, and certainly not cowardly men. Courageous men blaze the trails on which cautious men may only dare to tread at a distance, and on which the cowardly will never step foot. Courageous men are on frontlines while cautious men only cheer from the sidelines, and the cowards remain silent. Courageous men make ripples in their own time while cautious men praise them later in their history books, and while cowards will pass through without notice. As the entire biblical story of God's redemption comes to a close in Revelation, after having been given all the substance and reason for confidence and courage in God's victory, the cowardly are the first to be condemned (21:8).

Rise up, oh men of God, and be the strong and courageous men that God has called you to be, for he has given you his Spirit for such a time as

---

30. Hammond, Peter. "95 Theses for Reformation Today." http://www.reformation-sa.org/index.php/component/multicategories/article/257-95-theses-for-reformation-today

this. "What then shall we say to these things? If God is for us, who can be against us?" (Rom 8:31). These are words that comfort us in our weaknesses and also confront us in our cowardice, but they are also the very words for the strong and courageous in Christ to live by!

—AARON B. HEBBARD

Bonus 96. Let Us Celebrate the Reformation as Part of our Reformational Efforts

He has caused his wondrous works to be remembered;
the LORD is gracious and merciful.

—PSALM 111:4

This is a bonus thesis. The idea for writing ninety-five theses is obviously reminiscent of Martin Luther's statements nailed to the church door five hundred years ago. Since we are celebrating this monumental occasion in 2017, this final thesis is not only to remember the inauguration of the Reformation, but also to instill a desire to replicate the outcome. And though all of these ninety-five theses have been built upon a full implementation of the Word of God in all of life, this particular thesis is not strictly commanded in Scripture. The Bible obviously does not say that we should celebrate Reformation Day along with other biblical celebrations, but still the biblical principle of remembering the mighty works of God through celebration and song are throughout Scripture all the way to the last book of Revelation.

Let us firstly deal with the conflict in our calendars. By and large the church has had cultural conflicts of conviction when it comes to celebrating the ever-growing-in-popularity Halloween. And this conflict has been nursed far too long. We try to redeem Halloween by having Christianized versions that christen the same nonsense with a slightly Christian flair.

Halloween has turned into Hallelujah or Harvest parties. The question is *why*? With such a great historically Christian event as the Protestant Reformation to celebrate on the very same day, why would we continue to attempt to give a little tweak to the pagan dominance of the day?

Let us secondly realize that avoiding the association of this pagan celebration is what we as a peculiar people, holy unto the Lord, are called to do (1 Pet 2:9). In a day and age when the culture is still being entertained by witchcraft, zombies, separatists, mediums, fortunetellers, idolatry, and occultic activity, we in the church still need to "come out from among them and be separate" (2 Cor 6:17). Avoiding Halloween, even baptized versions, is a matter of being set apart, and refusing to accommodate the very things the Lord has commanded us to detest and not tolerate amongst us (Deut 18:9–14).

Let us thirdly enter the culture war more ferociously on this point. As Halloween continues to grow in popularity and as a revenue giant in the seasonal celebration industry, the church is being marginalized as a non-player for that day in particular. For weeks leading up to Halloween, decorations are almost as prolific as Christmas décor. We need to celebrate the day, not just in our quiet corners, but in the center of town with as many churches as possible coming together to make an ostentatious presentation. Let the Halloween celebrators stop and take notice of our grandiose Reformation celebrations. Let our paraphernalia producers sell wares reflecting Reformational themes that will line the streets of our neighborhoods as a witness to the world that we are reclaiming the day. Let the world come to know and say, "We celebrate Halloween, but *all those* Christians celebrate something else"; and eventually, if we give clear and proper witness, they'll come to identify exactly what we are celebrating. Perhaps our celebration will lead them to investigate the Reformation; perhaps our overt celebrations will draw some in to join the celebration; and by the power of the Holy Spirit, perhaps some will come to the knowledge of the truth of the gospel through our celebratory witness.

With respect to Catholics, who obviously have less to celebrate on Reformation Day than do Protestants, they too can participate in redeeming the day by launching their own battle in the culture war by redeeming the day that was more strictly robbed from them (or vice versa?). Going against the grain of modern Halloween, let the Catholics reclaim what they traditionally celebrate as a religious memorial. In the end, I believe we would much rather debate the value of the day with Catholics who celebrate All Hallows' Eve than with pagans who see the day for witches, goblins, and jack-o-lanterns.

The time is now. The five-hundredth anniversary of the Reformation only comes once, and by God's providence it happens in our lifetime. Let this be a definite identifiable time documented in church history when the church abandoned the uneasy celebration of Halloween and fully embraced the celebration of the Reformation. And in so doing, let us pray we experience God's revival and consequent reformation in our own day.

—Aaron B. Hebbard

Epilogue

Pray for Revival; Prepare for Reformation!

Restore us again, O God of our salvation,
and put away your indignation toward us!
Will you be angry with us forever?
Will you prolong your anger to all generations?
Will you not revive us again,
that your people may rejoice in you?
—Psalm 85:4–6